A Pregnant Princess?

The tranquility of Princess Diana's final resting place contrasted with the tempest of rumors, myths, and interrogations that swirled up in the wake of her death. Even before her body was laid in the ground, word began to spread that she had been pregnant at the time of her death. Under normal circumstances, that would have been a purely private matter—an additional cause for sadness if true, pointless and idle gossip if not. But the violent death of the Princess of Wales was not a normal event. And the question of whether or not she was pregnant is potentially one of the most explosive elements in the investigation, because a pregnancy would give greater credence to the assassination plot theories that began in the Middle East and soon proliferated around the globe . . .

DEATH OF A PRINCESS

THE INVESTIGATION

**THOMAS SANCTON
AND
SCOTT MacLEOD**

St. Martin's Paperbacks

DEATH OF A PRINCESS: THE INVESTIGATION

Copyright © 1998 by Thomas Sancton and Scott MacLeod.

Cover photograph © Patrick Demarchelier/Camera Press/Retna.

ISBN: 0-312-96933-3

Printed in the United States of America

St. Martin's Press hardcover edition / February 1998
St. Martin's Paperbacks edition / September 1998

St. Martin's Paperbacks are published by St. Martin's Press, 175 Fifth Avenue, New York, NY 10010.

10 9 8 7 6 5 4 3 2

For Sylvaine and Susan

Contents

	FOREWORD	ix
	AUTHORS' INTRODUCTION TO THE REVISED	
	EDITION	1
1	NO ESCAPE	9
2	FIGHTING FOR LIFE	32
3	POSTMORTEMS	50
4	PARALLEL LIVES	60
5	DODI	71
6	THE PHARAOH OF KNIGHTSBRIDGE	94
7	ST. TROPEZ	117
8	THE KISS	135
9	THE LAST DAY	158
10	THE DRIVER	174
11	THE PAPARAZZI	198
12	THE INVESTIGATORS	221
13	IN SEARCH OF LOST MEMORIES	251
14	SKIDMARKS AND DEBRIS	262
15	WAS IT MURDER?	284
	EPILOGUE	311

Foreword

ON THE PLACE DE L'ALMA IN PARIS, THERE IS A STATUE OF a golden flame. It is a replica of the torch held by the Statue of Liberty. But it has taken on a different and powerful meaning for Parisians since Princess Diana and her boyfriend Dodi Fayed* died in a car crash in the Alma tunnel in the early morning hours of August 31, 1997. The flame is now the focal point of a Diana cult, its base piled high with cellophane-wrapped flowers, and plastered with scrawled messages such as "Farewell, England's Rose," and "Diana, you gave meaning to my life."

When a princess dies, and an enthralling one at that, the circumstances of her life and death take on a mythical quality in the popular mind. So it has been with Diana, Princess of Wales. Already she has become the stuff of legend. Some conspiracy theorists say she was the victim of a plot by Britain's MI-6 secret service, destined to prevent the embarrassment of her marriage to an Arab Muslim. Others believe Diana was hounded to her death by a rapacious band of paparazzi, ironically falling victim to the very personality cult she had tried so hard to promote when it suited her needs. Still others say the whole thing was the result of the random chain of improvisations and stupidities that put Diana in the back of a car driven at excessive speed by an improperly licensed driver high on a lethal cocktail of booze and antidepressants.

---

*While his father Mohammed styles his name with the "Al" honorific, Dodi did not.

Myths don't interest the hardworking French investigators assigned to the case. Their job is to find the truth in shards of glass, flecks of paint, stacks of depositions, and in the noncommittal physics of trajectory, velocity, and momentum. This book similarly seeks to get at the truth, partly through the same investigative and scientific methods as the French magistrates and detectives, but also by delving into the broader story of how Diana came to be in the car that night with Emad "Dodi" Fayed, sometime Hollywood producer and son of the controversial Egyptian-born tycoon Mohammed Al Fayed.

The more the authors dug into that side of the story, the more they realized that the caricaturish view of Dodi as a superficial playboy, macho womanizer, and cocaine-sniffing deadbeat had missed the essential fact that drew Diana into his arms: an alluring human warmth and fragility rooted in a childhood filled with vast material wealth but also much loneliness and melancholy.

And behind Dodi stood Mohammed Al Fayed, the larger-than-life father who deeply loved his son but had often neglected him as a child and dominated him as an adult. Mohammed wanted the best for his son, and actively encouraged his budding romance with Diana. Did he cynically play the matchmaker, as many critics charged, in order to wreak his revenge on the British Establishment that had snubbed him? Or did he merely promote his son's pursuit of happiness at the side of a young woman with whom he had maintained an avuncular relationship and whose late father had counted among his friends?

All those questions mesh with the grittier police-blotter aspects of the case to produce an investigation, in the broadest sense of the term, into the circumstances that led to the death of a princess in the Alma tunnel. Working in parallel— with Sancton reporting the French side and MacLeod focusing on the Fayed aspects—the authors have sought to weave their findings into a single, coherent work.

Both authors had been following the case virtually nonstop since 1:30 A.M. on August 31, when MacLeod, who lives only blocks away from the accident site, arrived on the scene with a notebook and a pair of binoculars. Sancton, woken up at 2:00 A.M. by a call from *Time*'s newsdesk in New York, worked the phones from his suburban Paris home. The results of that reporting went into the crash cover story that the magazine's far-flung staff produced in a mere twelve hours for an edition that hit the streets on Monday, September 1.

Over the next few weeks, the authors teamed up on several major follow-up stories in *Time,* then embarked on this independent book project in early October. The authors consulted thousands of pages of documents, books, and press stories, and interviewed scores of witnesses, lawyers, medical experts, automotive engineers, investigators, and associates of Dodi and Diana in Britain, France, Egypt, and the U.S. It is thus hoped that the book you are holding in your hands is the most authoritative account to date of the events surrounding the tragedy.

As far as possible, we have identified our sources directly in the text, using footnotes to amplify on certain points or add explanatory information. Inevitably, on a story like this one, many people requested anonymity and have therefore not been named. A number of eyewitnesses who gave their accounts to investigators are identified only by their first names and last initial. Despite a conscientious effort to contact all these witnesses directly, only a relatively small number accepted to be interviewed and quoted by name.

French medical sources presented a special problem: it is against French law, and rigorously prohibited by the Ordre des Médecins, the powerful professional association, for any physician to discuss details of doctor-patient relationships—even where the patient is not his own. As a result, it was impossible to find a single French doctor who would accept to go on the record discussing any aspect of Diana's treatment, or even to discuss in general terms the nature of the internal injuries that ultimately killed her. So strict is the gag rule on publishing medical details that the Ordre des Médecins even sent a stern letter of reprimand to the director of Pitié-Salpêtrière hospital for issuing a terse, five-sentence communiqué on Diana's cause of death!

Several French doctors were extremely helpful in elucidating these matters, and the details of French emergency medical procedures, but would only do so under the cloak of anonymity for fear of legal and professional sanctions. For this reason, the only medical experts who would go on the record were American physicians, whose information, combined with the anonymous French medical input, led to some stunning conclusions about Diana's treatment and raised the explosive question of whether her life could have been saved.

The book's medical findings may be shocking to many readers, and can be expected to unleash heated polemics in France. It was not the authors' purpose to open a finger-pointing debate or attack the excellent French medical system. Lest any French medical professional take umbrage at our conclusions, and suspect they are motivated by some nationalistic crusade against procedures that differ from standard American practice, it must be stressed here that such was not the authors' intention. If no French voices were willing to speak up in defense of French emergency medicine, it is not the fault of the journalists who wrote this book and made every conscientious effort to include those voices.

A few practical words are in order about the presentation of measurements, currencies, and hours. In many cases, measures have been converted from the metric system to the English system for the benefit of English-language readers. This has not been done in the case of precise scientific or technical measurements, but the reader who is so inclined can easily make the conversions himself (1 km. = 0.62 miles; 1 m. = 39.37 in.; 1 cm. = 0.39 in.; 1 kg. = 2.2 lb.; 1 g. = 0.035 oz.; 1 liter = 1.057 quarts; 1 cl. = 0.338 fl. oz.; 1 metric ton = 1.1 U.S./U.K. tons, etc.). Monetary amounts have been given variously in dollars, pounds sterling, and French francs, using the rough conversion rate of $1 = £0.62 = FF 5.5. Times have mostly been given using the French hour, which is one hour ahead of British standard time and, during the summer season when the accident took place, two hours ahead of Greenwich Mean Time.

In addition to the sources named (and unnamed) in the text, the authors wish to extend their thanks to the many people who contributed in various ways to make this project possible. Thanks first of all to Time Inc. Editor-in-Chief Norman Pearlstine, *Time* Managing Editor Walter Isaacson, and Deputy Managing Editor James Kelly for their encouragement and for granting us the time to undertake this book.

Particular thanks are owed to our research assistants in France, Elizabeth Angell and Elisa Dethomas, whose hard work in helping report and fact-check was invaluable. We were greatly helped by the efforts of Patricia Strathern in Paris, who pitched in with reporting on the photo industry and typed more than a hundred pages of interview transcripts, and Amany Radwan in Cairo, who provided insights and reporting on the Al Fayed family background in Egypt as well as on the conspiracy theories prevalent in the Middle East. Editorial Assistant Claire Senard of the *Time* Paris bureau encouraged and supported the project from the outset. Thanks also to the London staff of Harrods for the courtesy and professionalism with which they responded to our requests for information.

Valuable assistance was offered by French colleagues, especially Nathalie Prévost of the *Journal du Dimanche*, who provided reporting on the investigation. Thanks also to Gilles Delafon of the *Journal du Dimanche* for his helpful suggestions, tips, and contacts, as well as to Frédéric Helbert of Europe 1 radio and British journalist Deirdre Mooney in Cannes. Sylvaine Sancton and Susan Hack read the entire manuscript and made suggestions for improving it.

In addition to those who helped us directly, we should salute our colleagues in the French, British, and American press whose articles provided a wealth of information. In particular, we would cite the excellent articles in the *Journal du Dimanche, Le Monde, Libération, Le Figaro, L'Express,*

Le Point, Le Nouvel Observateur; The Sunday Times, The Times, The Guardian; The New York Times, The Washington Post, The International Herald Tribune, Newsweek, People, and *Vanity Fair.* We should also mention the excellent television specials on the accident, including those that appeared on the BBC's *Panorama,* CNN's *Impact,* ABC's *20/20,* and TF1's *Droit de Savoir.*

Finally, thanks to our agent, Andrew Wylie, whose original faith in this project made it happen.

—THOMAS SANCTON AND SCOTT MACLEOD
Paris, Christmas 1997

DEATH OF A PRINCESS

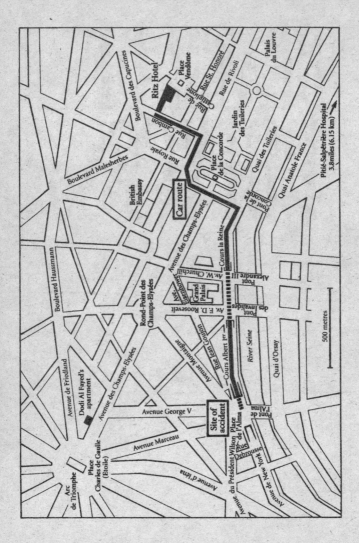

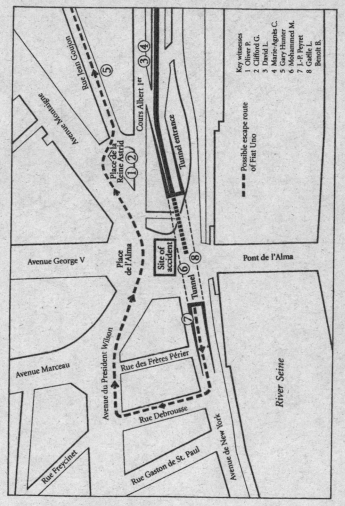

Rue Jean Goujon

Avenue Montaigne

Cours Albert 1er

Place de la Reine Astrid

Tunnel entrance

Avenue George V

Place de l'Alma

Site of accident

Pont de l'Alma

Tunnel

Avenue Marceau

Avenue du Président Wilson

Rue des Frères Périer

Rue Debrousse

Rue Gaston de St. Paul

Avenue de New York

Rue Freycinet

River Seine

Key witnesses
1 Oliver P.
2 Clifford G.
3 David L.
4 Marie-Agnès C.
5 Gary Hunter
6 Mohammed M.
7 J.-P. Peyret
8 Gaëlle L.
9 Benoît B.

- - - Possible escape route
of Fiat Uno

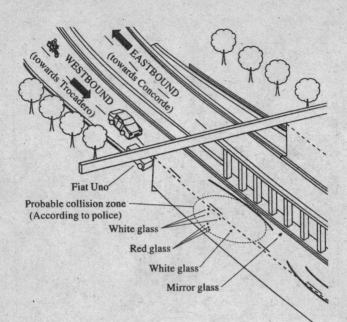

WESTBOUND (towards Trocadero)

EASTBOUND (towards Concorde)

Fiat Uno

Probable collision zone (According to police)

White glass

Red glass

White glass

Mirror glass

THE DEATH SCENE

12:25 A.M. 31 August 1997: The Mercedes S280, driven by Henri Paul and bearing Princess Diana, Dodi Fayed, and their bodyguard, collides with a Fiat Uno near the entrance to the Alma Tunnel, showering debris on the roadway. After the glancing blow against the Fiat's left-rear fender, the Mercedes swerves around it, leaving a single 19-meter skidmark, then heads back towards the center of the road. Finding the right lane blocked, Paul jerks the steering wheel to the left and hits the brakes, causing a fatal 32-meter skid into the 13th support pillar. The Mercedes spins around 180 degrees and comes to rest against the north wall of the tunnel. Witnesses Gaëlle L. and Benoît B. (Renault 5), Grigori R. (VW Passat) and Mohammed M. and Souad M. (Citroën BX) later gave key testimony. The Fiat mysteriously disappeared from the scene.

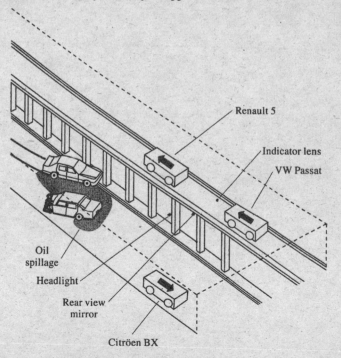

Renault 5

Indicator lens

VW Passat

Oil spillage

Headlight

Rear view mirror

Citröen BX

Authors' Introduction to the Revised Edition

A YEAR AFTER PRINCESS DIANA'S DEATH, SHE REMAINS A PO-
tent image in the popular consciousness. Her hauntingly
beautiful face still peers out from book jackets, magazine
covers, and television screens. The tragedy became the most
widely reported news event in history, generating more columns of print than the entire journalistic output on World
War II, and more hours of broadcast time than any single
story since the invention of television. Diana's sad saga will
forever be an emblem of our tumultuous *fin de siècle*.

The French investigation into the auto crash on August 31,
1997 that took the life of Diana, her lover Dodi Fayed and
driver Henri Paul, will probably not be wrapped up until late
1998 or even 1999. Legal claims in the case will continue
well afterwards. No official findings are likely to end the
widespread speculation—much of it far-fetched and ill-in-
formed—about the true causes of the tragedy. But as the
reader of this book will discover, there is little evidence to
support the idea that Diana's death was anything but an accident. Barring surprising new evidence, the investigators
will almost certainly conclude that a drunk driver, excessive
speed and a dangerous stretch of road are sufficient to explain
why the black Mercedes crashed into the 13th pillar of the
Alma tunnel. The authors of this book fully share that conclusion. Yet there remain a number of questions—first and
foremost, who was driving that mysterious "second car",

and why didn't he stop?—that may make it impossible to rule out other factors categorically.

Since the first edition of *Death of a Princess* went to press in January 1998, investigators have made no progress in identifying the white Fiat Uno believed to have collided with the Mercedes near the tunnel entrance. Nor have they made any breakthrough discoveries to explain the exact circumstances surrounding the crash, despite some tantalizing new leads.

On February 2, for example, Britain's *Mirror* published photos of a white Citroën AX, roughly the same size and shape as a Fiat Uno, speeding away from the entrance to the Ritz Hotel shortly after Diana and Dodi departed from a rear exit. But after studying the images, taken from the vacation video of a visiting Australian couple, investigators concluded that the Citroën was following two decoy cars and could not possibly have wound up in front of the Mercedes at the moment of the accident.

At about the same time, sources in the French justice ministry leaked word to the press that they had found more than 1 million francs ($180,000) in the bank account of driver Henri Paul, who had made cash deposits totaling tens of thousands of francs just prior to his death. The presence of such sums in the account of a man whose salary from the Ritz Hotel was only about $40,000 a year prompted the conspiracy-minded to speculate that Paul might have been paid off to crash the car in a suicide mission and leave the money to his parents. Investigators later concluded, however, that the money was the accumulation of a lifetime of saving by a frugal bachelor who frequently received large cash tips from wealthy Ritz clients.

On February 4, the French daily *Le Parisien* published an article claiming that the Mercedes' airbags may have inflated prematurely, causing Paul to lose control of the car. But investigators denied reports that they were re-examining this possibility after initial inspections of the car indicated the airbags had functioned normally.

In mid-February, private investigators hired by Dodi's father Mohammed Al Fayed, owner of the Ritz and the world-famous Harrods department store, alerted French police to the existence of a white Fiat Uno that had recently been repainted and resold. Fayed lawyers claimed that the car's previous owner was a French journalist who had photographed Diana in the past. French investigators examined the car in a garage near Tours, some 120 miles southwest of Paris, but found that its white paint did not match samples from the crash site.

In April, Austrian police arrested a man who was trying to sell Mohammed Al Fayed documents purporting to prove that British intelligence murdered Diana with the help of the CIA. The man, an Austrian-born U.S. citizen named Oswald Lewinter, alias George Mearah, 67, had demanded $15 million for the documents. Fayed's security chief John MacNamara contacted Austrian authorities, the FBI and the CIA, and enticed Lewinter to a rendezvous at the Ambassador Hotel in Vienna. There Austrian police arrested him on fraud and forgery charges and seized his papers. The incident prompted the CIA to take the highly unusual step of issuing a statement denying any involvement in Princess Diana's death.

Though his documents appear to have been fakes, Lewinter was correct in thinking Fayed might be in the market for evidence of a plot. When Fayed met the authors of this book in December 1997, for his first interview since the tragedy, he made it clear that he did not believe Diana and Dodi died by accident and hinted that his enemies in the British establishment might be behind the crash. Fayed later made a more explicit accusation in an emotional interview that ran in the London *Mirror* on February 12. "I believe in my heart, 99.9 percent, that it was not an accident," he said. "There was a conspiracy and I will not rest until I have established exactly what happened. I will find the person who caused this accident. I believe there were people who did not want Dodi and Diana together."

Fayed's sensational claims, for which he offered no proof, triggered fresh attacks from a British press that had long treated him as a pariah. A rival tabloid, the *Sun*, led the scathing reaction, denouncing the interview as "claptrap" and "crackpot speculation." Wrote royal correspondent and Diana friend Richard Kay in the *Daily Mail*: "Has he no idea how this hurts the boys?" The *Daily Telegraph* accused Fayed of using conspiracy theories to "escalate his war against the British Establishment and to embarrass members of the Royal Family." Buckingham Palace itself weighed in, with a spokesman complaining that such speculation was "causing a lot of stress to the family."

The following month, the *Mirror* produced another scoop in the form of an exclusive interview with Trevor Rees-Jones, Dodi's bodyguard and the only survivor of the accident. After suffering from trauma-induced amnesia, Rees-Jones now claimed that sessions with psychiatrists had partially revived his memory of the moments following the impact. "I have flashes of a female voice calling out in the back of the car," he said. "First it's a groan. Then Dodi's name is called. It could only have been Princess Diana. I was conscious and so was she." The claim that Diana was awake and speaking after the crash added credence to the idea (advanced in this book, and elsewhere) that the Princess might possibly have been saved had she been taken to a hospital sooner. It also appeared to give some backing to Fayed's claim, widely disbelieved, that a nurse had reported Diana's "final words" to him at the Paris hospital where she died.

Meanwhile, back in Paris, Judge Hervé Stephan, the French magistrate who is heading the crash probe, decided it would be better to hear Rees-Jones' new revelations in person than to read them in the British tabloids. The bodyguard was summoned to the Palais de Justice on March 6 for what would be his fourth interrogation in the case. But in spite of his new "flashes" concerning the post-accident phase, the bodyguard's memory of the critical moments preceding the crackup had still not returned, and his testimony added nothing of substance that could help explain the causes. On April 20, explaining that he needed to "move forward" with his life, Rees-Jones announced that he was leaving Fayed's employ.

Mohammed Al Fayed flew to Paris on March 12 for his first face-to-face meeting with Stephan. Fayed, a civil plaintiff in the investigation, asked the judge to carry out "complementary investigations" into the role of the Fiat Uno—a question that was already at the very center of the probe. Stephan, for his part, was reportedly displeased by Fayed's conspiracy claims and by the parallel investigation he was conducting. The two-hour meeting apparently cleared the air. When he emerged from the session, looking dapper in a double-breasted plaid suit, Fayed beamed at reporters from the courthouse steps while his lawyer Georges Klejman voiced his "confidence and his thanks for the work done to date." As for the plot theories that Fayed had so conspicuously broadcast in the *Mirror*, Klejman said simply, "Nothing has been ruled out. Nothing has been established."

The possibility that the Ritz might bear some liability for the accident was hardly the only legal problem Fayed had to worry about. On March 2 he was arrested and released on bail, but not formally charged, in connection with his long-running feud with his archrival R.W. "Tiny" Rowland. The flamboyant British tycoon, whom Mohammed had defeated in winning control of Harrods in 1985, filed court papers in December claiming Fayed had ordered his staff to break into a safe-deposit box that Rowland kept at the department store. According to an exclusive account in *The Times* of London, the court papers claim that Fayed was seeking documents that might help him clear his name, which had been badly tarnished by Rowland's allegations during the battle to control Harrods. Rowland's allegations about Fayed's murky business dealings and misrepresenting his past possibly had been a major factor in the government's longstanding refusal to grant Fayed British citizenship.

A Harrods spokesman said Al Fayed had voluntarily gone to talk to the police, categorically denied the "false and malicious" allegations, and hoped to "bring this matter to a speedy conclusion." Nonetheless, the timing could not have been worse for the Egyptian: in December, 1997, Home Secretary Jack Straw had announced that the government was reconsidering Fayed's citizenship application. The latest legal tussle, and the uproar over his conspiracy claims, were not likely to weigh in Fayed's favor.

In the often bizarre aftermath of Diana's death, controversy was hardly limited to the house of Fayed. Charles, the ninth Earl Spencer, who had pilloried the media in his emotional eulogy for his sister, found himself the target of repeated press attacks over everything from his messy South African divorce to his plans to sell tickets to Diana's gravesite, organize a memorial rock concert and turn his ancestral Althorp House into what critics scornfully dubbed "Dianaland." In the sleepy little town of Great Barington, where Althorp is located, residents feared that their peace would be shattered by busloads of tourists lining up to gawk at Diana's island resting place (from across a lake), trek through a Diana museum (built in a converted 200-year-old stable), and buy Diana memorabilia at the Althorp gift shop. Harold Brooks-Baker, the publisher of *Burke's Peerage*, called on Spencer to explain how he intended to spend the roughly $1.5 million raised from the sale of 152,000 tickets to the estate for the July 1 to August 30 visits. Spencer has promised a full accounting.

The Diana memorial fund, of which the Princess' sister, Lady Sarah McCorquodale, is a trustee, was criticized for putting its imprimatur on products ranging from scratch-off lottery cards and tubs of margarine to garish purple teddy bears. (Other products awaiting official approval include an "England Rose" lager beer, a Barbie-doll-style effigy of the Princess and a new line of dog food!) The fund also came under fire when it was reported that a law firm connected to one of the trustees had billed the organization more than $800,000 in legal fees.

By the end of this year, the Diana fund is expected to have raised some $160 million for worthy causes ranging from AIDS and cancer research, to the homeless, the ballet and the anti-landmine campaign. But Earl Spencer and his mother Frances Shand Kydd issued a public statement in April calling for the fund's activities to be phased out. Prince William, 15, heir to the throne, was reported by the *Sunday Times* to be upset over the "commercial exploitation" of his mother's death. Even Diana's buddy Elton John, whose "Candle in the Wind 1997" became the biggest-selling single in history and has earned more than $30 million for the fund, complained that it was time to give all the Diana commemorations "a rest."

The backlash was not confined to emotional expressions from Diana's supporters. Many in Britain who witnessed the near-hysterical outpouring of grief following her death wondered if the country had not gone a bit over the top. In April the Social Affairs Unit, a conservative British think tank, published a book called *Faking it: The Sentimentalisation of Modern Society,* "Today's Britain is not 'modern,' let alone 'cool.' It is a fake society with fake institutions," it declared. "The society's defining moment was Princess Diana's funeral, in which sentimentality—mob grief—was personified and canonized, the elevation of feelings above reason, reality and restraint." In a vitriolic chapter entitled "Diana, Queen of Hearts," Professor Anthony O'Hear wrote: "In the Diana story, duty is a notion which is entirely absent. Nor in the version according to Diana and the tabloids are we even to entertain the thought that Diana's obsession with her own feelings and her self-development might have done damage to the monarchy, to her marriage, to her children and ultimately to herself."

Naturally, Diana's admirers sprang to her defense. "The idea," said Tony Blair, "that because we express our emotion, in a way frankly that was felt all around the world, about Princess Diana, the notion that . . . this is un-British, I just regard that as absurd." In an attempt to put the Princess back on her pedestal, Lord St. John of Fawsley, a former Conservative minister, called her "one of the great figures of our time. Her appeal lay precisely in that she elevated feeling to the highest position. That's why people responded to her—they know she really cared."

It is for historians, and ultimately the British people, to

pass judgment on the meaning of Diana's short life and untimely death. The aim of this book is to provide as much factual information as possible about the circumstances immediately surrounding her death, the events that led up to it, and the people who shared the stage with the Princess in this modern-day, real-life tragedy.

1

No Escape

"DO YOU HAVE A MERCEDES FOR A DISCREET DEPARTURE?"

Jean-François Musa was taken aback. His Etoile Limousine company keeps a fleet of six luxury cars at the Ritz hotel for the exclusive use of its clients. This was an unexpected request, but he had to take it seriously: it came from one of the hotel's most senior officials, Claude Roulet, assistant to Ritz president Frank J. Klein.

The purpose of the Mercedes was to allow Diana, Princess of Wales, and her boyfriend Emad "Dodi" Fayed, son of Egyptian tycoon and Ritz owner Mohammed Al Fayed, to leave from the back of the hotel without being seen by the hordes of paparazzi who had been stalking them all afternoon and were now jamming the main entrance along with a hundred gawkers and curiosity seekers.

Musa had spent much of the day driving Fayed's Range Rover as a security backup while Dodi's regular chauffeur, Philippe Dourneau, drove the couple around Paris at the wheel of a black Mercedes 600. Those two vehicles were now parked in front of the hotel's main entrance on the Place Vendôme, where Musa and Dourneau stood waiting for the couple to finish their dinner. Musa was expecting Dodi and Diana to leave in the same two-vehicle convoy.

But orders were orders. Musa went to the key closet located to the right of the main entrance and opened the mirror-covered door. Rummaging through the brown envelopes inside, he found the key to the only extra vehicle he had available: a black Mercedes S280, license number 688 LTV 75. It was a lighter, less powerful car without tinted windows—not ideal for fending off paparazzi—but it would have to do.

There was just one hitch: at that hour, close to midnight on Saturday, August 31, he had no chauffeurs on duty. The car was registered as a *grande remise* vehicle, meaning that it could only be driven by a licensed chauffeur. Musa therefore offered to drive the S280 himself since he possessed the required permit. He was told that wouldn't be necessary.*

Alexander "Kes" Wingfield, one of Fayed's two bodyguards, came out of the revolving door and surveyed the crowd from the colonnaded portico. There were at least 30 photographers standing with cameras at the ready, including some particularly aggressive types who had scuffled with security guards earlier in the day.

Wingfield hailed Musa at the curbside and explained the plan. "You and Philippe are going to create a diversion," he said. "Rev the engines up, turn on the lights, and pretend to be preparing a departure with the Mercedes and the Range Rover. Meanwhile, Dodi and the Princess will leave from the rear with Trevor." Trevor Rees-Jones, the second bodyguard, had remained inside the hotel with the couple.

"Who's going to drive?" Musa asked.

"Henri," said Wingfield.

Musa knew Henri Paul well. As the assistant head of security for the Ritz, Paul had frequent dealings with Musa concerning the comings and goings of the hotel's well-heeled customers. But, as Musa later said, "It was not customary for M. Paul to drive vehicles for his clients." Nor did he possess the license required for that job. Moreover, something did not seem quite normal about Paul that night. As Musa put it, "He seemed chattier than usual."

---

*This is based on Musa's account to investigators. Roulet later told police that he was unaware of the circumstances leading to the change of chauffeur and the rental of the second Mercedes.

More than chatty. Paul was strutting around in front of the hotel, uncharacteristically grinning and gesturing to the photographers, treating them with irony and feigned complicity. As the departure time approached, he emerged to tell the journalists, "Ten more minutes," then, "five minutes." Some of the paparazzi, used to being handled by Paul with cold disdain, found his behavior frankly "bizarre."

Not all of the journalists were in the Place Vendôme. A handful, suspecting a possible rear exit, were waiting on the sidewalk of the Rue Cambon behind the hotel. One such was the Sygma agency's Jacques Langevin. A veteran war photographer who had won prizes for his photos of the tanks in Tiananmen Square, Langevin, 44, found himself saddled with this unlikely assignment simply because he was the agency's weekend duty man. His editors had called him away from a dinner party after receiving a tip from their correspondent in London.

"I didn't personally know Henri Paul," he says, "but some colleagues who did told me, 'He's not in his normal state. He's been drinking.' He seemed euphoric. He was teasing us, grinning and acting the smart alec." According to some of the photographers, Paul had taunted them by saying, "You won't catch us tonight. Don't even try."

It was a pleasant summer night, clear and 77 degrees, and the journalists waited patiently for the couple to make their move. Langevin recounts that he had parked his metallic gray VW Golf in the Rue Cambon and stood vigil behind the hotel along with several other journalists. Among them were Serge Benhamou, 44, Fabrice Chassery, 30, and Alain Guizard, 30, a writer from the Angeli agency.

"We were standing on a sidewalk in the Rue Cambon," says Langevin, "a bit up the street because repair work was blocking the area just in front of the exit. Henri Paul came out and waved at me. He strutted around like a star. It was not necessarily a drunkard's behavior, he was just hamming it up."

Inside the hotel, Dodi and Diana were just making their way down the long, richly carpeted corridor from the second floor Imperial Suite, where they had dined, to the rear staircase. When the couple arrived at the back service exit, located at 36 Rue Cambon, they waited a few moments while Paul and Dodi discussed the final details of the plan.

At 12:19, a Ritz employee drove the Mercedes S280 up to the door. "Henri Paul came out," says Langevin, "then another guy came out and made us a thumbs-up sign as if to say, 'They're coming.' Then a bodyguard [Rees-Jones] emerged. Diana came out before Dodi and entered the car first. I took several pictures of her, then a few of the car from three meters away with a telephoto lens. The car pulled away rapidly."

According to the Ritz security cameras, the time was precisely 12:20. Langevin did not give chase. His car was parked 30 meters away, and he decided to call it a night. But others were determined not to let their prey escape so easily.

Benhamou started up his green Honda Lada scooter and followed the Mercedes as it headed down the Rue Cambon towards the Rue de Rivoli and turned right. Alerted to the departure via their portable phones, other photographers in front of the hotel began to scramble for their vehicles. Romuald Rat, 24, of the Gamma Agency hopped on his Honda NTV 650 behind his driver, Stéphane Darmon, 32, roared down the Rue de Castiglione one block to the Rue de Rivoli, and made the obligatory right turn.

They caught up with the Mercedes in the Place de la Concorde, a vast open expanse whose central Egyptian obelisk, brilliantly lit at night, is one of Paris' best-known landmarks. The limousine had stopped for a red light at the corner of the Rue Royale, near the Hotel Crillon. Rat and Darmon were not alone. Serge Arnal, 35, from the Stills agency, was at the wheel of his black Fiat Uno; at his side sat the Angeli agency's Christian Martinez, 41, one of the toughest and most dogged paparazzi in the business. Benhamou was just behind the Mercedes' left fender, revving his Honda and waiting for the light to change. Other vehicles had also joined the convoy.

According to one of the pursuers, Paul took off just before

the light changed, catching the photographers off guard. He passed up the Champs-Elysées, the most direct route back to Dodi's apartment near the Arc de Triomphe, and headed towards the westbound riverfront express road known at that point as the Cours la Reine. Without stopping, he swung onto the expressway and floored the accelerator.

"The car was going faster and faster," says one of the photographers following the Mercedes on a motor scooter. "We said to ourselves the driver was going really too fast. We couldn't follow him anymore. One thing is clear: it was not normal the way he was driving. I never saw anyone take off like that. He drove like a gangster. Unbelievable!" Gamma motorcycle driver Darmon, himself no stranger to quick accelerations, described Paul's takeoff as "almost supersonic."

The Mercedes steadily picked up speed on the 1.2 kilometer straightaway leading to the Alma tunnel. The photographers claim that they were left far behind the car, at a distance of at least 200 meters. Other witnesses, however, described seeing motorcycles much closer. Brian Anderson, a California businessman, told CBS News that he was riding in a taxi along the express road when he was passed by a black Mercedes closely tailed by two motorcycles. The first one, mounted by two people, seemed headed "in a direction to get in front of the car," said Anderson. "I felt that the one motorcycle, certainly without hesitation and any doubt whatsoever, was driving aggressively and dangerously."

Other witnesses later interviewed by police also spoke of motorcycles tagging close behind—and of the dangerous speed of the Mercedes. Thierry H., 49, a Paris-based engineering consultant, reported that he had been driving in the right lane of the express road near the Alexander III bridge, some 800 meters before the Alma tunnel, when he was "passed by a vehicle moving at a very high speed. I estimate its speed at about seventy-five mph to eighty mph [the speed limit at that point is 30 mph]. It was a powerful black car, I think a Mercedes . . . This car was clearly being pursued by several motorcycles, I would say four to six of them. Some were mounted by two riders. These motorcycles were tailing the vehicle and some tried to pull up alongside it.''

Clifford G., a 34-year-old professional chauffeur, was catching a breath of fresh air on the Place de la Reine Astrid, a grassy triangle near the tunnel entrance. His attention was drawn to the express road by the loud whine of an automobile engine. He immediately identified a Mercedes heading towards the tunnel at an estimated speed of more than 60 mph. ''I also saw a big motorcycle pass. I can't tell you how many people were on it . . . The motorcycle was going fast. I would put the motorcycle at thirty or forty meters behind the Mercedes.''

These witnesses lost sight of the Mercedes when it entered the tunnel but heard the horrific crash that followed.

The driver and passenger of a car coming in the opposite, eastbound direction saw the final instants from close range. ''As we entered the Alma tunnel,'' said the passenger, Gaëlle L., 40, a production assistant, ''we heard a loud noise of screeching tires . . . At that moment, in the opposite lane, we saw a large car approaching at high speed. This car swerved to the left, then went back to the right and crashed into the wall with its horn blaring. I should note that in front of this car, there was another, smaller car. I think this vehicle was black, but I'm not sure. Behind the big car there was a large motorcycle. I can't be sure how many riders were on it.''

The Mercedes had apparently lurched to the left to avoid hitting a slow-moving car in front of it. The limousine grazed the curb of the central walkway and nicked the third support pillar, swerved back to the right, then lost control and skidded head-on into the 13th pillar. The violence of the crash left a rectangular cookie-cutter imprint of the post in the car's front end, showered the pillar with motor oil, and sent debris flying into the opposite lane. The car then rebounded, spun around 180 degrees, and crashed into the right-hand wall. The time was 12:25.

The Mercedes had been transformed in a millisecond from a sleek luxury sedan into a tangled hulk of gnarled metal. Paul was killed instantly, his spinal cord severed and his chest crushed by the steering wheel. The pressure of his inert body set off the horn, producing an ear-splitting wail. Clouds of grayish smoke, apparently caused by motor oil spilling onto the hot engine, filled the tunnel.

Some of the cars in the opposite lane pulled over and stopped. Occupants leapt out and stared at the horrific scene. Gaëlle and her boyfriend Benoît B., 27, parked just outside the tunnel and ran to the westbound lane to flag down oncoming vehicles. From the driver of one car, Gaëlle borrowed a cell phone and called the *sapeurs-pompiers,** the fire department's specialized emergency squad. According to their logs, the call came through at precisely 12:26.

At virtually the same instant, a 32-year-old man called the civilian rescue unit, known as the SAMU,† on a portable phone. Speaking on condition of anonymity, he said in an interview that he heard the accident from the apartment he was staying in, just 50 yards from the tunnel entrance. "I heard screeching tires followed by three shocks," he recounted. "I looked out the window and saw a commotion around the tunnel, so I ran down to see what was happening. I was there within a minute of the accident."

Entering the tunnel on foot, he advanced to within a couple of yards of the Mercedes. "The guy in the front passenger seat [Rees-Jones] was badly injured but conscious," he says. "The lower half of his face was ripped off and hanging loose; it was hard to look at. I told him not to panic, help was on the way. He looked at me and struggled but could say nothing. The driver didn't move. The man in the backseat

---

*The sapeurs-pompiers, under military authority, are a firemen's unit specially trained and equipped to deal with automobile accidents, explosions, bombings, and other emergencies. Among other things, they operate ambulances manned by medical teams specialized in on-site resuscitation. On the night of the accident, three *sapeurs-pompiers* units (Courbevoie, Malard, and Champerret) were present in the Alma tunnel.

†The service d'aide médicale urgente [SAMU] is a civilian emergency service that is directly attached to the state-run hospital system. It operates a 24-hour-a-day network consisting of mobile hospital units (ambulances fully equipped for intensive on-site care) manned by doctors specialized in emergency medicine. Each SAMU center is backed up by SMUR [service médical d'urgence et de réanimation] units with resuscitation ambulances and other support vehicles.

was also lying still, his legs obviously broken." This witness did not see Diana, who was slumped on the floor behind a closed door. When two people tried to open the door, he shouted, "Don't do that! If you move the bodies you can kill them!"

Malo France, a taxi driver from Bénin, passed through the eastbound lane of the tunnel with his customers moments after the accident and stopped briefly to gaze on the devastation. "It was horrible," he said, "the worst accident I have ever seen. I made the sign of the cross over my heart. I thought, God save them, and God protect us from these types of accidents. In the front seat there was a man. I also saw a woman with blond hair. She was crying, very loudly. There were two different voices, one a man and one a woman."

The photographers had arrived within seconds of the accident. The first on the scene were Rat and his driver Darmon. Rat later told police that they had lost sight of the Mercedes after it went through the first tunnel, under the Alexander III bridge, and had given up the chase. They continued along the express road in order to return to their photo agency, said Rat, and happened upon the wrecked car. Witnesses reported seeing a motorcycle with two riders much closer to the Mercedes, but nothing proves they were Rat and Darmon. Yet even if they were more than 300 meters behind the Mercedes, as they claim, Rat and Darmon would have gotten to the Alma tunnel within 10 to 30 seconds after the crash at the speed they were traveling.

They were followed almost immediately by Arnal and Martinez in Arnal's black Fiat Uno and Benhamou on his Honda Lada scooter. Next came the Sola agency's Fabrice Chassery in his anthracite gray Peugeot 205 and his colleague David Oderkerken, 26, in his beige Mitsubishi Pajero 4×4. Among the stragglers were Langevin, the Sipa agency's Nikola Arsov, 38, and independent photographer Laszlo Veres, 50, who was called by Benhamou. Police have determined that several still unidentified photographers were also on the scene.

Darmon drove slowly past the smoking, wailing vehicle and parked his Honda 20 meters down the road. "I jumped off the motorcycle and ran towards the car," said Rat. "At that time, I thought they were all dead. I was shocked. For several seconds I stayed back from the car. After a moment, I got ahold of myself and went to the car to open the door, because I wanted to see what I could do to try to help them. I saw that for the chauffeur and M. Fayed, they were obviously dead, and I could do nothing. So I leaned over the Princess to see if she was alive . . . I tried to take her pulse and when I touched her, she moved and breathed. So I spoke to her in English, saying, 'I'm here, be cool, a doctor will arrive.' "

Shortly before the crash, decoy drivers Musa and Dourneau received word from a Ritz staffer that the couple had left from the Rue Cambon. That was their cue. Musa took off in the Range Rover with Wingfield at his side and Dourneau following close behind in the Mercedes 600. But the diversion was a flop. Most of the paparazzi had already caught on to the couple's rear exit and headed after them. Only a handful of photographers, including Arsov and Pierre Suu, followed the decoy vehicles as they headed down the Rue de Rivoli, through the Place de la Concorde, and turned onto the Champs-Elysées.

The convoy's destination, like that of Dodi and Diana, was 1 Rue Arsène-Houssaye, near the Arc de Triomphe, where Fayed had a ten-room apartment with a spectacular view of the Champs-Elysées. To avoid the usual Saturday night traffic jam along that famous thoroughfare, Musa and Dourneau turned left on the Avenue Churchill and headed for the express road along the Seine. They had thus rejoined Henri Paul's itinerary without realizing it.

As they approached the Place de l'Alma, they noticed people running out of the tunnel and making signs to stop. So they exited before the tunnel and headed up the Avenue Marceau in the direction of the Arc de Triomphe. Suddenly Dourneau got a call on his cell phone. It was Dodi's butler,

René, asking if he had time to walk the dogs before the couple arrived at the apartment. Dourneau was surprised. "They're not there yet?"

"Aren't they with you?" asked René.

"Negative," said the chauffeur. "I'm driving a decoy car." Wingfield thought Dodi had perhaps changed plans again, so he tried to beep Rees-Jones. No answer.

"When we got to the apartment," said Dourneau, "we saw that there was no one there yet, so we waited. There were several paparazzi. Then suddenly one of them received a call on his portable phone. He turned white. François [Musa] and I realized that he had just learned some terrible news. We had to insist before he told us that Dodi had just had an accident under the Alma bridge. François and I drove there immediately in the Range Rover." Wingfield remained at the apartment and phoned his superiors in London at precisely 12:45.

The bodyguard's call was taken by Dave Moody, who had been monitoring the couple's movements from the Park Lane control room, the 24-hour nerve center of Mohammed Al Fayed's 40-strong security force. Moody immediately phoned Paul Handley-Greaves, the man in charge of all close protection operations.

"There's been an accident involving the two principals," Moody told him, using the code names for Dodi and Diana. Handley-Greaves rushed from his home to Park Lane, arriving just in time to get Wingfield's second call. By that time, the bodyguard had spoken to police and received confirmation of the accident, but not of Dodi's death.

Handley-Greaves, 32, a former military police officer in the British army, called Mohammed Al Fayed just after 1:00 A.M. "Sir," he said, "there's been an accident involving your son and the Princess. We're not sure of the extent and have no details on injuries at this point."

Al Fayed, who had been sound asleep at his estate in Oxted, Surrey, reacted with surprising calm. "Okay," he told Handley-Greaves. "Get as much detail as you can and get back to me as quickly as possible."

At about that time, the phone rang in Dodi's apartment. René thought it was his boss calling about a change of plans. It was Dourneau. *"Dodi est mort,"* he said. "Dodi is dead, he's gone."

"What?" stammered the butler. "That's not possible!"

"He's dead. They tried to revive him for twenty minutes, but there's no sign of life. Nothing." Dourneau was calling on his cell phone from the tunnel. His voice choked up as he described the dreadful scene to René. The butler sank into a chair and wept. According to a French official on the scene, Dourneau was "devastated" and kept repeating that he blamed himself for not insisting on driving the couple.

Back at the Place de l'Alma, meanwhile, bedlam reigned. When he heard the crash, Clifford G., the off-duty chauffeur who had been standing near the express road, ran into the tunnel on foot. "As soon as I arrived," he later told investigators, "I noticed four or five men around the wrecked Mercedes taking photos with professional equipment ... None of these men did anything to help the wounded people in the Mercedes. It was obvious that the four occupants were wounded. There was blood, their bodies were sprawled every which way inside the Mercedes. Yet these men photographed the car and the wounded from every angle. Seeing this spectacle, I shouted, 'That's all you can do instead of calling for help?' "

Clifford was not the only witness who was outraged by the conduct of the photographers. Jack Firestone, director of an ad agency in Hewlett Harbor, N.Y., was returning to his hotel in a taxi with his wife and son after some late-night sightseeing. When they saw the wrecked car in the Alma tunnel, they stopped briefly in the eastbound lane. The photographers, Firestone later told the Associated Press, were like "sharks after raw meat." There were "clicking away like mad, running around the car, snapping from every position they could ... It was obvious these paparazzi knew they had struck gold."

A sound engineer who drove through the tunnel eastbound

at about the same time provided investigators with one of the most vivid descriptions of the photographers at work. "After parking my car, I saw photographers leaning into the interior of the car through the back door and taking photos. Before taking pictures, I saw one of the men doing something inside the car. I think he was moving the body of M. Al Fayed or the Princess in order to take better pictures. I approached the Mercedes and distinctly heard a groan. I think it was a man's voice."

At this point, says this witness, about a dozen men entered the tunnel on foot carrying cameras, one of which was a U-matic video camera. (American tourist Michael Walker also described someone filming with a video camera, but investigators never located the cameraman.) There followed a scuffle in which a young man, apparently of North African origin, went after Rat for leaning into the car. "God damn it! Why did you do that?" he demanded. Rat, according to this witness, replied, "We can't do otherwise, we had to do it like that." The youth then charged at Rat and tried to hit him, but the photographer fended him off by twirling his heavy camera on its strap while others moved in to separate the two men.

The photographers also fought among themselves. Rat, deeply shaken by the sight of the wreck, screamed at his colleagues that they must not take any close-up photos of the victims, only of the car. The others obeyed at first, then began to move closer and shout back at Rat. "Go screw yourself!" said one photographer, according to a witness later interviewed by police. "I'm doing my work, too, just like you." Another witness reported hearing one of the photographers tell another: "It's your fault!" The sharpest disputes seem to have been between Rat and Martinez, who has admitted that he took pictures of the inside of the car. Rat took no photos inside the car, and no close-ups of the victims, as his confiscated film would later attest.

Gamma motorcycle driver Darmon stood off at a distance and watched the scene in utter amazement. "The photographers lined up on the right-hand side of the wreck," he later told the *Guardian*. "All the bodies were in the car. The underpass was white with electronic flashes. The cameras were going like machine guns. It was so dazzling that, for a while from my vantage point at the exit of the tunnel, I could not see the Mercedes."

Apart from Arnal, who tried to call for help, and Rat, who claims to have first-aid training and tried to take Diana's pulse, none of the other photographers appears to have done anything to help the victims. Their argument, not unreasonable, is that people without proper training would only make things worse if they touched seriously wounded victims.

That did not stop others from doing what they could. Clifford, the off-duty chauffeur, did his best to help the injured. "I went to the passenger in front, who was trying to move," he told investigators. "His mouth and tongue were ripped off. He had passed through the windshield and was trying to get out. I held up his head and told him not to move, to await help."

Clifford had not noticed the blond woman in the back until he saw her head move behind the bodyguard's seat. "I saw her face, and a voice told me, that's Lady Di," he said. "I understood then who it was. I repeated the same words to this young woman in English. Lady Di tried to speak. She opened her mouth to tell me something but no sound came out. She was bleeding from the forehead and tried to get up."

The first doctor on the scene was Frédéric Mailliez, 36, a physician with the private medical service S.O.S. Médecins. Mailliez and his companion, Mark Butt, 42, a native of Baltimore, were driving home from a birthday party and entered the Alma tunnel via the eastbound lane within a minute of the accident. "I was pretty sure that the car had just crashed because the smoke was still in the tunnel and the horn was still going on," Mailliez said in an interview with CNN's Art Harris and *Time*'s Thomas Sancton. "People were just walking towards the car. I saw the severely damaged car and I saw four people inside. Two were apparently dead and two severely injured."

Mailliez went back to his car, a white Ford Fiesta bearing

a prominent blue S.O.S. Médecins logo, and placed a magnetic beacon light on its roof. On his cell phone, he called the firemen's emergency unit. "There is a severe car crash here at the Pont de l'Alma," he told the dispatcher. "There are two people severely injured. I need two ambulances." Mailliez also requested a specially equipped vehicle, a sort of mobile can-opener, to cut through metal and liberate trapped accident victims. He then grabbed his medical bag and returned to the Mercedes. A volunteer fireman was already attending to Rees-Jones in the front seat, so Mailliez turned to the blond woman in the rear (whose identity he did not learn until he saw it on CNN the next morning).

He found Diana slumped on the floor with her left leg up on the rear seat and her right leg folded under her. She was leaning against the back of Rees-Jones' seat with her back towards the door and her chin tucked against her chest. She was in a position that made it difficult to breathe, says Mailliez, so he carefully raised her head and put an oxygen mask over her face. In an interview published in the *Impact Quotidien*, a daily journal for physicians, he described his actions in these professional terms: "I helped her to breathe with a mask and I attempted to liberate the upper respiratory passage by bending her head back slightly. I sought to unblock the trachea and prevent the tongue from blocking the oropharynx. She seemed to be a bit more agitated, thus more reactive, once she was able to breathe better."

Mailliez said that the woman seemed to be in the best shape of anyone in the car, though it was not apparent to him at the time that she suffered from serious internal hemorrhaging. "At the beginning, from the outside, she looked pretty fine," Mailliez later told CNN's Larry King. "But the internal injury, as you know, was already starting . . . I thought this woman had a chance. I didn't know about this internal problem." Someone behind him said the car's occupants spoke English, so Mailliez asked her a few questions and, as he put it, "tried to make her feel more comfortable."

During all this time, Mailliez reports, photographers continued taking pictures, but they in no way hindered him in his work. Mailliez's companion, Mark Butt, confirmed that the photographers stayed out of the way. "I think people imagined there were twelve or fifteen paparazzi huddled around the car, and it wasn't like that at all," he said. "They were at various distances, some keeping their distance, some going very close. But just at times. They didn't stay close. They weren't just all huddled around."

On the key question of whether Diana spoke to him, Mailliez's numerous interviews give rise to conflicting interpretations. In his August 31 deposition to police, he described the Princess as being "unconscious and moaning." In his interview with the *Impact Quotidien,* he said she was "unconscious . . . agitated and moaning" and that when he spoke to her he "obtained no response." Appearing on CNN's *Larry King Live* show on September 23, Mailliez was asked point-blank: "Did she say anything to you?" Answer: "No." Then on November 22, in a front page interview in the *Times* of London, Mailliez was quoted as saying that the Princess had indeed spoken to him: "She kept saying how much she hurt as I put a resuscitation mask over her mouth."

The following day Mailliez called the Associated Press and complained that he had been misquoted by the *Times*. "I never said she was crying in pain, that she spoke to me of her pain," he told the wire service. "She was semiconscious, muttering but never saying anything precise." But Bill Frost, the *Times* reporter who wrote the story, firmly stands by it. In an interview at his paper's London headquarters, he said that Mailliez not only told him Diana had spoken, but that the doctor had explicitly quoted her as saying "I'm in such pain" and "Oh, God! I can't stand this!"

In any event, there is no doubt that Mailliez played an active and important role in treating Diana during the first critical minutes after the accident. Photos of the scene show the boyish-looking, brown-haired physician, dressed in a white T-shirt and white trousers, leaning far into the car. With his left knee on the backseat, he is seen first cradling Diana's head, then administering oxygen. To his right, a volunteer fireman, dressed in blue jeans and a blue T-shirt, is supporting Rees-Jones' bloody head in his hands.

Other photos show Diana in profile, quite recognizable with her elegantly coifed blond hair. There is blood on her forehead; trails of blood also trickle from her nose, mouth, and left ear. Apart from the blood, her face is not disfigured. In at least one photo she appears to have her eyes open. Dodi's left leg, horribly bent and deformed by multiple fractures, lies on Diana's lap. His jeans are ripped open from the knee to the lower abdomen. Diana's left arm is draped listlessly over his kid-skin boot. In the front, one sees the body of Henri Paul slumped over to the right, his right hand pressed against the wheel, his left arm extending through the shattered windshield. Though the front end of the Mercedes is thoroughly smashed, the back passenger area is intact; the roof is only slightly deformed and the rear end of the car looks in pristine condition, apart from the torn-off muffler lying on the road behind it.

"When I saw Diana in the backseat, I got shivers up my spine," says photographer Nikola Arsov, who had followed the decoy cars and arrived at the scene some time after the accident. "You can't imagine how beautiful she was. It was devastating!" The sight was more than some journalists could bear. Speaking anonymously on German TV, a photographer who fled the scene (possibly Benhamou) later described how disturbing the experience was. "It was true that Diana was still alive," he said, his voice disguised and his face in shadow. "She was moving about . . . she had her head on her breast. Her arms were still moving. But I believe she was not conscious, like she was in shock. It was simply horrible."

Photos of the overall scene show a chaotic situation, with photographers and large numbers of passersby milling randomly around the car. There is glass and debris all over the roadway. Two young men who appear to be Japanese tourists are standing on the central median. One fat, bald man in shorts, sandals, and a striped T-shirt is bending over and gawking into the right rear door at the face of the dying

Princess. Some tourists and curiosity-seekers can be seen snapping pictures with their cameras.

Witness Mark Butt described seeing "people taking photos out of their [car] windows of the accident." One American tourist, Michael Walker of Mansfield, Ohio, who passed through the eastbound lane in a taxi, shot photos that he later offered to sell to Sygma, CNN, and other networks. (CNN and Sygma, finding the photos to be of poor quality, turned him down, but one of his grainy shots was later published by Britain's *Sunday Times*.)

Hailed by passersby while patrolling in the area, the first two policemen reached the scene within five minutes. They seem to have been overwhelmed by the situation and had great difficulty pushing back the feisty photographers. In his initial report on the accident, dated August 31, officer Lino Gagliardone described the situation in these terms:

"We immediately went to the scene and observed a Mercedes, license plate number 688 LTV 75, with a severely damaged front end lying across the roadway facing the opposite direction, as well as a large number of people, mainly photographers, who were shooting pictures of the right rear of the vehicle, whose door was open.

"Officer Sébastien Dorzée rushes to the site, trying to move back some photographers who put up resistance. They are virulent, pushy, and continue to take photos, intentionally preventing him from aiding the victim. One of them declaring, while pushing the officer back, 'You piss me off, let me do my work: in Sarajevo, the cops let us work. You should go get shot at and you'll see what it's like . . .'

"I observe that the occupants of the vehicle are in a very grave state. I immediately repeat the call for aid and request police reinforcements, being unable to contain the photographers and aid the wounded.

"Very rapidly, a BAC 75 [anti-criminality brigade] vehicle arrives to help us push back photographers and passersby . . . The first vehicle of the firemen's emergency unit arrives, begins treating victims, asks officer Dorzée to try to keep the right rear passenger awake by talking to her and tapping on her cheek, and also asks me to hold up the head of the front right passenger. Very quickly reinforcements from the *sapeurs-pompiers* and SAMU arrive to assist the medical units already present.''

Questioned as a witness that night, officer Dorzée gave his own account of the situation. ''There reigned a great confusion,'' he said. ''The journalists were busy taking photos and insulting one another. I even heard one tell another 'It's your fault.' I first tried to push back the journalists from the wrecked car. I found this task difficult because the photographers were very excited ... Finding myself alone in the face of numerous journalists [his partner had left the tunnel to radio for help], I had a great deal of difficulty gaining access to the vehicle. I had to push back repeated assaults by the photographers ... Although these journalists insulted and pushed me, I did not strike any blows. But I want to stress that they were very aggressive towards one another and towards me.

''I finally got to the vehicle,'' he continued, ''and I observed that the driver was dead, trapped against the steering wheel, and that it was the same for the rear passenger on the driver's side. The front passenger was grievously injured. He had a large wound on his face. He did not move, but I could see signs of life in his face. The rear passenger was also alive ... She seemed to be in better shape. However, blood flowed from her mouth and nose. There was a deep gash on her forehead. She murmured in English, but I didn't understand what she said. Perhaps 'My God!' This person was conscious and I tried to maintain her in that state until help arrived.''

At 12:32, seven minutes after the crash, an ambulance and a technical support vehicle arrived from the *sapeurs-pompiers* station in Rue Malar, just across the river. Eight minutes later, the first of three SAMU ambulances, each one carrying a doctor and nurse on board, arrived from the Hôpital Necker some three km away.

*   *   *

Paris police chief Philippe Massoni was reading in bed when he received a telephone call at 12:40 informing him of the accident. Within minutes, he was en route for the tunnel in an official car with lights flashing and sirens blaring. From the car phone, he called Interior Minister Jean-Pierre Chevènement. The minister wanted to come to the tunnel, but Massoni convinced him to go directly to the Pitié-Salpêtrière hospital, where the emergency team was preparing to send the Princess and Rees-Jones.

At 1:00, Massoni telephoned the Elysée Palace. Christine Albanel, the weekend duty officer, took the call. "There's been a very grave accident in the Alma tunnel involving the Princess of Wales and Dodi Al Fayed," said Massoni. "The President should be informed." Albanel, however, decided not to wake Jacques Chirac immediately, heeding his standing orders not to bother him at night unless some major decision or other presidential action was required. Instead, she decided it was more urgent to alert the British embassy, just down the street from the Elysée on the Rue du Faubourg-St. Honoré.

The British duty officer was stunned. "The Princess of Wales?" he repeated. "My God! What a shock." It was getting on to 2:00 by the time British ambassador Sir Michael Jay received the news. Press attaché Timothy Livesey arrived at the ambassador's residence shortly afterwards in his red Renault Laguna to drive Jay and his wife Sylvia to the hospital. At about the same time, Prime Minister Lionel Jospin was awakened at his hotel in the Atlantic port city of La Rochelle, where he was hosting a weekend gathering of his Socialist Party. His staff began making tentative plans to fly him to Paris.

In Antibes, where he was just winding up a ten-day vacation with his family, Ritz president Frank Klein was called by the hotel's night manager and informed of the accident just before 1:00 A.M. Klein reached his assistant Claude Roulet on his cell phone just as he was arriving at the Alma tunnel. Roulet confirmed the worst.

Klein then called Al Fayed's estate in Oxted. "I apologize

for disturbing you," he said when Mohammed came on the line. "I am sorry to tell you that there has been a terrible accident. Dodi has passed away and the driver is dead."

Al Fayed, who had already been informed of the accident, sounded incredulous. "Dodi passed away?" he repeated. "What about Lady Diana?"

"She is badly injured," Klein replied. "Roulet is there. Dourneau and Musa are there. They are trying to get more information." Al Fayed immediately voiced his suspicion that the death may not have been an accident.

At his home in Suffolk, meanwhile, Al Fayed family spokesman Michael Cole received a call from Clive Goodman, royal editor of the *News of the World*. Goodman told him Dodi had died. Cole exploded on the phone. "That's disgusting!" he shouted. "Why don't you leave these people alone? Look what you've caused." Cole was unsure whether or not to believe the report. "I have nothing to say to you," he growled and slammed down the phone.

Still, Cole felt he had to call the elder Fayed and let him know what he had just learned. Fayed's reaction was calm and stoical. "Michael, I know. Frank Klein just called from Antibes with the news. I am going to Paris immediately. Let's just find out what's happened. Let's find out."

At about that time, Dodi's half sister Jumana was awakened by the telephone in her Paris flat, not far from the Place de l'Alma. She had flown in from the U.S. that evening with her husband Hisham and their children. They had planned to meet with Dodi and Diana on Sunday to celebrate Jumana's 32nd birthday. The caller was a relative in America who had heard a television report of Dodi's death. The relative had then phoned the Ritz, where an official confirmed the awful news. Jumana was so badly jolted by the call that her husband was afraid to leave her side.

As soon as he arrived in the Alma tunnel at 1:15, Massoni took charge of the police operations. He ordered his men to set up a security cordon, closing off the area behind barriers of red and white tape. Police cars, their blue lights swirling and blinking, blocked off the tunnel entrance. Powerful flood lamps were brought in to facilitate the work of rescue units and police.

The investigative phase began with the arrival of Patrick Riou, director of the Paris judiciary police, and Martine Monteil, head of the criminal brigade. Deputy procurer Maud Coujard, roughly the equivalent of Paris' assistant district attorney, arrived shortly afterwards on her motorcycle. After hearing the first accounts from police and witnesses on the scene, Coujard quickly decided to assign the case to Monteil's criminal brigade. The choice of Paris' elite detective unit was the first sign that French authorities were determined to treat the road accident as a possible criminal case.

The prime targets of the nascent investigation were the photographers who continued to snap pictures after the arrival of police and medical workers. ''The police first told us to push back but didn't prevent us from working,'' says Langevin, who had happened on the scene some 10 minutes after the accident as he headed to a friend's home from the Ritz. ''Plainclothes cops checked our press cards, then said, 'Okay, fine. Do your work, but stay back.' They seemed not to know who the victims were at first. Then the police chief arrived. We were in the middle of the tunnel, under control of the police. I didn't even take ten photos, then it was all over. They said to stop and asked us to go out of the tunnel. Then they took us away, saying nothing, but forbade us to use our telephones. They frisked us, confiscated our equipment, and took our film. I realized then that this was serious, that they were going to interrogate us.''

Six photographers and the motorcycle driver Darmon were piled into a paddy wagon and taken to a police station in the Rue de Courcelles, where they were strip-searched and booked. That was only the beginning of a harrowing ordeal. But at least three photographers slipped through the net that night: Chassery, Benhamou, and Oderkerken, all of whom had left by the time the police rounded up their colleagues.

Commissioner Monteil's first report from the accident

scene, dated August 31 at 2:00 A.M., states the reasons for the photographers' arrest:

"According to the first witnesses, the Mercedes, proceeding down this portion of the road at high speed, appears to have swerved [because] the chauffeur was being pursued and interfered with by the vehicles of the journalists who had given chase. The driver must have lost control of his vehicle and failed to recover. Again according to the first witnesses, the 'paparazzi' who were pursuing the Mercedes hastened to take photos after the accident, neglecting the elementary gestures of assistance to people in danger. Based on these observations, the first policemen on the scene proceeded to take the photographers in for questioning."

Forty-eight hours later, after undergoing numerous interrogations and spending two nights in prison, the seven were charged with involuntary homicide (equivalent to manslaughter) and nonassistance to people in danger, a violation of France's so-called Good Samaritan law. As the investigation proceeded, however, the facts about the photographers' role would prove more complicated and less clear than they appeared to the first witnesses in the heat of the moment.

Medical workers, meanwhile, were frantically trying to save the accident victims. Henri Paul was killed instantly. Dodi showed no signs of life, but medics pulled him out and laid his broken body on the road several meters behind the car in order to attempt a last-ditch external heart massage. To no avail. He was officially pronounced dead on the scene at 1:30.

SAMU workers had taken charge of Diana at 12:40. According to one SAMU doctor, she was in a "class 1" coma, meaning a state of semiconsciousness in which a patient moves and murmurs, but does not speak coherently or respond to questions. Her pulse and blood pressure were weak. Doctors decided it was too dangerous to move her until her condition was stabilized.

A police captain observing the scene described Diana laid out on a stretcher near the car while the medics attached tubes to her body. She had an "open wound on her forehead and also a bleeding cut on her right arm." Another police report gave a more complete medical assessment at that point: "Head injuries, lethargic coma, multiple fractures of the right arm, bleeding wound on the head as well as the right buttock, chest injuries, very grave condition." There was no specific mention at that point of internal injuries.

After getting the emergency team's assessment, Massoni immediately called back the Elysée. "Her condition is very, very grave," he told duty officer Albanel, filling her in on the medical details he had just learned. "I could hear the sirens behind him," recounts Albanel. "His voice sounded very tense." Following initial reports that the Princess had only been injured, the latest news sounded ominous. Albanel still decided not to wake the President, but called Chirac's chief diplomatic advisor Jean-David Levitte at home. Whatever the outcome, the incident would require close cooperation between the French and British governments. Overseeing those delicate contacts was Levitte's job.

Meanwhile, emergency workers had cut the roof off the car and extracted Rees-Jones. He was gravely injured, and looked in far worse shape than the Princess. Witness Mark Butt vividly described the bodyguard "moaning in agony." He was bathed in his own blood with his jaw ripped off and his tongue nearly severed. In addition, he suffered from serious head and chest injuries and a broken right arm. But Rees-Jones was lucky: he was the only one wearing a seatbelt.

2

Fighting for Life

THE SAMU AMBULANCE BEARING DIANA LEFT THE TUNNEL at about 1:25 escorted by two motorcycle policemen with sirens blaring. On the doctors' instructions, however, the ambulance proceeded slowly in order to avoid bumps and accelerations that they feared might harm a patient in such a fragile state. Due to the convoy's snaillike pace, Diana's ambulance did not pass through the gates of Pitié-Salpêtrière until 2:05, some forty minutes after leaving the tunnel and an hour and 40 minutes after the crash. At that time of night, the drive from the Alma tunnel to the hospital normally takes between five and ten minutes. According to photographer Pierre Suu, who followed the ambulance from the tunnel, it stopped near the Austerlitz bridge for about ten minutes, apparently to perform some emergency maneuver. Press reports, later denied by hospital officals, claimed that doctors on board the ambulance had injected adrenaline directly into Diana's heart to counter a sudden cardiac arrest.

There were other hospitals nearer to the accident site. But Pitié-Salpêtrière, 3.8 miles southeast of the Alma tunnel, was chosen because it was the closest of the four Paris hospitals with specialized 24-hour-a-day emergency services. It was also to Pitié-Salpêtrière that Rees-Jones was dispatched shortly after the Princess.

The duty physician, Dr. Bruno Riou, an anesthesiologist, was making the rounds of the intensive care unit at about 1:00 A.M. when he was beeped and told to prepare for a seriously injured accident victim. He immediately headed for the operating room in the basement of the hospital's Gaston-Cordier wing and began suiting up.

There, he was met by Dr. Jean-Pierre Bénazet, head of emergency surgery, and Dr. Pierre Coriat, head of the hospital's anesthesiology–intensive care department. Joining them was Dr. Alain Pavie, one of France's foremost cardiovascular surgeons, who happened to be on duty that night. By the luck of the draw, the operating team included four of France's very best. They were joined by four senior nurses and four other surgical staffers. By 1:30, the operating room was ready. It was only at that point that they learned the identity of the patient they would soon receive.

Meanwhile, Police Chief Massoni had joined Interior Minister Chevènement at the hospital. Chevènement, who had grabbed the first clothes he could find and dashed over, was dressed casually in a polo shirt and light jacket. The two officials greeted Britain's ambassador Jay and his wife on the ground floor of the emergency unit, then ushered them up to a corridor on the second floor, where offices had been cleared for them and international phone lines installed. There, Massoni and Chevènement briefed Jay as fully as possible on Diana's condition, and also mentioned the role of the paparazzi as a possible factor in the accident.

The ambassador then called Robin Janvrin, the Queen's deputy private secretary, who was staying with the royal family at Balmoral Castle. Janvrin woke Prince Charles with the news. Charles told his mother immediately, but decided not to wake his sons until morning. By then, he hoped, Diana might be out of danger.

While Sylvia Jay held the address book and dialed the numbers, Sir Michael made other essential phone calls. "We called the Foreign Office and asked them to inform 10 Downing Street," says a British official. "Then we contacted Foreign Secretary Robin Cook, who was in Manila. He held up his plane so he could remain in touch. All we could do at that point was wait."

Back in England, Michael Cole was also working the

phone. One of his first calls went to the Ritz hotel's president, Frank Klein, in Antibes. Klein had already been informed of the accident and was making arrangements to return to Paris. Cole also spoke with Klein's assistant, Claude Roulet, who had been left in charge of things and who was on duty at the Ritz that night. Roulet had rushed to the scene of the accident and been briefed by one of the police investigators. Among other things, they told him their initial findings indicated that hot pursuit by the paparazzi was a key factor in the accident.

Armed with the latest information, Cole decided he must now inform Raine Spencer, Diana's stepmother, who was on the Harrods board and was thus an acquaintance of Cole's. Raine Spencer was staying with friends in a palazzo overlooking the Grand Canal in Venice. She had gone to bed at 3:00 A.M. after a gala night and was sound asleep. Her groggy American host answered the phone and was reluctant to wake her guest. "Put her on," Cole barked. "This is important." Raine finally came to the phone. She reacted, Cole recounts, with "stiff upper lip and backbone."

Diana was wheeled into the operating room shortly after 2:05. Police Chief Massoni, who witnessed her arrival, was shocked by her pallor. "I no longer recognized the woman I had seen in the tunnel," he said. At that point, Dr. Riou noted, "She suffered from very grave thoracic hemorrhaging, quickly followed by cardiac arrest." It was immediately decided to open up her chest and examine the extent of internal injuries. The doctors discovered that her chest cavity was filled with blood from a tear in her left pulmonary vein, the vessel that carries oxygenated blood from the left lung into the atrium chamber of the heart. Backed-up blood had pooled in the lungs, making it impossible for Diana to breathe without the support of the heart-lung machine that she had been hooked up to upon entering surgery. Blood loss had starved her internal organs of oxygen and fluids and damaged the heart muscle.

While Pavie sutured the lesion, other doctors took turns

squeezing the Princess' heart in their hands in an attempt to restore a heartbeat. Drugs and electric shocks were also administered. Still the heart refused to pump. After nearly two hours of fruitless efforts, the doctors turned off the heart-lung machine and sewed up the chest cavity. There was nothing more to be done. The Princess of Wales was declared dead at 4:00 A.M. on Sunday morning.

The doctors summoned Chevènement. Accompanied by Massoni, the minister descended two flights of stairs to the operating unit. Riou and Pavie met them in the hallway in their green surgical gowns. "We tried everything," they said. "She died at four o'clock."

Chevènement went back upstairs, pulled Ambassador Jay aside, and told him the news. Shortly afterwards, Riou and Pavie, still in their operating greens, came up and personally briefed Sir Michael. "They were soft-spoken, thoroughly sensitive to our feelings," says a British official. "They gave their information in a professional way. Obviously, they were moved and saddened that their efforts had not succeeded. But they indicated that the injury was so serious that there had been little hope."

According to a French official present at the hospital, several members of the operating team told him that Diana may have actually died before reaching the operating room. They noted that, after the first half hour under the tunnel, she had stopped moving and moaning and slipped into a deep coma. "What's troubling," says this official, "is that it took more than an hour from the time of the accident to the time the ambulance left the tunnel, and then it rolled very slowly."

Had the patient not been Diana, this official confides, doctors might have pulled the plug and pronounced her dead long before they did. Instead, they worked frantically into the night to find a spark of life. "They did absolutely everything they could to save her," said hospital spokesman Thierry Meresse to the *Sunday Times*. "They went far beyond the bounds of duty, far beyond anything that has been done before. It was a superhuman effort."

Superhuman? Far beyond anything that has ever been done

before? Even allowing for the emotion of the moment, the language sounds a bit excessive, as if to dispel any suspicion that, had things been done differently, Diana might still be alive today. It's a legitimate question.

According to the French medical examiner's report, the Princess died of "internal hemorrhaging due to a major chest trauma and a phenomenon of deceleration which caused a rupture of the left pulmonary vein." Diana was not autopsied in France, and the results of the autopsy that was performed by British authorities in the London suburb of Fulham for now remain a tightly guarded secret.* Thus it is impossible at this point to know the precise details of her injuries, the size of the rupture, the extent of other possible internal lesions that could also have contributed to the hemorrhaging. But since the published and unpublished reports have focused on the torn pulmonary vein as the central cause of death, it is worth examining the precise nature of this kind of injury and the chances of survival.

"The pulmonary vein is a large vessel that empties into the left atrium of the heart," says a thoracic surgeon on the staff of a public hospital in Paris. "It's the vessel that feeds oxygenated blood back into the heart. It is a large vein, with a heavy blood flow, which can be ripped in the case of a major shock, or deceleration. This produces a pulling on the vein, which can cause it to snap and rip off. That provokes a hemorrhage in the chest that is very quickly fatal. If it is really torn off, there is virtually no chance of survival. The blood empties out very quickly, with a compression of the heart, the lungs, followed by a heart attack and cardiac arrest. The person dies very quickly."

---

*According to British law, the coroner must hold an official inquest into the death of any British subject who dies overseas of nonnatural causes. Its purpose is to evaluate the time, place, and cause of death, not to assess blame. But the inquest, by law a public hearing, cannot be held until the French investigation is over. In Diana's case, the inquest is being headed by Dr. John Burton, official coroner to the royal family, who has complained of a lack of cooperation from French authorities. It is the first royal inquest since the Queen's cousin, Prince William of Gloucester, died in a flying accident in 1972.

The condition is rarely diagnosed, however. The reason, says this specialist, who insists on anonymity, is that people with such injuries usually die before they can be treated. "They are usually dead on arrival at the hospital, because they die en route. Like all the lesions affecting the large blood vessels, this one causes such massive hemorrhages that you don't have time to get the victims to the hospital and operate. Such people can die in several seconds or several minutes, so when help arrives and they are transported, they often die before they reach the operating table."

But not always. "That depends," this surgeon continues, "on the extent of the hemorrhaging. If you have a big hole or a small hole in a vessel, the blood doesn't flow out at the same rate. Those who arrive [alive] are the ones who have incomplete ruptures of the vein. That can happen. The proof is that this patient arrived alive at the hospital, so there must not have been a complete rupture."

Another French physician, the head of emergency services at a large Paris hospital, says the fact that Diana did not die immediately of a massive hemorrhage indicates that the tear in the pulmonary vein was "either a small one" or that it was partially closed, "perhaps by a bone fragment from a fractured rib." Thus it might have been possible to save her "with some luck and intelligence"—if that was her only internal lesion.

These physicians are careful to point out that they do not have enough precise information about the nature and extent of Diana's injuries to come to any definitive conclusions about her case. Moreover, they are restrained from doing so by law and by the strict code of ethics of France's powerful Ordre des Médecins, which forbid physicians to discuss details of doctor-patient relations.

Freer to analyze and speculate is Dr. John Ochsner, 70, chairman emeritus of surgery at Ochsner Clinic in New Orleans, and one of America's preeminent cardiovascular surgeons. "A ruptured pulmonary vein is a rare, rare injury," says Ochsner. "The much more common deceleration injury is to the aorta. There's a ligament that attaches from the pulmonary artery to the aorta and that tends to tear the aorta as it moves back and forth in the mediastinum. Once that ruptures—pow!—death is instantaneous.''

Ochsner says that is not necessarily the case with the pulmonary vein. ''Because the pulmonary vein is a low-pressure system, the bleeding is less rapid and can kind of clot and form a pseudoclosure. The pressure going in there is almost a negative pressure, because of the inspiration from the heart [i.e., the left atrium is sucking the blood in from the left pulmonary vein]. So the lowest the pressure ever is is when the blood is flowing into the heart. In contrast, when it's going out of the heart [through the aorta], it's the highest pressure. So the reason [Diana] didn't bleed out right away is that the tear was probably clotting and because the pressure there is so modest.''

Would a person in that state have any chance of survival? ''Sure,'' says Ochsner, ''depending on the size of the rent, or tear. If it wasn't too big, they could put the patient on a heart-lung machine and just go in and do [the repair] electively. It's pretty obvious: with that lesion, if you can get them in the hospital and on a heart-lung machine early enough you can save them. But time is of the essence.''

Precisely. It took an hour and 45 minutes from the time of the accident to the time the Princess entered the operating room. What was going on during all that time? First, it took 15 minutes for the first fully equipped SAMU ambulance and its onboard doctor to reach the scene. Second, it was a slow, delicate operation to get Diana out of the car; even though the door was open, emergency workers had to cut through metal to free her because one of her legs was pinned under the seat. Third, she received extensive treatment on-site, lasting between 30 and 45 minutes, before the ambulance ever rolled. Once inside the large, boxlike SAMU ambulance, which was fully equipped as a mobile hospital unit, Diana was put on an IV drip (essentially liquids and dextrose), intubated, attached to a respirator, and given external cardiac stimulation. What saves many lives in the aggregate, though, may have been ill-adapted to this particular case. It is very different in the United States, where accident victims are quickly scooped up and rushed to the hospital.

"The philosophy here is to try to stabilize the patient as much as you can, because traveling with this kind of status can be very dangerous for a patient," said Frédéric Mailliez, the first physician to treat Diana and an experienced emergency doctor. "So we try to restore a little bit of blood pressure and some other things before we start to drive." Similarly, says Mailliez, it is not uncommon for emergency doctors to tell ambulance drivers to go slowly. "If you are braking or accelerating," he explains, "it can be very bad for the blood pressure, so you have to be very careful while you're driving." A spokeswoman for the French hospital system confirms that Diana's ambulance "slowed down and rolled gently. It's common sense: any person in a SAMU vehicle is already receiving medical treatment, so they don't drive at [high] speed."

Dr. Ochsner takes issue with such reasoning. "You couldn't try to repair that injury on the scene, you'd have to be in the hospital," he says. The external chest massage would probably be "the worst thing that could happen," he argues. "Once you start beating on the chest you increase pressure in all the chambers at one time. If anything, that would hurt her." As for the go-slow driving technique to avoid shocks and bumps, Ochsner bristles. "Shocks and bumps? You know, if you're trying to save a life, you have to get them to the operating room quickly."

So could the Princess of Wales have been saved if she had reached the hospital earlier?

"I can't second-guess anybody," says Ochsner. "What I'm saying is if it was a small rent, a patient would have plenty of time. But if it's big enough where it's slowly bleeding, as hers was—something between a minor tear and a complete bleed-out—there had to be some resistance of flow, with a clot or something. Otherwise she would have bled out. What I'm saying is this: given that she was still alive after nearly two hours, if they'd have gotten her there in an hour, they might have saved her.''*

Ochner's view is supported by Dr. David Wasserman, 45, an American physician with nine years' experience working in the emergency rooms of some of the country's busiest urban hospitals, including New Jersey's Hackensack Medical Center. ''If they had gotten her to the operating room sooner, she would have had a far greater chance. You could never diagnose that kind of injury in the field, never. In the U.S. there'd be hell to pay in a case like this—lawsuits, internal investigations. Spending all that time on on-site treatment was absolutely the wrong approach for this patient.''

While not accusing any individual medical worker of professional errors in treating Diana—indeed, they clearly followed standard French procedures—Dr. Wasserman argues that the fault lies with the whole French approach to emergency medicine. ''Stabilizing patients in the field is a mistake we made for decades in the U.S. before we abandoned it in favor of the scoop-and-run method about ten years ago,'' he says. ''Before that, we found we were losing more patients by messing with them in the field than by getting them to the hospital. All kinds of studies have found a major negative correlation between the time spent in the field and a patient's prognosis. In most cases, the only thing we do to trauma victims on site is to stabilize the spine and start an IV drip. Then we get them to the hospital fast.''

It seems that Fate was not kind to the Princess of Wales during her last visit to Paris: it put her in the path of the pursuing paparazzi, in the hands of a drunken driver, and in the care of an emergency medical system that—despite its

---

*A more mundane step that might have saved the Princess was attaching her seatbelt. ''We know that the impact speed with the post was survivable because the bodyguard survived,'' said Richard Cuerden, head of the University of Birmingham's Accident Research Centre. ''We expect that people in the rear have as good chance, if not better, of making it.''

overall high quality—may have used the wrong method for dealing with her kind of injury.*

At 4:15 A.M., the phone rang in the second floor apartment reserved for the Elysée duty officer. Christine Albanel had been waiting anxiously for word from the hospital. "It's all over," said Police Chief Massoni. "She's dead." Albanel, herself the mother of an eight-year-old boy, thought instantly of the young princes and felt a pang. But there was no time to dwell on this. She set about drafting a statement for the President and contacted the head of the Paris hospital system to discuss arrangements for Chirac and other dignitaries to pay their respects at Pitié-Salpêtrière.

At about that time, the Queen's private secretary, Sir Robert Fellowes, telephoned the hospital from Balmoral Castle. A British embassy official took the call and broke the news. "He was gutted," says the official. It was Fellowes, the husband of Diana's sister Jane, who informed Prince Charles at 4:30 A.M. With the royal family thus alerted, British officials and their French counterparts set about planning how to break the news to the world media. It was decided to organize a press conference.

Like Sir Robert, Raine Spencer received word from British embassy officials at the hospital. She called Michael Cole in

---

*As the authors predicted in the preface to the first edition, our analysis of Diana's medical treatment set off heated polemics in France, where Health Minister Bernard Kouchner (who had refused all our interview requests) and other French medical officials accused us of unfairly criticizing the French emergency services and vaunting the superiority of American methods. This nationalistic reaction is absurd, as is the charge that we relied only on "cooperative" American doctors to make our case. The reader of the above passage can clearly see that two French specialists are quoted—albeit anonymously because of France's rigid medical secrecy laws. Subsequent to the first edition's publication, moreover, several eminent British specialists have voiced support for our conclusions. Among them: Dr. Andrew Mason, spokesman for the British Association of the Accident and Emergency Medicine; Dr. Peter Craig, former chief of surgery in the British Army; and Dr. Stephen Miles, a specialist in emergency medicine at Royal London and Homerton Hospital, who declared in the *Daily Telegraph* on February 10, 1998 that "All the resuscitation in the world at the roadside wouldn't have saved her. The only way she could have been resuscitated was by operating." Moreover, as Kouchner himself admits, there is a long-running debate within the French medical community on the merits of on-site stabilization versus scoop-and-run.

Suffolk. "I sank to my knees," Cole recalls. "This was more horrible even than the news of Dodi's death. We had lived for a couple of hours with the hope that she would survive. The first reports had not been unencouraging."

Mohammed Al Fayed's Sikorsky S-76 helicopter landed at Le Bourget airport, 10 miles north of Paris, at about 3:30 A.M. after a one hour and 20 minute flight from Oxted. Chauffeur Philippe Dourneau and Kes Wingfield picked him up in the Mercedes 600. Wingfield confirmed Dodi's death, but said Diana was still alive. Instead of proceeding directly to the morgue to view Dodi's body, Al Fayed decided to go first to the hospital and try to see the Princess. Upon arriving at Pitié-Salpêtrière, he was met by Sir Michael Jay, Chevènement, and Massoni, who informed him that Diana had just died.

Meanwhile, in the hospital's basement, a Paris medical official performed an external examination on Diana's body. The report showed a three cm wound on the forehead, a cut over the lip, crushed ribs, a fractured right arm, an eight cm cut on the right thigh, bruises on both hands and feet, and a cut on the right buttock. The body chart did not detail the internal injuries, however, since the Princess' chest had already been sewn up by the surgeon.

Before leaving the hospital, Al Fayed says, he was approached by a French official he knew. "There is someone who must speak with you," said this official. He introduced Al Fayed to a medical worker who claimed to have treated Diana. As Al Fayed recalls the story, this person told him that the Princess had drifted in and out of consciousness and that at one point she had spoken. What Diana had said, Al Fayed was told, was this: "Tell my sister Sarah to look after my children." Al Fayed received Lady Sarah in his London office the following Thursday and repeated to her Diana's alleged last words.* He also gave her a silver plaque, which

---

*Al Fayed's "last words" story, which he repeated in his controversial interview with the London *Mirror* in February 1998, was widely criticized in the British press as implausible. The authors' decision to relate the claim in this book, exactly as it was told to us, is not intended to endorse or impugn its credibility but to add it to the record and let the reader draw his own conclusions.

Dodi had had inscribed with a love-poem, and which a maid had found under Diana's pillow at Dodi's Paris apartment.

At 5:00, in the Lassay wing of the hospital, Riou and Pavie took their places next to Chevènement and Ambassador Jay at a table bristling with microphones. By this time, the doctors had changed into spotless white medical tunics; Chevènement was wearing a black suit and tie that he had sent for so as not to appear in front of the cameras in his polo shirt.

The opening statement, read by Riou and co-signed by Pavie, summarized Diana's case in five terse sentences:

"Last night in Paris, the Princess of Wales was the victim of a high-speed road accident. She was immediately taken under the care of the Paris SAMU, which carried out initial resuscitation efforts.

"Upon her arrival at the Hôpital La Pitié-Salpêtrière, she manifested an extremely grave hermorrhagic shock originating in the chest, quickly followed by cardiac arrest.

"An emergency thoracotomy revealed an important wound in the left pulmonary vein.

"In spite of the closing of that wound and an external, then internal, heart massage of more than two hours, no circulation could be reestablished and she was pronounced dead at 4:00 A.M."

CNN, which had been covering developments throughout the night, conveyed the news immediately via the voice of Christopher Dickey, *Newsweek*'s Paris bureau chief, whom the network had reached by cell phone. Within minutes, other TV, radio, and wire services were broadcasting the information around the world.

Before dawn, crowds began to gather at the Place de l'Alma and continued to swell throughout the dazzlingly sunny day that followed. Mounds of flowers and teddy bears and hundreds of handwritten notes soon appeared at the base of the golden flame, a replica of the torch of the Statue of Liberty. The flame became the focal point of a Parisian Diana cult that mirrored, on a smaller scale, the multitude of flowers and humankind that accumulated in London around Kensington Palace in the days following the accident. Across the river from the Alma Bridge stood the Eiffel Tower, which is illuminated at nighttime in a flood of golden light. It was perhaps one of the last images the Princess saw before entering the tunnel.

Meanwhile, people began flocking to the hospital. Michel Souvais, 40, a Parisian artist, laid a dozen white roses at the hospital entrance shortly after 6:00 A.M., the first of thousands who would pay a floral tribute. "Diana was a princess of legend," he said, his voice breaking with emotion. "She was beautiful, exuberant, full of life, almost a fairy."

At 7:00 A.M., Christine Albanel called the President on his private line. Wakened from a sound sleep in his third floor Elysée bedroom, Chirac had difficulty comprehending what his aide was telling him. "Lady Di? You mean the Princess of Wales? Place de l'Alma? She was in Paris?" Once the news sunk in, the President was deeply moved. "I will tell my wife immediately," he said. "She will be shattered. She knew the Princess and liked her very much. And she is a mother, too."

The President then said he wanted to send a communiqué to the press. Albanel had already drafted a statement and read it to him over the phone. Fifteen minutes later, he called her back with some word changes and ordered the text sent to the wire services immediately. "I have learned with deep emotion of the brutal death of Lady Diana," said Chirac's statement. "She was a young woman of our times, warm, full of life and generosity. Her tragic death will be deeply felt because she was a familiar figure to all of us. In these terrible hours, I think of her family and especially her children."

At 7:30, the President called Albanel again. He had decided to send his wife, Bernadette Chirac, to the hospital immediately to pay respects on his behalf. That afternoon, Chirac would be at the hospital to greet Prince Charles and Diana's two sisters when they came to collect the body. Mrs.

Chirac arrived at the hospital at 8:45, followed by Prime Minister Jospin at 9:15.

By this time, Diana had been brought up from the basement operating room where she died to a room on the second-floor intensive care corridor where French and British officials had set up their crisis center. Nurses had cleaned the body and covered her with a white sheet up to the shoulders.

Diana's personal valet Paul Burrell, 39, the one she always referred to as "my rock," arrived at about 1:00 P.M. to help prepare her for her final voyage. He brought with him a suitcase containing makeup and a long black dress. Working with hospital staff and French undertakers, he dressed her, arranged her hair, and applied color to a face that had turned ashen.

Plainclothes policemen mounted a permanent guard outside the door. Inside, the hospital's Roman Catholic chaplain, Father Yves Clochard-Bossuet, sat by Diana's bed and quietly prayed for her soul. Wakened in his hospital apartment at 3:00 A.M., the priest had been ushered into the dead Princess' room shortly after the body had been brought upstairs. When Mrs. Chirac arrived at the hospital, she joined him in prayer at Diana's bedside. The priest later ceded his place to the Rev. Martin Draper of St. George's Anglican church in Paris.

With Prince Charles and Diana's two sisters expected in the afternoon, French and British officials held a 2:00 P.M. planning session in their impromptu crisis center, just 15 meters away from the room where Diana lay. The meeting included French government protocol chief Bernard Grasset, a British protocol officer, British embassy press attaché Timothy Livesey, Elysée deputy spokesman Jérôme Peyrat, Elysée press coordinator Evelyne Richard, Paris police chief Massoni, Dr. Riou, Dr. Pavie, and four employees of the Paris funeral home that had provided the casket and hearse. The undertakers were carrying lugubrious greenish suitcases containing the makeup and other accessories with which they had prepared the body.

The discussion centered on protocol issues: who would do what in what sequence, who would stand next to whom, where Chirac would greet Prince Charles, how the cortège would leave the hospital. But the conversation was quickly diverted onto such morbid questions as, "What state is the Princess in? How is she dressed? Is her face damaged? Does Prince Charles want to see the coffin open or closed?"

In fact, Diana was not yet in the coffin. She had been made up, coifed, and dressed and lay on a hospital bed. The windows had been shuttered and the curtains drawn to block the prying cameras of journalists, some of whom had rented balcony and window space across the street from the hospital. The room was lit only by a small wall lamp. "Her face was not at all damaged, she looked impeccable," says an official who saw the Princess at about 3:00 P.M. "It was a bizarre moment. I was filled with an infinite sadness before this beautiful woman, adulated around the world, who lay dead in this humble hospital room." Before the royal party arrived, the undertakers slipped discreetly into the room and lifted Diana into her coffin. According to Prince Charles' express wishes, the lid was left open.

There had been much discussion about whether the hearse should leave from the main entrance, where a huge crowd stood vigil behind police barricades, or from a discreet rear exit. Charles' instructions were unambiguous: "Don't hide the departure of the coffin. Let it be filmed inside and outside the hospital. Let it be seen by the people."

The Prince's decision came as a relief to French authorities, who feared an upswell of public rage if the people could not see the hearse wind its way through the streets of Paris. "People would have been furious," says a French official. "The atmosphere in the streets that day was crazy. Thousands of people had converged on the Place de l'Alma. Multitudes jammed the road from the Austerlitz bridge to the hospital. It took three companies of CRS [paramilitary police] to hold them back from the entrance. They had to see the hearse."

Emotions were running high among the public, gripped by

a mixture of grief and rage. Once Charles' wishes were known, French and British press attachés went to the barricades and hastily assembled a pool of 12 journalists—six cameramen and six print reporters—to come inside and cover the event. When the journalists entered the courtyard, a volley of shouts, catcalls, and whistles rang out. Patients and visitors, standing at the windows of the hospital, insulted the cameramen with cries of ''Killers!'' ''Assassins!'' Police had to be summoned to quiet them down.

At 5:00 P.M. a BAe 146 of the Royal Flight touched down at the Villacoublay military airfield, 20 miles southwest of Paris, where they were met by British ambassador Michael Jay. When the royal party arrived at the hospital with a French police motorcycle escort at 5:40, President and Mrs. Chirac were waiting at the entrance with an honor guard of France's ceremonial *Gardes Républicaines,* resplendent in their dark blue uniforms with red and gold trim, white gloves, and red plumes on their parade caps.

Charles emerged from the ambassador's silver-gray Jaguar with a rather daffy smile frozen on his face. He greeted the Chiracs in his flawless, but heavily accented, French: *''Monsieur le Président, Madame Chirac, merci d'être là.''* The presidential couple then accompanied the Prince and Diana's two sisters, Lady Jane Fellowes and Lady Sarah Mc-Corquodale, to the intensive care unit. While the Chiracs waited in the corridor, the Prince and his ex-sisters-in-law entered the room.

Diana was in the coffin now with her hands folded over her black evening dress. The Reverend Martin Draper said prayers with them, then left the room. Charles and the sisters remained several minutes silently contemplating this young woman who, only hours earlier, had been brimming with life. Though it had not been planned by the protocol chiefs, Charles asked to remain alone with the body for a moment.

When the Prince came out, his eyes were red, and he had obviously been crying. He quickly recovered his aplomb and stepped towards Riou and Pavie to thank them for their efforts. The first words he uttered were *''Mes félicitations!*

[Congratulations!]'' A rather incongruous remark under the circumstances, but an understandable lapse for a man in a state of emotional shock. Chirac, who had viewed the body with his wife shortly before Charles' arrival, was no less moved. "The President looked positively devastated," says an Elysée aide.

Following the script worked out by the two protocol officials, the clergyman led the way down the stairs in his black robes with white lace trim. He was followed by the casket, draped under the purple, red, and gold royal standard, borne by four black-uniformed pall bearers from the French undertaking firm. Then came Charles, followed by the two sisters, Mr. and Mrs. Chirac, Ambassador and Mrs. Jay, protocol officials, and police officers.

The dignity of the moment was slightly marred by the filthy state of the corridors and stairway, which were littered with cigarette butts, plastic coffee cups, and discarded fast-food wrappings. An Elysée staffer had grabbed a broom and swept out the entrance hall just before Charles' arrival, but had not had time to tidy up the stairs and hallway.

When the cortège reached the ground floor, the silence was shattered by a high-pitched voice: "You bitch! You're not ashamed to have come here?" An elderly woman visiting the hospital had mistaken Lady Sarah for Charles' mistress, Camilla Parker Bowles (whom she in fact resembles). When an Elysée aide quietly explained to the woman that it was Diana's sister, she burst into tears over her faux pas.

Charles may not have noticed. By that time, he seemed to be totally detached from reality. His face was expressionless, his movements stiff and mechanical. After the coffin was placed into the gray and black hearse, the Prince took his leave of the Chiracs. Then he got into the back of the ambassador's Jaguar and waited. Chirac and his wife stood nearby. The 12 Gardes Républicaines stood at attention. For more than a minute, nothing happened, because neither the French nor the British side knew who would give the order to depart.

During this awkward pause, a British embassy employee

dashed down the stairs and ran to the car in which Lady Jane and Lady Sarah were seated. He opened the trunk and placed a plastic bag inside. Tears were streaming down the young man's cheeks. These were the clothes Diana had been wearing on her last night in Paris.

At 6:15, the vehicles finally started to move. Chirac, his eyes brimming, saluted the departing cortège. When the hearse reached the hospital gate and turned right onto the Boulevard de l'Hôpital, applause suddenly swelled up from the crowd, punctuated by cries of "Diana! Diana, we love you!" The cortège continued at a stately pace through the streets of Paris, then picked up speed on the highway en route to Villacoublay, where Diana's coffin was placed aboard the BAe 146 by a Royal Air Force guard of honor. At last, she was going home.

3

Postmortems

ON SATURDAY, SEPTEMBER 6, 1997, IN BRITAIN'S LARGEST public funeral since the death of Winston Churchill, the flag-draped coffin of Princess Diana rolled through central London on a horse-drawn gun carriage flanked by 12 red-jacketed Welsh Guards and followed on foot by her sons, William and Harry, Prince Charles, Prince Philip, and her brother, Earl Spencer. The somber procession to Westminster Abbey was watched by more than a million people lining the route and some 2 billion more around the world on live television. After a funeral service attended by some 1,900 mourners, powerfully marked by Elton John's rendition of "Candle in the Wind 1997" and Spencer's uncompromising eulogy, Diana was laid to rest on a peaceful island in the middle of a lake at her ancestral home Althorp House, some 70 miles northwest of London.

The tranquility of her final resting place contrasted with the tempest of rumors, myths, and interrogations that swirled up in the wake of her death. Even before her body was laid in the ground, word began to spread that she had been pregnant at the time of her death. Under normal circumstances, that would have been a purely private matter—an additional cause for sadness if true, pointless and idle gossip if not. But the violent death of the Princess of Wales was not a normal event. And the question of whether or not she was pregnant is potentially one of the most explosive elements in the investigation, because a pregnancy would give greater credence to the assassination plot theories that began in the Middle East and soon proliferated around the globe.

For the mother of the future king of England to bear the child of a Muslim Arab, a child who would be the half sibling of the heir to the throne, would be embarrassing in the eyes of the royal family and the ruling Establishment. If a pregnancy were confirmed, the conspiracy theories would be uncontainable. There could theoretically be consequences for Britain's relations with the Arab world and some resentment among the 1.5 million Muslims living on British soil. Thus what would normally have been another poignant detail in a personal tragedy took on a far greater significance.

Most of the "proof" of Diana's alleged pregnancy is circumstantial. Some photos of her in St. Tropez, for example, do show a little roll in the belly, which some have attributed to a pregnancy. It could just as easily be the normal midriff of a 36-year-old woman in a bathing suit. For a pregnancy to be visible, the fetus would have to be at least three or four months old. Diana and Dodi only got together in mid-July, making it unlikely that any conception could have taken place longer than six weeks previous (unless the father were someone other than Dodi). Stories that the couple had started dating as early as 1996 are totally untrue, according to sources close to both of them.

It is also pointed out that on August 30 Diana told her friend, journalist Richard Kay, that she was reducing her official duties and clearing her calendar as of the month of November. That could add credibility to the pregnancy theory, since a pregnancy begun in July or August would be obvious to the whole world by that time. Then there was her provocative statement to the British journalists in St. Tropez: "You will have a big surprise coming soon, the next thing I do." Some have suggested that the "surprise" could have been wedding plans—perhaps accompanied by a pregnancy. But Diana's impromptu remark was made before Dodi even showed up in St. Tropez.

Concrete evidence is more difficult to come by. There was a document, purportedly a confidential letter addressed by

Dr. Pierre Coriat, head of anesthesiology at Pitié-Salpêtrière, to Interior Minister Jean-Pierre Chevènement, stating that Diana was nine to ten weeks pregnant. A photocopy of this letter circulated around the editorial offices of several French publications. But the document, apparently of dubious authenticity, was denounced as a fake by both the Interior Ministry and the hospital. Consequently, no French news outlet ever published it.

But there were allusions to a possible pregnancy in the mainstream press. *Time* magazine, in its edition of September 22, 1997, stated that a SAMU doctor claimed to have been told by a colleague, who treated Diana in the tunnel, that she had made a rubbing gesture on her belly and informed him that she was "six weeks pregnant." Though the magazine had carefully couched this second-hand anecdote in a paragraph on "lies, conspiracy theories and outrageous tales," the passage was taken out of context and widely misquoted as "proof" that Diana was pregnant. In fact, *Time* had merely relayed what a reporter was told by the second SAMU doctor; there was no way of knowing if he, or his anonymous colleague, was accurately quoting the Princess' words. Given the conflicting accounts about whether she even spoke at all after the accident, this doctor's story does not seem entirely convincing.

Also under the heading of second-hand accounts, a well-known and respected French journalist related to the authors the following story: a physician he knows personally, who works at Pitié-Salpêtrière, told him that blood tests taken upon Diana's arrival showed she was indeed pregnant. This physician, who identified his source as one of the doctors who operated on the Princess, then said that when he looked in Diana's medical dossier several days after her death, all the test results had been removed. The journalist was unable to corroborate the story and therefore did not report it. His medical source, who may or may not be telling the truth, refused to be interviewed for this book. Thus there is no way of verifying this potentially explosive account.

But it is possible to examine the extent to which it may

be considered plausible. It is necessary to know, first of all, whether doctors would have drawn blood and tested for pregnancy while fighting desperately for a trauma victim's life. The answer to the first half of that question is yes: they would systematically have taken blood samples in order to identify the blood type (for transfusion purposes) and measure the degree of hemorrhaging with an NFS test* that counts the different kinds of blood cells. In most cases, other tests would normally be done, for example, to evaluate the coagulability of the blood, measure the level of electrolytes in the blood serum, and, for women of childbearing age, a Beta-HCG test for pregnancy.†

In the U.S., according to Dr. David Wasserman, an experienced American emergency room physician, the Beta-HCG would be pretty standard in a case like Diana's. "The doctors would want to know if a patient was pregnant or not," says Wasserman. "It wouldn't stop them from giving her life-saving treatment, but it would stop them from doing elective procedures that might harm the fetus."

According to a high-ranking French specialist in emergency medicine, obliged to speak anonymously because of the medical secrecy required by French law, it would be "reasonable and rational," though not obligatory, for French emergency physicians to do the Beta-HCG. He stresses, though, that for "an emergency doctor with a medical catastrophe on his hands, his primary concern would not be to know if the woman was pregnant or not."

This French specialist, however, notes that another standard, obligatory, measure could reveal the presence of a fetus. In addition to a brain scan and an X ray of the thoracic region, he says, the emergency room doctors would necessarily have done a sonogram. This technique, which examines internal organs via the reflection of ultrasonic waves,

---

Numération formule sanguine, performed by centrifuge, and known in English as the CBC test.

†The Beta-HCG (for "human choriopic gonadotropin") measures a hormone from the placenta that is found only in the blood of pregnant women.

would be performed primarily to identify lesions and check the accumulation of blood in bodily cavities. But, as any woman who has been through prenatal care in a modern medical facility in the past two decades knows, a sonogram will also produce the recognizable image of the fetus, with the head and folded-up body clearly visible even to the layman. (Though a fetus younger than three weeks could only be detected by a specialist.)

This specialist cautions that under emergency medical conditions, a doctor would not necessarily see a fetus on the sonogram screen unless he was looking for one, which could be obscured by massive hemorrhaging. At six weeks, however, the fetus would probably be visible. It is possible, says this doctor, that photos were made from the sonogram screen that might show a fetus. If a permanent image was made, it would necessarily be included in the medical dossier, along with all the blood test results.

Thus, if Diana was pregnant, there is a very strong chance that the evidence would be in her medical dossier at the hospital. As for the current whereabouts of the medical file, this physician, who is not connected with Pitié-Salpêtrière and claims no first-hand knowledge, speculates that "it is probably locked up in a safe in the hospital director's office. I can't see it being archived like an ordinary file."

In addition to hospital officials, it is likely that the police also have a copy of Diana's file. In cases of violent or suspicious deaths, where an official investigation is opened, copies of the victim's medical records are usually requisitioned by the prefecture of police, currently headed by Philippe Massoni and under the ultimate authority of Interior Minister Jean-Pierre Chevènement. Thus the evidence of Diana's pregnancy, if it exists, could well be in the hands of police investigators.

According to sources with access to the official investigation dossier, none of Diana's medical records are included. There is only a succinct report on the pathologist's external corporal examination. The French medical examiner, Dr. Dominique Lecomte, did not perform an autopsy on the Princess and, according to what a police report describes as "instructions received," drew no blood sample from the body. In Britain, the autopsy on Diana's body was carried out by the Fulham coroner's office, a procedure that would quite likely have discovered the presence of a fetus. When questioned about pregnancy reports, a coroner's office spokesman replied with an evasive "No comment. That's part of the investigation."

A full-scale public inquest by Royal Coroner Dr. John Burton will be held upon completion of the French investigation. But Burton has the right to hold any part of the proceedings in camera and thus avoid revealing details he deems too sensitive. It seems highly unlikely, therefore, that he would reveal any information confirming a pregnancy.

While falling short of concrete proof, the information available at this point leaves open the possibility that Diana may have been pregnant. In the future, the release of documents or testimony now withheld may answer this key question one way or the other. But one thing is virtually certain: the evidence does exist to prove or disprove a pregnancy.

Questioned by the authors about the claim that blood tests taken on Diana's arrival confirmed her pregnancy, officials of the Assistance Publique, which administers all public hospitals in France, refused to deny or confirm the account. Also contacted by the authors, Health Minister Bernard Kouchner declined to comment.

The reason advanced for this official silence was the legal obligation to maintain "medical secrecy." On December 29, however, French authorities suddenly saw fit to lift that veil of secrecy in order to respond to an article in the Spanish magazine *Interviu.* The article had reproduced the purported letter from Dr. Corial to Interior Minister Chevènement saying that blood tests revealed "a state of pregnancy of 9–10 weeks." Pitié-Salpêtrière spokesman Thierry Meresse denounced the letter as a counterfeit and stated, "No tests were taken in this regard. The role of the doctors was to save Diana's life, nothing else." Coming nearly four months after Diana's death, that terse denial raised the inevitable question:

if the answer was that simple and that categorical, why had it not been given sooner? Nor did Meresse's statement provide any proof that Diana was not pregnant. Thus the speculation continued.*

For "reasons of hygiene and decency," according to a police report, the bodies of Dodi Fayed and Henri Paul were taken directly to the Institut Médico-Légal—the Paris morgue— near the Austerlitz bridge on the right bank of the Seine. The autopsy on Paul was held Sunday morning on orders of prosecutor Maud Coujard. As with Diana, Dodi's body did not go under the knife in France.

A source in the prosecutor's office explains this apparent lapse in investigative rigor. "In the case of an accident like this," he says, "an autopsy would have been carried out only on the driver. The passengers cannot have caused the accident. Furthermore, because this involves a personality like the Princess of Wales, it is unthinkable to order an autopsy. The idea of us cutting Princess Diana or Dodi Fayed into little pieces is unimaginable. As for blood tests, their levels of alcohol or drug consumption are simply not relevant."

Instead of an autopsy, therefore, Dodi's body received an external corporal examination. The report by Paris medical examiner Dominique Lecomte attributes death to "internal hemorrhaging, caused by a massive chest trauma with multiple trauma of the lower limbs (4 fractures on the right leg, 3 on the left)." In addition to those injuries, the coroner's diagram indicates serious damage over the right eye and multiple lacerations on the face.

Mohammed Al Fayed arrived at the morgue at about 5:00 A.M. Interior Minister Chevènement had called ahead, so Al

*Writing in the *Sunday Telegraph* on February 15 1998, Rosa Monckton, who had vacationed in Greece with Diana from August 15 to 20, maintained that it was "biologically impossible" for the Princess to have been pregnant at the time of her death. If Monckton's statement refers to a menstrual period, which is the clear implication, it would seem to discredit the notion that she was pregnant at that time. The authors would have been happy to have included Monckton's information in our first edition had she not refused our repeated requests to interview her.

Fayed was expected when he appeared at the main entrance of the lugubrious one-story building on the Quai de la Rapée along the banks of the Seine. Dodi's body was rolled out on a gurney. Al Fayed peered into his son's face and prayed silently. "I could see that Dodi was at peace," Al Fayed later confided to friends. "He had such a beautiful smile. He looked like a little boy again. For a moment, he looked so alive that I thought the soul had come back into his body, and that he would live. But when I saw the injuries to the back of his head, I realized that was impossible." Al Fayed also viewed the body of Henri Paul, then headed to the Ritz to seek more information on the accident.

Frank Klein landed at Le Bourget at 9:30 A.M. on board Al Fayed's Gulfstream IV. Also on board were Mohammed's brother Salah and Salah's son Moody, who had driven to Nice from Monaco to rendezvous with the plane. Upon arriving at the hotel, Klein went straight to his ground-floor office. Mohammed's brother and nephew took the heavily guarded private staircase leading to the owner's second-floor suite.

Mohammed later sent for Klein. "I went up to give my condolences," recounts the German-born hotel executive, his gray hair, dark blue suit, and blue patterned Hermès tie reflecting the quiet elegance one associates with the Ritz. "He was sitting in his office in tears, just heartbroken, heartbroken," says Klein. "When you see a man as strong as Mr. Al Fayed, a man like a rock, so tough in everything he achieved, suddenly hit by a thing like that—losing his eldest son—there is nothing you can say."

While Al Fayed grieved upstairs, his staff pursued the complicated process of securing export and burial permits for Dodi's body—no easy task on a Sunday, in August, when the French bureaucracy was virtually closed down. Since Muslim tradition requires the dead to be laid in the ground within 24 hours, it was first feared that Dodi might have to be buried in Paris. Due to the persistence of Claude Roulet at the Ritz and Al Fayed personnel in London, however, the permits were delivered in time to take Dodi back to England.

But the complications were just beginning. At Le Bourget, Al Fayed was told that the door to the Gulfstream IV was too narrow for the coffin, so it was suggested that it be placed in the cargo bay. Al Fayed wouldn't hear of it. It was finally decided to transport the coffin by helicopter, where it could just barely be squeezed into the aisle between the two rows of seats. Al Fayed sat next to it the whole way back.

Henri Paul would have to wait much longer before he could rest in peace. For three weeks, until his burial in his home town of Lorient on September 20, his nude, broken body lay on a morgue slab with ID tag number 2147 on his left ankle, his head bent at an improbable angle, his shattered legs as misshapen as a frog's, his torso sewn up with rough sutures running like a railroad track from his breast to his lower abdomen.

The autopsy was performed on August 31, starting at 8:30 A.M. The medical examiner's report, dated September 1, graphically describes the effects of the horrific frontal shock he received as the 13th pillar rammed the steering wheel into his chest. Excerpts:

"The lesions observed are essentially traumatic with a severing of the spine along with the displacement and rupture of the spinal cord, rupture of the lower aorta.

"The multiple fractures observed, essentially of the spinal column, rib cage, pelvis and of lower limbs, are consistent with a traumatic shock."

The diagram of Paul's body shows serious facial damage, numerous crushed ribs, multiple fractures in the pelvic area, three fractures in the right leg, one in the left leg, and crushed testicles. The only positive thing to emerge from this chilling report is the fact that poor Henri Paul, with his severed spinal cord, surely felt no pain.

Not the least important of the medical examiner's tasks was to collect samples of blood, internal organs, bile, urine, eye fluid, and hair. Also collected were Paul's stomach contents, consisting only of 20 cc of a "clear brown liquid."

Duplicate batches of each sample were sent to a police lab and a private lab for toxicological analysis.

The first results, published on the afternoon of Monday, September 1, were stunning: the police lab put Paul's blood alcohol level at 1.87 g/l; the private analysis showed 1.74 g/l. In other words, the man who had driven Diana and Dodi to their deaths had consumed the equivalent of eight or nine shots of straight whiskey—more than three times France's legal driving limit of 0.50 g/l. All on an empty stomach.*

There was more to come. On September 10, a communiqué from the prosecutor's office stated that further blood tests showed Paul had also consumed two antidepressants: fluoxetine (the active ingredient in Prozac) and tiapride, a combination of drugs commonly used in the treatment of alcoholism. Taken in conjunction with alcohol, they would multiply its effects, slow down reflexes, and create an impression of euphoria. Users of both drugs are cautioned to exercise "prudence while driving cars or operating machines."†

Whoever put Henri Paul at the wheel of a car on the night of August 30, 1997, had clearly made a disastrous decision.

---

*Another troubling fact that emerged from Paul's postmortem: his blood was found to contain an abnormally high level of carbon monoxide. One possible explanation, though purely speculative in the absence of supporting evidence: exhaust fumes may have been leaking into the interior of the Mercedes.

†According to the well-known French pharmacology manual, the *Dictionnaire Vidal* (1996 edition), tiapride (marketed by the French firm Synthelabo as Tiapridal) is generally prescribed to treat "a state of agitation and aggressiveness, especially in an alcoholic patient; intense and persistent pain; abnormal, spasmodic movements." The manual stresses that alcohol "increases the neuroleptic sedative effect. Alteration of vigilance can make it dangerous to drive vehicles and use machines. This product should be used with caution by drivers or users of machines." Fluoxetine (marketed by Eli Lilly & Co. as Prozac), says *Vidal*, is prescribed for "major depressive episodes, or obsessional and compulsive disturbances." Its use in conjunction with alcohol is "discouraged." It is noted that "since Fluoxetine can modify blood pressure and reflexes, it is advisable to warn drivers and users of machines of this risk."

4

Parallel Lives

THE FIRST TIME DODI FAYED LAID EYES ON DIANA SPENCER was July 29, 1981. She was getting married to Prince Charles in St. Paul's Cathedral before a worldwide television audience of more than 750 million people. Dodi was sitting in front of a TV set in a Monte Carlo hotel suite.

Dodi, then 25, had been spending the summer on the Côte d'Azur with his cousin Mohammed Khashoggi. The two young men had everything to keep them amused: fast cars, open-air cafes, topless girls, ear-pounding nightclubs, wild parties, sun, and sand. They also had the use of the *Nabila*, a 282-ft. yacht owned by Mohammed's father, Saudi billionaire Adnan Khashoggi.

On that day, however, Dodi wasn't interested in boats, girls, or discos. At a time when satellite television was not available shipboard, he had booked a suite at a luxury hotel in order to see the historic event. "I got bored," Mohammed recalls, "but Dodi watched the whole thing, from beginning to end."

It is safe to say that Dodi did not fall in love with Diana that day. Yet for those who believe in fate and destiny, there is an undeniable symmetry, a sort of closing of the circle, in the fact that these two people from such seemingly different backgrounds fell into each other's arms on that same southern French coast 16 summers later. And that their improbable relationship seemed headed for the same event that the young Dodi was so intent on witnessing that day: a wedding.

*   *   *

Diana Frances Spencer was the daughter of a British aristo-crat from Althorp in the English midlands; Emad Fayed was the son of an Egyptian trader from Alexandria. In London, they moved in social circles, having initially met at a polo match sponsored by Dodi's father Mohammed, chairman of the Harrods department store, in 1986. They crossed paths again briefly in 1991 at the London premiere of Steven Spiel-berg's *Hook,* which Dodi had helped to finance, and in the spring of 1997 at a dinner party hosted by Raine Spencer, Diana's stepmother. By the time they renewed their acquain-tance at the Al Fayed villa in St. Tropez, both were divorced and seemed like two planets whose orbits were finally in alignment.

The story of Diana's life is a fin de siècle morality tale. Born the year before the Beatles recorded their first album, she was the product of Britain's provincial landed aristoc-racy. But that world of privilege afforded her no protection from the emotional blows of a childhood buffeted by parental infidelity, scandal, and divorce. Diana's mother, Frances Shand Kydd, had walked out on her father, Earl Spencer (Johnnie to his friends), when the girl was six. The earl raised his children the old-fashioned way—with nannies—and spent little time looking after Diana and her younger brother, Charles. (Her two elder sisters were already off at boarding school.) The eighth Earl Spencer later married Raine, the divorced Countess of Dartmouth and daughter of best-selling romantic pulp novelist Barbara Cartland. Raine was quickly cast as the evil stepmother, and nicknamed Acid Rain.

Undereducated and unsophisticated, Diana got Ds on all four of her O levels, and despite being well-liked at the West Heath School in Kent, she had no hopes of university. At 16, she spent six months at the Institut Alpin Videmanette, a finishing school in Rougemont, Switzerland, near Gstaad, where she could perfect skiing if little else. She was miser-able and begged to be allowed home. Within a year, she had taken cookery classes and was living with two girlfriends in a flat in London bought for her by her father. But it was her love of children that led her to work part-time at the Young England nursery school, and as a nanny for an American family living in London.

But Diana had one crucial thing going for her: she belonged to the high-born genetic pool from which the future monarch might—and did—choose his consort. The royal wedding was a marvelous fairy-tale stage set. But for the 19-year-old Diana Spencer—Shy Di, the tabloids called her—the unhappiness of her parents' divorce led seamlessly into the unhappiness of her own semiarranged marriage.

If nothing else, the extravagant wedding gave a much-needed public relations boost to the ever-remote British monarchy. But it placed a burden on Diana that no young woman could have been prepared for. Her constitutional duty to produce an heir to the throne was hardly humanized by her discovery of her husband's long-running affair with Camilla Parker Bowles. Not many years after the births of William (Wills) and Henry (Harry)—"an heir and a spare," as the saying goes—her marriage was on the rocks. And all the world knew it, thanks to the obsessive media interest in everything that Diana did.

The intense press coverage, ironically, was in large part the result of Buckingham Palace's own hyping: first, via the internationally televised wedding, then through the countless scenes of the "happy" couple criss-crossing the globe to burnish the glory of an empire that no longer was.

The illusion was shattered in 1992, the annus horribilus, Queen Elizabeth said, by the publication of *Diana: Her True Story*. Secretly cooperating with author Andrew Morton, she used the book to reveal the depths of her personal misery: an unfaithful, distant husband, a decade-long struggle with the eating disorder bulimia, and suicidal bouts of depression. While Diana convincingly portrayed herself as a victim of the cold and bureaucratic House of Windsor, her search for comfort plunged her into public relations nightmares. They included the tabloid exposure of her flirtations with a variety of men, including James Gilbey, a friend from Diana's Sloane Ranger days in the late seventies; James Hewitt, her riding instructor; and Will Carling, a former England rugby captain.

Diana and Charles separated in 1992. By the time her divorce became final on August 28, 1996, just more than one year to the day before she died, she had moved deliberately to construct a new life for herself, one without Charles, without a royal title (Her Royal Highness was stripped by the Queen) and largely without Wills and Harry, who were now at Eton and Ludgrove Preparatory School, respectively.

Despite Diana's frequent complaints about the media attention, her new agenda seemed calculated to keep her in the limelight. The Princess was a royal rebel who never fitted in with her former husband's aristocratic cliques, yet had none of her own. Nonetheless, the kindergarten teacher–turned–fairy-tale princess had evolved into one of the world's best-known celebrities. After her separation from Charles, she would spend more and more time with rock stars, fashion designers, and magazine editors. In what turned out to be the final year of her life, if the actor Kevin Costner is to be believed, she had planned to star in a sequel to the Hollywood motion picture *The Bodyguard*. She would have played a princess.

Diana's other passion was her carefully crafted identity as a humanitarian. Having cut a million red ribbons at factory openings and clinics as the wife of the Prince of Wales, she now longed to embark on a more personal crusade in support of social concerns. On June 23, she paid a visit to Mother Teresa's AIDS hospice in the South Bronx, where the tiny nun gave the Princess a rosary with which Diana would later be buried. But the cause which preoccupied most of her charitable energy in her last year was a much hoped-for ban on antipersonnel land mines.

She even devised a way of combining her interests in glamour and giving. At Wills' suggestion, she had Christie's auction 80 of her designer dresses for the benefit of the AIDS Crisis Trust and the Royal Marsden Hospital Cancer Fund. At 212 pages, Christie's produced more of a fanzine than an auction catalogue including 66 glossy pictures of her wearing many of the gowns being sold.

But there remained something conspicuously missing in Diana's new life: a new man. One recent flirtation was Royal Brompton heart surgeon Hasnat Khan. They dined several times, but both had denied a romantic liaison. When Diana visited Khan's parents on a May goodwill trip to Pakistan, the reticent doctor merely shrugged.

"Diana" is the goddess of the hunt. "Emad el Din," Dodi's given names, mean "pillar of faith" in Arabic. When Diana once again met Dodi in June 1997 he had several things going for him. Slightly older than Diana, he was not married and had no children. That spared any embarrassment about a younger man, or an older man with potentially messy family problems. His family was also very wealthy. That meant that Dodi could take care of her in the manner to which she had grown accustomed: planes, helicopters, limousines, palaces, country homes, secluded holiday estates. Unlike former boyfriends who kissed and told, Dodi was discreet, even secretive.

Moreover, they were kindred spirits whose personalities and backgrounds were strikingly similar. Both were superficial when it came to intellectual pursuits. Neither had been a good student. They shared an infatuation with the stars of fashion and entertainment. They loved the movies, especially silly comedies, although Dodi was also fond of action films. Dodi, like Diana, was the lonely child of a broken marriage. He too longed for somebody to love and be loved by. A gentle and sensitive man, Dodi could easily empathize with the Princess. In her, he found an outlet for his huge capacity to love—and a chance to prove himself to a successful and powerful father, who both adored and doubted him. "I didn't know that life could be so wonderful," Dodi told his press agent, Pat Kingsley, during the last month of his life. "The psychological attraction between them must have been as powerful as the undertow between two ships," says Dodi's friend, movie director Roland Joffé.

*   *   *

The roots of Dodi's melancholy go back to his childhood in Alexandria, "that strange and evocative city," as Lawrence Durrell, who lived and was inspired to write novels there, called it, "a place for dramatic partings, irrevocable decisions, last thoughts." Dodi was born on April 15, 1956. He was the only child of Mohammed Al Fayed, a handsome and tenacious young trader from Alexandria, and Samira Khashoggi, a pretty and talented Saudi girl attending school in the city.

Mohammed Al Fayed arose from simple but respectable origins as the son of an Egyptian schoolteacher. Dodi's maternal grandfather, Dr. Mohammed Khashoggi, lived in Mecca, Islam's holiest city. He was the royal physician to King Abdul Aziz Ibn Saud, founder of Saudi Arabia. With the end of the war in 1945, and a peaceful and prosperous era of history beckoning, Dr. Khashoggi decided to send his children off to boarding school to get a first-rate education. For his sons Adnan, Essam, and Adil, he selected Victoria College in Alexandria, the elite academy of the Arab world, whose courses were taught in English and attended by the offspring of kings and prime ministers.

An enlightened man, Dr. Khashoggi—the name means "spoon maker"—also sent his daughters, Samira and Assia, to Alexandria's English school for girls. Because Samira, the elder daughter, was so anxious about being far from home without her parents, Dr. Khashoggi's wife decided to establish a second family residence in Alexandria even as her husband remained in Saudi Arabia. Eventually, a sixth child came along, Soheir, who was born in Alexandria.

A neighbor introduced Mohammed Al Fayed to Adnan Khashoggi, who hired him to help manage a fledgling import-export business. One day on the beach in Alexandria, the story goes, Mohammed was introduced to Khashoggi's sister Samira, then just 19, and not long afterwards they married. They lived in a small house near the much larger dwelling where the sprawling Khashoggi clan stayed. Mohammed was deeply in love with Samira, and was proud when she bore him a son. The arrival of the new baby was an exciting event for all the Khashoggis: he was the family's first grand-child. The boy was named Emad el Din Mohammed Al Fayed. When little Emad was learning to speak, he had difficulty with all the letters D in his name, and he would make a stuttering noise that sounded like Do-di. His father playfully called him "Dodi," and the nickname stuck.

But the happiness was short-lived. When Emad was scarcely two, the 22-year-old Samira stunned Mohammed and her family by asking for a divorce. She felt she had made a mistake by marrying Mohammed. Apparently, she had fallen in love with Anas Yasseen, who was another of her brother Adnan's business partners, also a cousin from Saudi Arabia. In Arab tradition it is not uncommon for a man to retain custody of his children following a divorce, but usually he waits until they reach the age of eight. Mohammed, understandably angry and upset, took little Emad away from his mother when he was still a toddler. Thus began a bitter family feud that would last throughout Dodi's life. At first, Mohammed apparently refused to permit his ex-wife even to see their son. Samira soon married Anas, and later moved to Beirut. Dodi's total separation from his mother, it seems, would last several years.

The painful truth that his mother had walked out on him and his father left Dodi with a lasting hole in his heart. "It is very hard for a little boy to be raised without his mother," says his aunt Soheir, now 50, a novelist living in New York. "I don't think my sister realized that Dodi was suffering without a mother. I admitted this to her: I told her that I loved her, but that I would never leave my children. That is my point of view. I always looked at Dodi's face and saw sadness in his eyes as a child."

Samira was a vibrant and talented woman whose subsequent unhappiness only seemed to torment Dodi further. At first, she had a wonderful life with Anas, who went into the Saudi diplomatic corps and became an ambassador to India, the United Nations, and later Turkey. In 1965, Samira gave birth to her second child, Jumana, or Gigi, as her mother nicknamed her after the film. Although Dodi was nine years older than Gigi, Samira did everything possible to bring her children together so they could know each other as brother and sister.

After Anas was killed in a road accident in the mountains of Turkey in 1974, Samira threw herself more deeply into her work. She soon founded *Al Sharkiah (The Oriental)*, one of the first magazines for women in the Arab world. She also wrote ten romantic novels, including two that were made into popular Egyptian films. Although she seemed careful to keep any references to her personal life as oblique as possible, the plots were about love and betrayal. She married a third time, to a Lebanese businessman. But he apparently ran off with another woman. In 1986, Samira died suddenly of a massive heart attack following what appeared to be a mild stroke.

Samira had grown so sad in her final years that some family members took to saying that she had died of a broken heart. Part of her unhappiness had to do with her only son. She came to regret not having been there for his childhood years. When Dodi became a teenager, some of his resentment toward her began to show. But they had reconciled before she died. "He knew how much his mother loved him," Jumana says. "When she died, he collapsed."

Although Mohammed Al Fayed doted on his son, his business responsibilities didn't leave him much time to spend with Dodi either. His shipping business prospered, and eventually he bought a redbrick Victorian villa in Alexandria's Ras el Sada quarter, a three-story dwelling in a walled compound that was large enough to accommodate his brother Salah and Salah's family. After King Farouk was toppled in a coup by Col. Gamal Abdul Nasser in 1952, Mohammed found the new socialist regime less favorable to his business interests and thus shifted much of his activity to Dubai, where he was to build his fortune. With both his parents gone much of the time, Dodi was effectively raised by Salah—a flashy dresser with an eye for beautiful women—and his Italian wife.

Dodi was a lonely and sensitive child. He would spend hours by himself gluing together model airplanes and automobiles. The villa had a vast garden with dozens of palm trees and bougainvillea, and Dodi kept a menagerie: two gazelles, a parrot, and a monkey.

His later career in entertainment was influenced, perhaps, by the games that would go on when he went to visit his grandmother Samiha. His aunt Soheir had a marvelous marionette theater, and he used to love to work the puppets with her. The children would act out little dramas together. Once, they put a wig on Dodi and dressed him up as a girl. Everybody laughed, and Dodi told his aunts he wanted to be an actor when he grew up.

Everyone who knew Dodi in Alexandria remembers two things about him: he was the boy who had everything, and he was painfully shy. He had such trouble making friends at school that his uncle worried about him. His best friend from those days, Nubar "Tika" Zarbhanelian, recalls how Salah approached him for help one day at the Alexandria Yacht Club. "He told me, 'Tika, my nephew doesn't know anybody, he doesn't go out. You go around, you know girls. Will you take him with you?' "

Tika was glad to oblige. Dodi's doting father spared him no amusement: cars, speedboats, anything he wanted. On one birthday he was presented with a metallic silver Opel convertible. The car caught fire due to an overheated engine, and was destroyed the same day. But Dodi had other means of transportation: he was driven to school every day by a chauffeur in one of the family cars; classmates recall that he would always wear a watch whose color matched the car. "My first impression of Dodi was, 'Lucky him, the sky is the limit,' " Tika says. "It was obvious that he had everything he asked for. But Dodi didn't know how to have fun. I knew how to have fun, but didn't have the means."

Despite the imposed dreariness of Nasser's socialism, Alexandria remained a cosmopolitan port city, with large communities of Greeks and Italians mixing with Arabs, and with much to offer a couple of wealthy and well-connected teenagers. In the summer, Dodi and Tika would hang out every day at the yacht club, where they would go sailing, swimming, and waterskiing. One day Dodi's Uncle Salah brought a new boat to the yacht club and christened it with the name "Dodi." From that point on, Emad was called Dodi by all his friends.

Tika remembers how he and Dodi would moor their sailboat in the harbor at 2 P.M., and wait for white-jacketed waiters in black bow ties to come out on motorboats and serve lunch on silver trays. Later in the day, they might head to the colonial-style Alexandria Club, once reserved exclusively for British expatriates, and go horseback riding. There were other amusements. Dodi had all the latest rock records and was crazy about movies—partly, says Tika, because they could kiss their girlfriends in the darkened cinema.

When it came to conquering the opposite sex, the shy young Dodi was hardly a budding casanova in his school days. Tika used to tease him in the clubhouse shower room that, his anatomy being what it was, he should have no trouble getting girls to like him. Tika realized that part of Dodi's problem was a longing for his mother. But the subject was so painful for Dodi that, even as his best friend, Tika never dared to bring it up. Tika was always falling in love with his girlfriends. But Dodi, he says, couldn't do that. He preferred just to have fun and remain aloof. "I had to shake him," Tika says. "Dodi would look at you as if he was waiting for you to tell him what to do. He had question marks in his eyes." Tika recalls how Dodi once asked him for advice about how to organize a party. Tika supplied the guest list and told Dodi what food and drinks to buy. "Dodi couldn't make decisions," he says.

Dodi's confidence didn't improve much with his coming of age. In Alexandria, he attended the boys' primary school at the elite College St. Marc, which had been run by French monks since 1922 for the children of the city's wealthiest businessmen and weightiest politicians. It was a harsh institution, where teachers thought nothing of disciplining a student, standing at attention in the regulation white shirt and blue tie, by slapping him in the face, or calling in a father to demand an explanation for a son's poor marks. A teacher at St. Marc's recalled that Dodi was "a quiet, obedient boy who displayed no rebellious behavior." He also showed no great flair for his studies, finishing 30th in a class of 38.

By 1969, Mohammed decided that it was time that Dodi left Alexandria. He enrolled him at the Institut Le Rosey, an exclusive boarding school in Rolle, Switzerland. Nestled near the quaint Swiss mountain resort of Gstaad, a winter playground of the rich and famous, the school is only miles from Diana's alma mater, Institut Alpin Videmanette, where eight years later the future Princess spent six months undergoing a little polishing. At Le Rosey, Dodi met the children of other jet-setters, and would begin to form his outer and inner circles of friends for the years ahead. But, according to Philippe Gudin, director general of Le Rosey, Dodi left after one year and did not graduate.

Members of the family draw a blank on exactly what Dodi did next, but when he was about 16 or 17, his father sent him for military training in the United Arab Emirates, where Al Fayed was on close terms with the country's rulers. It is customary for the emirs of the gulf to send their brightest sons to Britain's Royal Military Academy at Sandhurst. And in January 1974, Dodi was packed off to Sandhurst for a six-month course as part of the regular intake from the U.A.E.

Afterwards, commissioned as a second lieutenant, he had the chance to join the U.A.E. air force. Instead, he became an attaché at the U.A.E. embassy in London. "Sandhurst gave Dodi some discipline in his character," says his uncle Adnan. "He was extremely respectful of his elders, a tradition that is dear to Arabs. Whenever an adult came into a room, he would rise."

5

Dodi

RICH ARAB. VULGAR JET-SETTER. CHAMPAGNE-SWILLING PLAY-boy. Cocaine-snorting party animal. Who could resist snide clichés after Dodi Fayed, the son of an "Arab shopkeeper," as one British commentator sniffed, became romantically involved with the Princess of Wales? Not the smug English aristocrats, who despised Diana already for her public confessionals about infidelities in the House of Windsor, which they believed had brought disgrace to the British monarchy.

"What on earth does she see in him?" Diana's biographer, Andrew Morton, wrote in *The Sun* three days before her death, posing a question that was on the lips of many in Britain and the rest of the world. "You can't help regretting," chimed in Sarah Bradford, Queen Elizabeth II's biographer, "that this beautiful woman, who could have been queen, has chosen someone so trivial." Columnist Glenys Roberts, writing in the *Mail on Sunday*, wondered whether Diana hadn't fled the confines of the royal family for another prison—"an Arab one."

After Dodi and Diana were dead, the pundits still couldn't help themselves. The notion was advanced that as a young Arab stud Dodi had worn a "slightly sinister" mustache, slapped and pushed his girlfriends and threatened them with a 9mm Beretta. (Actually, the mustache made him look more like a doe-eyed Omar Sharif than a tough guy.) One writer, William Safire of *The New York Times*, went so far as to blame Dodi's machismo directly for Diana's death. Perhaps wanting to impress Diana with "his power," Safire surmised, an angry and frustrated Dodi ordered his chauffeur to lose the pursuing paparazzi by stepping on the gas.

The Dodi who died with Diana in Paris was in fact not very much different from the lonely little boy with the searching brown eyes in Alexandria. Sure, he was rich, and in time he had learned how to enjoy the company of attractive women, who in any case were drawn to his wealth. But, at least to those who knew him best, his habit of throwing his wealth around—and his women away—had far more to do with insecurity than insincerity.

As Dodi crept past his 41st birthday, his neurosis about health and safety made it inconceivable, as far as his closest friends are concerned, that he would have indulged in drugs, much less dangerous car chases. In Diana, he had found, at last, the love of his life. If he did tell the driver to step on it that night in Paris, it would have been out of the gentler and nobler desire to spare Diana, not to mention himself, the flashbulb frenzy he had come to loathe during their brief romance. If he did give that instruction, it went terribly wrong. But nobody who knew Dodi well describes him as the sort of daredevil who would risk his life—or that of his lover—to attempt a tire-smoking getaway.

The caricature of Dodi as high-living playboy is based on his Hollywood days, the roots of which go back to his Egyptian childhood. When he and his friend Tika would take their girlfriends to the Metro or Royale cinemas in downtown Alexandria, it was often to see a James Bond film. Tika recalls how he and Dodi went to see both *Goldfinger* and *Thunderball* twice. A shy and insecure kid on the verge of puberty, Dodi adored the flashy cars, the curvaceous girls, and the suave ways of Ian Fleming's 007. And he eagerly indulged his growing fantasies.

A few years later, while staying with his father in London on a break from Le Rosey, Dodi met a group of American kids whose parents were expatriates residing in Britain. One of them was Barbara Broccoli, the youngest daughter of Albert R. "Cubby" Broccoli, producer of the James Bond movies, many of which were filmed at Pinewood studios to the west of London. At the time, Dodi was the cute little rich kid with his own flat in his father's apartment house at 60 Park Lane overlooking Hyde Park. He even had his own Rolls-Royce and chauffeur. The Broccolis lived around the corner on Green Street, Mayfair. Over the years, they became Dodi's adopted family.

One day in 1971, Cubby Broccoli was shooting *Live and Let Die* when Barbara invited Dodi, then 15, to come along to Pinewood and watch. From that day on, Dodi was hooked. "My father built this huge soundstage, one of the largest stages in the world, with model submarines, the works," says Barbara, now producing the Bond films after her father's death in 1996. "Dodi was knocked out by all this. He couldn't believe what could be achieved on a movie set." Throughout the rest of his life, Dodi would always tell friends how the fabled Bond producer had given him the moviemaking bug. He learned to recite every Bond film scene by scene, and went out of his way to meet the two best-known James Bonds, Sean Connery and Roger Moore.

As a teenager, Dodi would hang around Pinewood with Barbara, whom he nicknamed Beebee after her initials as well as the affectionate word for friend in Arabic *(habibi)*. She vividly remembers how Dodi could spend an entire weekend at the cinema, munching popcorn and riveted to the latest adventure film. "At times, he was lonely, and films filled a void for him," she says. "It was because they gave him such pleasure that he wanted to make them."

Noticing his budding interest in the business, Barbara's mother Dana suggested that Dodi join her son Tony at a summer school course in cinema at Loyola University in New Orleans, where they would be looked after by a Broccoli family friend. When he and Tony arrived, Dodi took one look at the student accommodations and frowned. Having had enough of dormitory living in Le Rosey, he checked into a luxury hotel.

When Dana learned of this, she phoned Dodi at the hotel and demanded to know why he had left his friend behind.

"It wasn't very comfortable," Dodi replied.

"Tony is there," the mother shot back.

"Well," Dodi said, sheepishly, "that Tony is a commando."

Wealthy, pampered, well-connected, and starry-eyed, Dodi was in the fast lane now, on his way to Hollywood.

Barbara Broccoli says it was in the midseventies when Dodi sat down and had a heart-to-heart talk with her father about launching his own career in the movies. Dodi admired Cubby, a former Twentieth Century-Fox mailroom clerk who went on to produce more than 40 motion pictures. In their chat, Cubby strongly suggested that Dodi join forces with an experienced film executive. He was concerned that, as a young kid with a lot of his father's money to spend, Dodi might be vulnerable to rip-off artists unless he had an old hand at his side.

Following Cubby's advice, Dodi and his father eventually set up a small independent company called Allied Stars Ltd., and hired one of Cubby's trusted associates. Incorporated in June 1979, two months after Dodi's 23rd birthday, it listed two parent companies, Allied Stars S.A., a Liberian company, and the Swiss firm Compagnie de Gestion et de Banque Gonet.

By most accounts, Dodi happily left the particulars to the old hands but used the new company to begin learning the trade. Allied Stars' first project was *Breaking Glass,* a new-wave film with a young Jonathan Pryce about a punk rock singer in 1970s London, which immediately made a few million dollars and eventually became an art cinema staple. Clive Parsons, a co-producer of the film, recalls that Dodi's involvement was minimal and his father made the financial decisions.

Good luck—something which Dodi seemed to have in abundance—was at work with the next project: at 25, Dodi won the 1982 Academy Award for Best Motion Picture as executive producer of *Chariots of Fire,* the stirring drama about a Scottish divinity student and his Jewish outcast team-mate on the 1924 British Olympics squad.

According to Barbara Broccoli, the movie came into being after the producer David Puttnam passed the *Chariots* script to her father's associate and he in turn passed it to Dodi. "I remember him telling me how moving it was, how important it was, how desperate he was to make it," says Barbara. "I asked Dodi, 'Why does this story mean something to you as an Egyptian?' And he said, 'It's about somebody who has strong beliefs. And who is an outsider.' "

Dodi, Broccoli says, lobbied his father to co-finance the $6 million project with Puttnam. Although Puttnam was once quoted as saying that Dodi's father "made all the decisions," Broccoli insists that "it was because of Dodi's interest that this film was made." Dodi received a typewritten note of gratitude signed "Puttnam" after the completion of the film in 1980, and Dodi had it framed and put on a wall of his Park Lane apartment.

Dated August 15 in the year before the film's release, the note thanked Dodi for placing an ad in *Screen* magazine praising Puttnam's work on the movie: "For the past several months it has been me who should have been thanking you for all you've done to bring about a minor miracle. Thanks once and for all for making it all possible."

Barbara Broccoli believes that Dodi's modesty fed the tendency for movie people to dismiss him as a dilettante. She recalls his excitement in early 1982, when the Academy of Motion Picture Arts and Sciences announced that *Chariots* had been nominated for seven Oscars, including one for Best Picture. It was also announced that Albert Broccoli would be given the prestigious Irving Thalberg award for lifetime achievement in the movie business. Dodi and Barbara rushed off to Harry's Bar in London to celebrate their good fortune, and wound up sitting next to each other at the Oscars a few months later. "When the Best Picture was announced and it was *Chariots of Fire,* I saw David Puttnam go up toward the stage," Barbara recalls. "I said, 'Dodi, go up! Go up! Go up with Puttnam! You belong with Puttnam!' He sat very shyly and said, 'No, no, no, I can't, Beebee. I'll go next time.' That is sort of how Dodi was. He was very shy and modest.''

In 1982, armed with his golden statuette, Dodi began to break out of his shell. He started to make the party scene and often enjoyed the hospitality of his uncle Adnan Khashoggi, the Saudi financier and one-time arms broker who was then at the peak of his notoriety as the "world's richest man." Dodi's dashing younger cousin Mohammed Khashoggi remembers celebrating Dodi's *Chariots* Oscar with a wild summer on the Côte d'Azur. "He liked the good life, no doubt about that," Mohammed says. "He was in that business where the chicks are running by. He has a plane, a boat, and a car. He was completely locked into this lifestyle."

And that included the conquest of famous and beautiful women, according to Mohammed. Dodi had already had some minor flings with actresses. There was Valerie Perrine, an older woman he met on the set of *Superman*. Also Brooke Shields, a Khashoggi family friend, who had portrayed a child prostitute in *Pretty Baby* and virgins on the verge of sexual awakening in *Blue Lagoon* and *Endless Love*. Now Dodi was ready to take on all comers. He called Tika back in Alexandria and told him he was with Ali MacGraw, star of *Love Story*. "Come and have some fun with me," he told Tika. "You are wasting your time in Egypt."

It was the glitzy eighties, Ronald Reagan and Margaret Thatcher were in power, big spending was fashionable, and Dodi lived the fantasy life of a nomadic millionaire. He jetted between family homes in London, Paris, Gstaad, and St. Tropez, and bachelor pads at the Beverly Hills Hotel in Los Angeles and the Hotel Pierre in New York. His favorite haunts, where he would be waved through to the V.I.P. section, to puff on a Cohiba and sip Stolichnaya, were Spago and the Ivy in Los Angeles, and Harry's Bar, Tramp and Annabel's in London. For a time he was a familiar figure around Hugh Hefner's Playboy Mansion, and the list of his girlfriends grew. It would eventually include names such as Britt Ekland, Koo Stark, Charlotte Lewis, Patsy Kensit, Mimi Rogers, Tina Sinatra, Tawny Kitaen, Winona Ryder—and many others.

During the 1982 Oscars, his uncle Essam Khashoggi in Los Angeles threw a big party and invited half of Hollywood. To Dodi, however, the real star of the evening was his mother, who had flown in from Paris for the proud occasion. Dodi cruised by other Oscar blowouts, too, including one at Sly Stallone's. On the party circuit in the early eighties, Dodi in all likelihood tried a few lines of cocaine—some former "friends" even claimed that he had bricks of the white powder at his own gatherings to please his guests—but nobody recalls that he had a drug problem. "Cocaine was everywhere," says Dodi's press agent Pat Kingsley. "I don't know that he ever did anything, but if he went to one party during that time, [cocaine] would have been visible." Questioned about Dodi's alleged cocaine use, a French woman who was his friend and sometime lover is evasive on the subject. "I never did it with him," she says, "and I wouldn't say so if I did. It's pointless getting into that now. Nobody's perfect." Film director Richard Donner, a friend of two decades, has a different view: "I don't remember him even smoking a joint, actually."

Dodi liked to think of himself as the suave and sophisticated ladies' man idealized in the pages of *Playboy,* a magazine that he received regularly right up until the month of his death. But there was another side to him that he tended to shield from his male acquaintances: he was also the type of guy who read self-help books, like the best-selling *Men Are From Mars, Women Are From Venus: A Practical Guide for Improving Communication and Getting What You Want in Your Relationship.* The book, a gift from former girlfriend Kelly Fisher, was on the nightstand of his Paris apartment the very evening he was headed there with Diana.

While Dodi struck many Hollywood types as the mysterious macho Arab straight out of central casting, his restless pursuits in fact said something rather different about him, which many of his women friends better understood: Dodi's lonely and uncertain childhood had bruised his soul, leaving him insecure and desperate for acceptance and approval throughout his adult life. "You could see in his eyes the sadness, because he didn't grow up between mother and father, you know, the same way as normal children," says his uncle Adnan. Another relative, familiar with a bout of depression that hit Dodi when his mother died, is more emphatic: "Dodi had a tenuous relationship with life."

Friends say that one reason he dated so many women was that, haunted by the image of his mother walking out the door, he feared rejection if he made a commitment to any one of them. When he met a girl he liked, he would invariably shower her with massive bouquets of roses, stuffed teddy bears from Harrods, and candlelit dinners (with live string quartets), eager to give his love and receive some. But then with an instinct for self-protection, he would invariably draw back, rather than risk an arrow through the heart. "Because of what happened between his mother and father," says his aunt Soheir, "Dodi was always worried about marriage."

Soheir remembers that Dodi was too sensitive even to attend the funeral of his beloved grandmother Samiha when she died. Throughout his life, he was shaken by the feud between the Al Fayeds and his mother's Khashoggi clan, and did more than any other family member to try to end it.

Dodi was extravagant to a fault. His propensity to lavish gifts on everyone around—sides of smoked salmon and bottles of perfume, a weekend in the Seychelles—seemed to spring from an impulse to please more than to impress others. (Diana, it turned out, had the same quality.) One night at Tramp, Dodi learned it was the birthday of the wife of owner Johnny Gold. He simply took off the Cartier gold chain he was wearing beneath his Versace shirt and draped it around her neck. "Dodi was more generous than anybody I have ever met," says his former wife Suzanne Gregard. "And it was always with no strings attached. He never expected anything in return."

A hypochondriac himself, Dodi constantly fussed about other people's health. A few months before he began seeing Diana, he heard that his aunt Soheir had a thyroid condition. "He told me, 'I need you around. I have a great doctor in New York,'" says Soheir. "When I went to the appointment, the doctor told me, 'This guy really loves you.' Dodi paid for everything and then called me every day to see how I was doing." "He was a good sweet friend," says Hollywood producer Lauren Shuler-Donner. "I knew if I ever really needed something, he would be there for me."

Women found Dodi's vulnerable side appealing. It was never the sex. Before he died, several former girlfriends stepped forward to testify that Dodi had been a flop in bed. One close female friend had a one-night stand with him and called it all off because, as she puts it, "it was too pathetic. Dodi was very flaky with women. He was not a tactile person, not touchy-feely. He was not someone you would walk down the street with holding hands. I think he was never in love because he didn't know how to love."

But in a town full of cynics, and in an age of materialism, he read poetry, and avidly wrote romantic verse himself. Despite his wealth, he had no discernible ego. He was especially attractive to women on the rebound from bad relationships. "He was an incredible listener," says Mohammed Khashoggi. "I remember one girl who fell in love with him. She said: 'He listened to every one of my problems from grade school on up.' When a woman is heartbroken and you have an open ear, it's an attractive quality."

Dodi's immaculate apartments in London and Paris perfectly reflected the persona of a he-man pretender who was really a kid at heart. They had exercise gyms, marble bathrooms with trays of cologne, and photos of Dodi with action-hero friends like Burt Reynolds, Jean-Claude Van Damme, and Christopher Lambert. But they were also filled with stuffed teddy bears, model airplanes and cars, a collection of sports caps, dishes of American candy bars and lollipops, and photos of his lovable dogs, Bear, Shoe, and Romeo. Adults still called Dodi "the kid" or "the boy."

You didn't have to be human to touch Dodi's heartstrings. He would pull his car over on the side of the road if he saw a stray dog in danger of being run over. One day, his assistant Melissa Henning was running down a list of contacts in search of a new pet schnauzer for Dodi when a vet informed her that he had a very abused dog in need of a good home. The Shetland sheepdog had been severely beaten by a previous owner, who had had the animal's vocal cords surgically removed so it wouldn't bark. "I told Dodi about it, and even though he wanted a schnauzer, he said, 'Melissa, go get her.' He nurtured her, and even sent her to doggie therapy for $100 a hour."

Dodi's tender love for his dogs, like his childhood fascination with his menagerie in Alexandria, was a mirror of his difficulty in forming bonds with humans. Often the wallflower at a party, Dodi was at his best when talking to people on the cell phone that never seemed to leave his hand. "He wasn't the kind of guy who told off-color jokes or ran around the room with a lampshade on his head," says Pat Kingsley. He was so reserved that staff members who attended meetings with him at Harrods considered him "boring."

Melissa Henning recalls the morning in 1989 when Dodi interviewed her for a job at Allied Stars. "He was so shy that I interviewed myself," she says. "I was surprised, because I thought he would be arrogant, wearing tons of perfume and gold chains around his neck. I didn't think I could work for a Middle Easterner because I didn't think they respected women's opinions. He was just the opposite. He asked me three questions, and one of them was 'When can you start?' "

Dodi's close relationship with his butler René Delorm, 55, typified his gentle and unassuming character. René is a Moroccan-born Jew whose family fled Rabat after French colonial rule ended in 1956. He served a stint in the French army before settling with his parents in Montreal. He hated the cold weather and wandered to California, where he spent 16 years as a waiter at two of the city's most famous celebrity hangouts, Ma Maison and later Spago. Whenever Dodi came in, René would have his favorite beverages waiting: "always a dry martini, and a bottle of Baron de L white wine."

One day in 1991 Dodi asked René to leave the job he loved and become his butler. Says René: "I told him, 'I am deaf, blind, and mute. I am a masseur. And I am Jewish.' I knew he was an Egyptian, and I didn't want to hide anything like that from him. He looked at me and smiled and said, 'Great!' "

René continued living in his own Santa Monica apartment, but three years later when Mohammed Al Fayed yanked Dodi back to Europe, Dodi asked René to join him in Paris. "I said, 'I am loyal to you, and to prove it I will come with you.' " René recalls. "I left behind my girlfriend and son and friends."

Dodi's death hit René as if he had been a member of his own family. "He was so easy to please," René says, choking back tears as he stands in the foyer of the third-floor apartment on the Rue Arsène-Houssaye where he awaited the arrival of Dodi and Diana in the early hours of August 31. "I could talk to him as a friend. It was the best job I ever had. Since Dodi left us, I have lost ten pounds. I don't sleep. I go to bed, and it all comes back—my life with him, what it could have been with the Princess. But the best doctor is time."

Dodi's deepest and longest lasting female relationships tended to be with sister figures like Barbara Broccoli; he never had to worry if they would walk out on him. In every city where Dodi lived there is a woman, or several, with whom he had a deep yet platonic relationship, and to whom he poured out the troubles of his life. Even his one marriage, to Ford Agency model Suzanne Gregard, turned out to be that sort of friendship. Gregard recalls that they "immediately hit it off" after meeting in 1984 at a restaurant on East Seventy-ninth Street during a dinner with a mutual friend, owner of Xenon, one of the hottest New York clubs of the moment. They began going out but did not date each other exclusively.

But then Dodi began pouring forth the impulses to romance and protect that would find echoes in his relationship with Diana a decade later. He showered Suzanne with affection, flowers, jewelry, and trips to the south of France. She continued to model in New York, but Dodi would fly her to London to visit him twice a month on the Concorde, protectively buying the seat next to her so she wouldn't be bothered by another passenger. Suddenly, a week before Christmas 1986, still in a funk over the unexpected death of his mother earlier in the year, he proposed to her on the spur of the moment. For Gregard, it was all intoxicatingly romantic. "He had the most beautiful brown Egyptian eyes," she says. "He was dark and handsome. I liked dark and handsome."

Dodi had already leased a house in Vail, Colorado, for the winter skiing season, so he and Suzanne simply got married at the chalet, before a local judge and 20 friends as witnesses. The union lasted all of 10 months before they decided on an amicable separation. But they remained good friends, and even continued to date when Dodi was back in town. Dodi tried for a reconciliation, but things didn't work out. A gold digger might have tried for millions, but Gregard says she did not seek or receive anything. Dodi had not insisted on a prenuptial agreement, and Suzanne politely returned the Bulgari wedding ring that had belonged to Dodi's mother. "It was very civilized, like, 'Do you want to file, or should I?' " says Gregard. "There was no financial settlement. That wasn't what the marriage was about. I didn't need Dodi's money. That would have ruined our friendship."

With most of the women Dodi dated, however, being rich often compounded his insecurity. "He always used to tell me that most of the girls were there for his money," says a platonic woman friend in London. "He was so sad about it. He didn't know who was there for love." That is one reason that many of Dodi's closest friends happened to be wealthy themselves; he didn't have to wonder about their motives. He had more than his share of bad luck with women out for the jackpot. Friends would warn him about a girl, but out of his desire to have a pretty woman around, and his fear of being the one to break a heart, he would allow a relationship to drift into ambiguity. It would often get him into trouble.

Dodi dated a 30-year-old model named Amy Brown in 1992. According to a suit he later filed against her, he handed over the deed to a $500,000 condo in L.A. after she "promised . . . she would continue to be his romantic companion." When she dropped him anyway, Dodi sued to have her evicted, claiming that she had "deliberately schemed" to get the property from him. They settled out of court and Brown moved out.

Another awkward relationship, one that would receive glaring publicity once his affair with Diana became known, was with Kelly Fisher, yet another 30-year-old model. Dodi met her during the summer of 1996 at the Ritz, where he would cruise the hotel's posh restaurants and bars for attractive girls. Over the next 12 months, they hopped around the jet-set circuit together, hanging out at Dodi's apartment at the Beverly Hills Hotel, his permanent suite at the Pierre in New York, and of course, the Ritz in Paris. He even took her on the same tour that Diana would later have of the Duke of Windsor's former villa in the Bois de Boulogne.

At Christmas, the couple took a Caribbean cruise. Dodi later gave her a ring, and Kelly would say that they had become engaged. None of Dodi's closest friends say they knew about any engagement. Dodi's butler, who probably knew him as well as anyone, doubts that Dodi ever had any intention of marrying Fisher. "He would have told me," says René. "She was not right for him." In fact, Dodi informed some of his friends that he told Kelly in February he wanted to cool down the relationship.

Dodi threw a birthday party at Annabel's in London on June 18 for Barbara Broccoli, who remembers a scene there involving Kelly. Barbara's husband, Fred, at one point asked Dodi, "So what is this, a serious thing between you two?" Dodi waved Fred off, saying, "I don't want to go into it." Kelly was kind of pushy and said, "Of course it's serious." Dodi replied: "Look, Kelly, let's not go into it." According to Barbara, in the middle of the dinner an infuriated Kelly got up and announced, "I'm leaving."

Dodi apologized to his guests and walked Kelly outside to her car. But even after such an outburst he could not let go of her. He continued seeing Kelly right up until the moment last July when he abandoned her on his own yacht in St. Tropez and—like Fitzgerald's Gatsby rowing out to meet his destiny in Lake Superior—began romancing Diana on his father's boat. In fact, he continued seeing Kelly afterwards, too. "Dodi had difficulty being alone," says Melissa Henning. "He would rather be with someone he didn't love than be totally alone. That was part of his insecurity."

Rosa Monckton, a friend of Diana's, said that the Princess "had a unique ability to spot the broken-hearted, and she could zero in on them." Barbara Broccoli suggests that Dodi fell for Diana, herself a wounded spirit, in part because he had precisely the same quality. "It made sense that they connected in a very profound way," she says. "Strangely, they had similar lives. One of the things Dodi said to me was 'It's so extraordinary that we don't have to *explain* anything to each other.' "

When it came to love, it was not only women who caused Dodi anguish. It was also his complicated relationship with his strong-willed father.

Dodi had lived a pampered and protected childhood in Egypt, Switzerland, and later Britain. Cars, boats, servants, toys, whatever he desired. But as the boy became a man, he discovered that his overprotective father had now become at times an overbearing one. Mohammed had sent Dodi to the Royal Military Academy at Sandhurst in 1974 to toughen him up. But Dodi's passion was moviemaking—he had inherited his mother's artistic sensibility rather than Mohammed's cutthroat business instincts—and it was that route that he was determined to follow.

In a career that spanned 18 years, apart from *Chariots*, Dodi never made a spectacular mark in the film industry. If Dodi lacked the ambition and genius for producing of a

Cubby Broccoli, he also never had the freedom to strike out on his own. For one thing, he did not have his own millions to be a major player. And although his father would come up with the cash on a project-by-project basis, the amounts tended to be small compared to the size of the family's wealth. What he put into Dodi's six completed pictures probably did not exceed a total of $10 million—hardly an extravagant sum by Hollywood standards.

Mohammed himself considered the movie business not much more than an amusing sideshow, perhaps something that could be used to dress up a commercial promotion at Harrods. He expected Dodi to devote more and more time to the trading empire that he had created in Britain. This was completely in keeping with the family-centered traditions of Arab culture, and as an Egyptian, Dodi accepted it. But as a jet-setter who had seen Americans worshipping at the temple of individualism, he did so with increasing reluctance.

The dichotomy frequently created discord with his father, and the two engaged in transatlantic shouting matches in Arabic, although cursing in English. "They did have a difficult relationship," says his aunt Soheir. "They had their ups and downs. But Dodi so much wanted the attention and love of his father, and Mohammed loved his son. He didn't want Dodi to be in L.A., but rather in London with him." "He didn't like going to Harrods," agrees a female friend of Dodi's. "He did it to please his father. Dodi just loved moviemaking." Moreover, she believes that the strong pull of his father dented Dodi's self-esteem. "When you are financially dependent on your father, told all your life what to do, and bought houses and wonderful things, people think you are good for nothing. Especially if you are a man."

Dodi and Mohammed went through estrangements from time to time. In 1986, the year he fell into a funk over his mother's death, he told British writer Andrew Stephen that he had not had much contact with his father for five years. "I don't want to see him," Dodi said. "I don't want to speak to him or anything like that." "His father didn't approve of his lifestyle and his show business connections," says an ex-girlfriend. "Dodi felt a lot of sadness because they were not able to understand and talk to each other. He felt like the black sheep of the family." Pointedly, he preferred to be known, even in his film credits, as Dodi Fayed, rather than Al Fayed, as his father more grandly styled the family name.

In about 1988 Dodi became a director of Harrods as well as another family business, the shirt-makers Turnbull & Asser in Jermyn Street. The following year he added a directorship of Modena Engineering, a Ferrari dealership near London just purchased by his father. But by the early 1990s, Dodi had quit his father's boards and was spending more time in Los Angeles. Although Dodi's associates tried to put the best face on it, his career after *Chariots* drifted along without notable distinction. When Dodi spoke to Andrew Stephen, he was well aware of the whispering behind his back. "People always assume that I'm just putting the money in and, you know, going off to the Bahamas or Switzerland or something. I'm not."

An associate at Harrods acknowledges father-son strains over Dodi's career path. "Mohammed loved Dodi, but he knew his son would never be another Mohammed Al Fayed, never a great businessman. It's not easy being the son of a successful father. Still, Dodi did his best. He got up every day and worked, when he didn't have to. And he did have a certain track record of success in Hollywood."

Indeed, in the milieu of ultrarich Arabs who made vast fortunes in the oil boom, Dodi stood out as someone who was not afraid of long hours. "How many producers in Hollywood have an Oscar sitting on their desk for Best Picture?" Pat Kingsley asks. Yet even she, his publicity agent, describes Dodi as a "part-time" producer. "Hollywood is a very tough town," says Kingsley. "It is hard to get a movie made. You have to find the material, a script, a director, and then financing. Dodi didn't have the time to put into it that other producers can devote. He had other obligations."

Dodi's main personal achievements were his two *F/X* films, released in 1986 and 1991, "my Bond movies," he called them. They were critically acclaimed thrillers about a

Hollywood special effects man involved in dangerous escapades, such as helping the government fake the assassination of an organized crime boss. Barbara Broccoli recalls that Dodi did all the things an involved producer has to do. He developed the scripts, hired the directors, and supervised the casting.

Dodi scored an executive producer's credit for *Hook*, the 1991 adaptation of the Peter Pan story, which starred Dustin Hoffman and Julia Roberts and was directed by Steven Spielberg. Dodi's role was essentially "finding" the material: Peter Pan author Sir James M. Barrie had bequeathed his copyright to London's Great Ormond Street Children's Hospital, which gave the Al Fayed family use of the story because Mohammed had made generous donations to the hospital. Dodi's last completed project, released in 1995, was *The Scarlet Letter* starring Demi Moore as Hester Prynne. Dodi's financing of the first draft of the screenplay earned him an executive producer credit in the film directed by Roland Joffé.

Around this time, Dodi's producing career was abruptly interrupted when a string of debts in L.A. upset his father and led him to bring Dodi back home to London. In all, at least 10 suits were filed against Dodi in the U.S., including several by landlords of luxury homes who claimed he failed to pay rent and some by ex-business associates who said he owed them money. He also got into assorted financial wrangles with American Express, the U.S. Internal Revenue Service, and the distributors of *The Scarlet Letter*. The financial card service reportedly sued Dodi for failing to pay a $116,890 statement; he apparently withheld payment after complaining about poor service from a jet-hire company he had paid with his Amex card.

Some of Dodi's problems stemmed from his notorious carelessness with cash. Even as a kid in Alexandria, Tika remembers, Dodi rarely had a piastre in his pocket, forcing his friends to pick up the tab time after time. "Dodi," explains an associate with dry understatement, "could be rather cavalier about money." According to friends in L.A., another

problem was Dodi's constant suspicions—often very justified—that people were taking him for a ride because he was
a rich man's kid.

"For all his worldliness and sophistication, in his soul
there was an innocent guy," says film director Richard Donner. "Everybody in this frigging town, if they wanted to stay
at the Ritz or get to his father, used Dodi in the worst way.
I would always say to him, 'Don't be so friggin' nice!' Just
tell 'em 'Screw you!' '' Matters weren't helped any when an
Egyptian named Mohammed Sead spent some time imper-
sonating him and running up debts. After hooking up as a
groupie with the rock band Duran Duran, Sead was caught
in Toronto and given a two-year prison sentence in June
1997.

Sometimes, according to some relatives and friends, Mohammed would get upset with Dodi and shut off his allow-
ance, purported to be $100,000 per month. "There is a big
difference between having a father turning the tap on and
off, and having your own money and making your own decisions," says one relative. "The ultimate control is money.
You don't bite the hand that feeds you, right?"

In 1994, the messy disputes with landlords became too
much for his father and he in effect ordered Dodi back to
London. "Mohammed is very conscientious about his
name," explains one of Dodi's closest friends. "He didn't
want his son incurring these liabilities. That was the straw
that broke the camel's back."

Back in Europe, Dodi began dividing his time between his
Park Lane flat in London and the Rue Arsène-Houssaye
apartment in Paris. He spent most of his working time on
product development at Harrods, setting up at an office
across the street from the store rather than in the fifth-floor
executive suite where he once had an office beside his father's. He came up with the idea for a Black Label line of
luxury goods, and got involved in hiring Hollywood actors
who traditionally open the semiannual Harrods sale.

He was also getting more involved in the management of
the Ritz in Paris. "He would talk to me about the hotel,"

says Ritz president Frank Klein. "If he had a problem with the way we did things, or a suggestion, he would tell me. He had helpful ideas. As he got older, and more involved in his father's business, he would have picked it up. In a different way from Mohammed, of course, but he would have been good at it. He had a way of telling you things without shouting."

By the summer of 1997, whatever tension existed between father and son seemed to be easing. Dodi's friends and associates spoke of how he was getting his act together. Dodi had kept his hand in Allied Stars, and since his move to Europe had supervised the development or acquisition of five projects: a live-action animated film tentatively called *Rock Hoppers*, a drama about the Holocaust, a family film about teddy bears, a time-travel family adventure comedy, and a spy thriller about a rogue intelligence network inside the CIA. In addition, he was going to produce a World War II submarine movie with Richard Donner.

For his 41st birthday in April, Dodi had dinner at Harry's Bar in London with Barbara Broccoli, and she remembers him being particularly philosophical that night. "He would talk about how he wanted to have kids and a proper relationship with someone," she says. "He really wanted to find someone he could love and who would love him."

By May, Dodi had decided to return to Los Angeles and begin the task of finding money for the new projects developed by Allied Stars. In Malibu's Paradise Cove, he bought the five-acre estate once owned by actress Julie Andrews and husband Blake Edwards, where Richard Gere, Barbra Streisand, and MGM chief Frank Mancuso were his immediate neighbors. A few weeks later, Dodi went to Paris and announced to his faithful butler, "René, you are going back to Los Angeles!" René later recalled: "He was so happy, too. He loved America. Most of his friends were there."

Then Dodi met Diana in St. Tropez. Nearly everybody who spoke to Dodi afterwards remarked on the change that had come over him, especially in the final week or two before his death. "Dodi had really come of age," says Pat

Kingsley, who spoke to Dodi throughout the summer. "Diana was an important element in that. His voice changed. He was more self-assured. He told me that he was going to make his father proud of him. He had always lived in Mohammed's shadow. Diana was giving him the confidence to challenge the world."

"Finally, the kid was going to be an individual," agrees Richard Donner. "He was his father's son. All he ever cared about was his father. He worried about his father's health. He would have been very proud to have his dad be proud of him. He was more and more serious about a hands-on attitude. He started to have more respect for himself that he actually could do it. It wasn't just titular. It wasn't just a name."

"He was stepping into life in a way that he hadn't before," says Roland Joffé. "There was a quality with Dodi of waiting in the wings. Dodi was getting to the point where he was going to be autonomous. He had tremendous respect for his father, and very much wanted to be a man his father could look up to." Adds Dodi's cousin Mohammed Khashoggi: "Diana was a strong, independent, and powerful woman. She complemented a side of Dodi that needed that. I don't think he would have given her up for anything."

Those dreams would be shattered minutes after Dodi organized his getaway plan at the Ritz to escape the pursuing paparazzi. Did Dodi order the driver to go faster? The question is a troubling part of the puzzle left by the terrible crash, and the answer may never be known. It is plausible that Dodi did give such an instruction, though probably not because of a macho impulse to prove his power. Nor because he was some reckless speed demon himself, or a bullying backseat driver. Dodi could have reacted because he felt under pressure, relying instinctively on his ever-present retinue of drivers and bodyguards.

Dodi was not with some forgettable starlet that night. Falling in love with the Princess of Wales was the most incredible thing that had ever happened to him. For a deeply insecure 41-year-old, she represented, all at once, the ultimate conquest of a beautiful and famous woman, the elusive soulmate of a lifetime's search, and the match that would make his father as proud as he could ever be. When Dodi arrived in Paris with Diana on August 30, it was the first time on land the couple had found themselves being chased by a pack of photographers.

Dodi himself may not have been reckless, yet he seemed to put blind faith in the chauffeurs and bodyguards his father had provided for him since his days in primary school in Alexandria. When a driver was at the wheel, he rarely if ever wore a seat belt in the back. Dodi's cocoon of bodyguards struck many of his friends as excessive. He would explain that his father insisted on the protection, fearing that Dodi could be kidnapped or killed for his money. But their presence was so intrusive, it caused Suzanne Gregard to resent the intrusion during their brief marriage. "He felt better," she says, "but we were never really alone."

A chilling preview of the tragedy in Paris seems to have occurred in a fast ride up Madison Avenue in New York in the mideighties. Dodi and Koo Stark, the then-girlfriend of Prince Andrew, were being chased by paparazzi and Dodi reportedly ordered the driver to step on it.

Roland Joffé believes that the illusions Dodi and Diana each lived played no small part in driving events toward the tragic destination. "Dodi had a deep streak of loneliness, and the world of bodyguards made him feel secure and protected," says Joffé. "You can feel the emotional buzz in the Ritz corridor that night: all that escape planning was a fantasy. Those trappings of invulnerability made them feel that they could speed through Paris and escape. Everybody became an actor. Somehow there was this privacy that had to be protected and photographs that had to be stolen. The emotions are very deep and that puts people in a strange state of heightened anxiety, as well as heightened delight. They want to go off to the press in one way, and they want to run from it in the other. I can see how under pressure you would begin to repeat all the things that you know made you feel safe. That's the strange thing about wealth, often, if it is used in a particular way, it also creates a great fantasy world that is self-perpetuating. That was the world they both lived in. In hindsight, those were tragic decisions. It made it easier for an accident to result.''

Dodi did have a ''thing'' about cars. Suzanne Gregard recalls that far from being a ''crazy race-car-driving sort of person,'' Dodi was actually uncomfortable even sitting in them. Dodi's mother's second husband had been killed in a frightful road accident in Turkey. At times, Gregard says, cars made Dodi claustrophobic.

He had a collection of luxury sports cars, including a Lagonda, an Aston Martin, and several Ferraris. Yet paradoxically he himself drove like the proverbial little old lady. In Los Angeles, he bought a $90,000 Humvee, a wide-bodied military vehicle used by U.S. forces in the Gulf War, about as secure a vehicle as one could find anywhere. His concern for safety was of a pair with a phobia about his health: he would carry around Handiwipes to clean his hands the instant he suspected contact with germs.

''From the experiences I had with him, Dodi was never, ever comfortable in cars,'' Gregard says. ''He liked beautiful cars. But he was not a fast driver at all. He really seriously was not comfortable in cars. I remember him pulling over a few times, he just wasn't comfortable. He had to pull over to the side of the road to sort of catch his breath, because he felt claustrophobic in the car. It is interesting looking back on how he felt in cars that he should die in the manner he died.''

Gregard says she is unsure what to make of Dodi's uneasiness, but believes it is fair to conjecture that Dodi might instruct a driver to lose pursuing photographers. ''When you are being chased by paparazzi, and you are trying to protect your privacy and her privacy, it is natural to say 'Step on it,' '' she says. ''If he did that, I don't think it makes him a bad guy, do you? I think I would do the same thing. But it doesn't mean 'Drive five hundred miles an hour and hit a wall.' ''

Barbara Broccoli says that Dodi was terrified of high

speeds, and would never have gotten in the car if he had smelled alcohol on the driver's breath. But she believes that Dodi would have wanted to shield Diana from any unpleasantness. "I think that he would have probably just wanted to protect her, to take care of her," she says. "A suggestion that he somehow would have enjoyed this is disgusting. He wasn't like that at all. I'm sure that he just wanted to get her somewhere safe."

That refuge, of course, was Dodi's third-floor bachelor apartment at 1 Rue Arsène-Houssaye, normally a 10- or 15-minute drive from the Ritz, depending on traffic, down one of the most romantic boulevards of Paris. Even if there had not been a paparazzo in sight, Dodi would have been anxious to get back. For he planned to ask Diana a very special question later that night.

6

The Pharaoh of Knightsbridge

"THEY ARE IN PARADISE NOW."

It was only hours after the crash when Mohammed Al Fayed uttered those fatalistic words to an associate in London. Millions around the world would share his feelings of shock and dismay when they heard the news that day. But who, perhaps apart from Diana's young boys, could feel the pain as acutely as he did? Not only had Al Fayed lost a beloved son, just when Dodi at last seemed to be finding his way in life, but he also grieved for the Princess he had come to regard almost as a daughter. Nor was he oblivious to the bitter irony that whatever the role of others in the crash, the pair had died under the protection of a driver and a bodyguard employed by Al Fayed's companies.

The holy Koran teaches Muslims that if they have conducted their affairs honorably in life, they will ascend to heaven, or Paradise, after they die. Paradise is above the visible sky and bestrides a number of blue-green seas. Looked upon by Allah from his throne and guarded by angels, it is a garden of bounteous fruit trees and rivers that flow with milk and honey.

Islamic tradition considers it merciful to bury a Muslim as soon as possible, before the corpse begins decomposing. But Dodi had died on the last day of France's summer vacation season, a Sunday no less, and a day when the government officials who were not on holiday would be frantically consumed by political and administrative fallout from the crash.

It was first feared that Dodi might have to be buried in France if the paperwork necessary to export his body to Britain did not come through in time. Some family members were arguing that Dodi's body should be transported to Alexandria and buried in the Al Fayed family plot there. But for Al Fayed himself, there was never any doubt: Dodi should be buried in Britain, the country where Mohammed had made the family home three decades earlier.

In London, senior members of the Harrods staff were summoned to work only hours after the first bulletins came from Paris; after struggling with police and judicial officials in Paris and local authorities in Britain, they secured the necessary permits allowing the body of Dodi, an Egyptian citizen at the time of his death, to be brought into Britain and buried there.

Already in London, ordinary Britons moved by Dodi's death had begun placing bouquets of flowers outside the 14 entrances of Al Fayed's famous department store in Knightsbridge. Before embarking from Paris in the company Sikorsky SK-76 helicopter, Al Fayed sent instructions back to Harrods on how the company should observe the tragedy.

The flags of the nations including that of his native Egypt were to be removed from the roof of the seven-story rust-brick Edwardian building, leaving only the Union flag flying at half mast. The 11,000 bulbs that illuminate the exterior of Harrods into a shimmering jewel box at night were to be darkened, and black drapes drawn over the store's colorful display windows. In window No. 20 facing Brompton Road, decorators put simple black-and-white portraits of Dodi and Diana, each in an 18-by-12-inch gold frame, resting beside an arrangement of white lilies. Within a month, at least a dozen books of condolence at Harrods had been signed, and Dodi's father had received 100,000 letters from all of the world expressing sorrow for his loss.

Six days later, the Princess of Wales would receive a grand funeral organized by Buckingham Palace, although not without some hesitation about its scale by the House of Windsor. The "unique service for a unique person," as the Queen called it, was a magnificent if sorrowful spectacle witnessed by more than a million people in London and two billion television viewers around the world.

Dodi received a hasty burial organized by a London company called Arab Cargo Ltd. and witnessed by only a few family members, cemetery employees, and an Egyptian imam.

While Al Fayed was still attending to matters in Paris, he called his friend Mohammed Shaker, Egypt's ambassador to the Court of St. James since 1988, and asked if he could help with some of the arrangements in London. Because time was of the essence, Shaker urgently instructed one of the embassy officials to contact Mahmoud Agha, a Palestinian who runs Arab Cargo, the firm most Arab embassies use when a national dies in Britain and the body has to be transported back to the Middle East.

Ambassador Shaker was waiting at Battersea heliport at 5:15 P.M. when Al Fayed's Sikorsky touched down. He embraced Al Fayed and his brother Salah, who had flown from Nice to join Mohammed in Paris. He then accompanied them to the Fulham mortuary in West London, where an autopsy was performed as required by law for British residents who die abroad.

Just as that grim task was being finished a few hours later, another hearse pulled up. Inside was a blond wood coffin bearing the Princess of Wales. By a quirk of timing, like a modernistic staging of *Romeo and Juliet*, the two caskets passed side by side on the way in and out of the mortuary.* At 7:30 P.M., with Al Fayed, his brother Salah, his brother Ali, who had now arrived from the U.S., a nephew, and Ambassador Shaker following in a cortège of three Mercedeses and a Range Rover, a black 1985 Daimler hearse took Dodi's coffin up Holland Park Road to the A40 and on to the London Mosque in Regent's Park, where a 20-minute

---

*As of this writing, nothing has filtered from the British autopsies except for the fact that Diana and Dodi showed traces of a "normal" level of alcohol consumption the night before.

prayer service was held. Escorted by three cars and six motorcycle outriders of the Metropolitan police, the convoy then sped through London's streets a final time, en route to an interfaith cemetery in Brookwood, Surrey.

The mourners arrived 90 minutes later at 10 P.M., after the setting of the late summer sun. They stepped through stones and weeds to reach a large plot in the Muslim section of the cemetery that had been hastily purchased by a family representative earlier in the day. Cemetery workers hoisted the coffin across from the hearse and then lowered it into the ground. In accordance with tradition, two attendants lowered themselves into the grave, opened the coffin, and gently shifted Dodi's linen-shrouded body so that it would face in the direction of Mecca.

Once the soil was shoveled back into the hole, the imam spent 15 minutes reading from Yasin, the 36th Surrah of the Koran. "On this day," he prayed, "no soul shall be unjustly treated, but neither shall you be rewarded but according to what you have wrought. On this day, the inhabitants of Paradise shall be taken up with joy."

Dodi proved to be restless in death as he had been in life. His family strictly observed the 40-day mourning period, repeatedly visiting his grave to say prayers over it, which Muslims believe will enable more sins to be forgiven. At 60 Park Lane, a tape player in Dodi's study piped Koranic readings throughout his apartment, which was empty and still, save for the flickering of candles in each room. But once the 40 days were up, his father had Dodi's coffin disinterred and transferred to a new family burial ground at his country estate in Oxted, Surrey. This, said a Harrods spokesman, was so the beloved eldest son would be nearer to his family.

There was another reason: Mohammed was upset with the owner of Brookwood cemetery. Al Fayed paid £30,000 for Dodi's plot, then landscaped it with flowers and shrubs and erected a 10-foot-square granite monument, with DODI cut into a large polished headstone. But when he sought to buy surrounding plots to provide better security for the site, which was receiving hundreds of visitors each day, he was informed that the price demanded was £500,000, a price the owner claimed was at the same rate but for more land. There were people, Al Fayed seemed to feel, who would still try to take a piece out of Dodi.

Mohammed Al Fayed's difficulties in securing his son a proper resting place on British soil ironically mirrored his own problems finding acceptance in the country he had immigrated to in 1965. Like some former colonial subjects, Al Fayed tended to admire rather than despise the masters who had once ruled his underdeveloped nation. An enthusiastic anglophile in his Savile Row suits and Turnbull & Asser shirts, Al Fayed was anxious to find a suitably lofty position in Britain's social heirarchy, aided by bank accounts stuffed with cash from arranging handsome Arabian deals for British construction companies.

Particularly after his spectacular takeover of Harrods in 1985, Al Fayed had come to consider himself a successful London businessman who had invested millions of dollars in the economy, paid millions more in taxes, employed thousands of workers, donated large sums to charities, and worked to preserve treasures of British heritage.

In addition to Harrods, he owned Balnagown Castle, the 16th-century-old ancestral home of the Clan Ross in Scotland, the Hôtel Ritz in Paris, 75 Rockefeller Plaza in New York, and various other residential properties in Britain and France. Another family trophy was Turnbull & Asser, the Jermyn Street shirtmaker to the Prince of Wales (and, of course, to Mohammed Al Fayed).

In time, however, some sections of the British Establishment came to view him as a disreputable Middle Easterner who lied about his business fortune, corrupted the country's politicians, and then betrayed them when he didn't get his way. Since 1995, the Home Office has denied his application for British citizenship without ever stating a reason. But a government investigation into his acquisition of Harrods said he had been untruthful about several things, including the source of the funds used for the purchase. Al Fayed's retort was that he was a victim of British racism, powerful businessmen, and corrupt politicians.

Certainly Al Fayed belonged to a bygone era of boisterous tycoons. A confidant of sheikhs and sultans, he had inhabited a mysterious world befitting a man who was raised in the demimonde that was Alexandria between the wars. When he paid £615 million in cash for Harrods in March 1985, he had the button-down financiers of the City shaking their heads in astonishment.

For all his bluster, Al Fayed possessed the undeniable (if slightly raffish) charm of a born salesman. At Harrods, he became the type of owner who would cheerfully leave the executive suite to throw some pizza dough for a restaurant promotion, escort a visiting dignitary through the maze of galleries, or assist Santa Claus with the children at Christmas time.

Al Fayed has been variously criticized for being extravagant, ingratiating, ruthless, secretive, and obsessed with security. Some of his troubles are certainly due to a clash of Arab and Anglo-Saxon styles. The title of his gilt-colored book about Harrods, *A Palace in Knightsbridge,* is perhaps a telling insight into a man who made his mark, initially, in a land where the truly powerful were the kings and emirs who lived behind grand edifices. In Britain, Al Fayed would receive scorn for cozying up to members of Parliament and even to the Princess of Wales. But in the East, he had well learned a maxim that is also current in the West: It's not what you know, it's who you know.

Nor, coming from a region known for its murky underworld of terrorists and spies, was it altogether surprising that the Egyptian multimillionaire arrived in Britain with a potentate's entourage of bodyguards and limousine drivers. (In a September 1995 article, *Vanity Fair* went so far as to allege that meetings and telephone calls at Harrods were bugged. Al Fayed sued for libel over the article, but withdrew his case in December 1997 without receiving a retraction.) But even paranoid people can have real enemies: since the Harrods takeover, Al Fayed has been almost continuously at war with business rivals and the British government over the acquisition.

Tragically, though, Al Fayed's penchant for "presidential security," as one of Dodi's former girlfriends calls it, in some measure helps explain how Diana wound up dying in that black Mercedes with Dodi on August 31. That irony would be cruelly compounded if, as some of his harshest critics have suggested, Mohammed had orchestrated the romance in order to have his revenge on a British Establishment he felt was racist and unjust.

After his takeover of Harrods, Al Fayed seemed to encourage accounts in London newspapers that he hailed from an old Egyptian cotton-growing family that had later moved into shipping. The family's origins were modest, according to an investigation into the Al Fayeds published in 1988 by the British Department of Trade and Industry. Al Fayed's father, a schoolteacher, was born in the Delta village of Al Rahmania in 1898. He married a local girl, Hanem Kotb, before moving to Gomrok, one of the poorer quarters of Alexandria, where the couple raised five children. Mohammed, the eldest son, was born on January 27, 1929 (though he listed his birthdate as 1933). When Mohammed was 10, his mother died and his father remarried.

According to the DTI report, Al Fayed never attended Victoria College, as some reports suggested, but went to work in his early twenties as a salesman for Singer sewing machines. Then in 1952, through a neighbor, he met Adnan Khashoggi, the future Saudi billionaire. Khashoggi, then a young go-getter right out of Victoria College, was starting up his first business, the Al Nasr Trading and Industrial Corporation. It was an import-export firm, sending Egyptian furniture and office supplies to Saudi Arabia for such customers as the ministry of health, where Khashoggi's father now worked as secretary general. Khashoggi and his cousin Anas Yasseen hired Mohammed to coordinate deliveries in Jeddah, giving him a small salary and 10% share of the profits.

It turned out to be a star-crossed arrangement. Al Fayed soon married Khashoggi's sister Samira, but the relationship cooled despite the birth of Dodi in 1956. At about this time, Al Fayed became entangled in financial disputes with Khashoggi, which became all the messier when his wife fell in love with Yasseen. According to the DTI report, a divorce settlement was agreed upon in December 1958 in which Adnan Khashoggi agreed to abandon a financial claim against Al Fayed "provided that Mohammed would give his sister her freedom from an unhappy marriage." Not surprisingly, ill feelings between the Al Fayeds and the Khashoggis continued for many years afterwards.

The year 1956 was a turning point for Britain, Egypt, Alexandria, and Mohammed Al Fayed. In October, forces from Israel, Britain, and France attacked Egypt in a transparent attempt to regain control of the Suez Canal and perhaps bring down Gamal Abdul Nasser's increasingly influential Arab nationalist regime. But the invasion prompted an international furor and brought down Anthony Eden's government, signaling a symbolic end of empire for Britain.

Just as the foreign troops were withdrawing in humiliation, a few months after the birth of his son, Al Fayed was starting up his first firm, the Middle East Navigation Company. It was an ambitious effort, considering how war had just sent tensions rippling across the region. But Al Fayed was able to capitalize on the political fallout from the conflict. With Egyptian Jews under threat for supposedly sympathizing with the Israeli attack, he reportedly got a bargain price for another shipping company being sold by a Jewish merchant in Alexandria. In the next few years, he expanded further, acquiring ownership in hotels and ships, including a 25% stake in a Genoa-based shipping company.

By the time Dodi was five, Al Fayed was wealthy enough to purchase a large house at 15 Khalid Pasha Street in Victoria, one of the smartest quarters of Alexandria. A touching studio photograph of the period shows Mohammed, proud, elegantly attired in a herringbone suit, cuff links, and a pinky ring, with a protective arm wrapped around a trusting Dodi, decked out for the occasion in a light summer suit and a little bow tie.

When Nasser nationalized some of the family's Egyptian holdings in the early 1960s, Al Fayed vowed never to return to Egypt. Despite cordial relations with Egypt's current government, headed by President Hosni Mubarak, he never has. It was in the city-state of Dubai that Al Fayed made his real fortune.

Dubai and the adjoining emirates of Abu Dhabi, Sharjah, Ajman, Umm al Qawain, Ras al Khaimah, and Fujairah, were still British protectorates, sharing the western shores of the Persian Gulf with Saudi Arabia. Dubai lacked the immense oil reserves of some of its neighbors. But with petroleum revenues throughout the gulf starting to take off, the ancient trading hub, whose dhow-filled harbor evoked images of Sinbad the sailor from the *Arabian Nights,* became a boomtown.

In mid-1965, Al Fayed established a small freight-forwarding company in London, General Navigation and Commerce Ltd., and began living in Britain. Apparently through contacts in the gulf, he became friendly with the emirate's ruler, Emir Rashid bin Said al Maktoum, at about the time that commercial quantities of oil were first discovered in Dubai. He soon formed profitable alliances with Emir Rashid's eminence grise, Mahdi al Tajir, who later served as an ambassador to Britain, and Richard Costain Ltd., a British construction firm with business in the Middle East.

Al Fayed thus established himself in the big league of Middle Eastern fixers, the highly prized facilitators at ease in both East and West, and able to bridge cultural and language barriers and arrange the lucrative deals between the two.

There were huge sums to be earned in Arabia, as emerging nations like Dubai suddenly found themselves puffed up with cash and strong ambitions to modernize. Channeling hundreds of millions of dollars in contracts for Costain and later Bernard Sunley and Sons Ltd., Al Fayed was instrumental in constructing the Dubai Trade Center, Port Rashid, and the Dubai Dry Dock, which have helped make Dubai the most active commercial port in the gulf. By 1975, Al Fayed had acquired a 20% share of Costain and won a seat on the board.

Overall, according to the DTI report, Al Fayed's business dealings in Dubai earned him no less than £85 million.

With undreamed-of wealth piling up, the streetwise salesman from Gomrok was developing a taste for the finer things of life. It was perhaps the builder in him that drew Al Fayed to architectural masterpieces in particular. He had all the impulses of every nouveau riche plus a fierce Egyptian pride rooted in his country's great pharaonic and Islamic epochs.

France, a nation that prides itself on the universal reach of its values and civilization, was a natural destination when Al Fayed began his quest for trophies. In 1979, he bought the fabled Hôtel Ritz from the daughter-in-law of the hotel's creator, the legendary Cesar Ritz. On a pistol-shaped piece of land in the Place Vendôme, Ritz built the hotel in 1898 and created the stately 142-room architectural landmark whose very name has become synonymous with luxury. (Starting price of a room in August 1997: 3,200 francs or $600 per night.)

When Al Fayed bought the hotel, it was in a woeful state of disrepair, with a manual switchboard, 50-year-old wiring and plumbing, and a pre–World War II kitchen. Al Fayed proceeded to spend $150 million—five times the purchase price—to modernize the hotel even as he restored its original grandeur. "Mohammed is a maniac about perfection," says Ritz president Frank Klein, whom Al Fayed hired away from the George V hotel in 1979 to help oversee the restoration. "He's one of those rare people with money *and* taste. He said, 'We have to build like a pyramid, starting from the basement and working up.' "

In 1985, a delighted Jacques Chirac, then mayor of the city, awarded Al Fayed the Médaille de Vermeil de Paris, a coveted municipal decoration. "Achieving a work of this importance is not a question of capitalism," Chirac told Al Fayed on that occasion. "You did it for reasons of prestige, and also because you were enamored of this exceptional hotel." In 1986, at Chirac's urging, President François Mitterrand made Al Fayed a Chevalier of the Légion d'Honneur. Seven years later, Mitterrand, himself a discreet but faithful customer of the Ritz, promoted Al Fayed to the rank of Officer of the Légion d'Honneur, one of France's highest civilian distinctions.

In 1986, Al Fayed embarked on another ambitious restoration project: the Windsor villa in the Bois de Boulogne. Located at 4 Route du Champs-d'Entraînement, surrounded by a 10-acre wooded park, the three-story 1900-era mansion had been the final home-in-exile of Britain's Duke and Duchess of Windsor. The duchess, American divorcée Wallis Simpson, for whom Edward VIII gave up his crown in 1936, lived alone in the villa from the ex-king's death in 1972 until she died in 1986. Impressed by Al Fayed's tasteful restoration of the Ritz, Chirac asked the Egyptian whether he would be interested in taking on the property, which belonged to the city of Paris.

Al Fayed, by now a resident of Britain for some 20 years, was intrigued by the love story of the ostracized Windsors. He quickly agreed to Chirac's suggestion and signed a renewable 25-year lease for the dilapidated property in 1987 for 900,000 francs, or about $163,000, a year, well under the going rate for such a grand and historic house in the poshest neighborhood of Paris. Al Fayed set about refurbishing the home at a personal cost of nearly $20 million.

Thinking of turning the property into a museum, Al Fayed purchased the Windors' personal belongings from the Institut Pasteur, sole beneficiary of the Duchess' will. Among the 40,000 items: the desk on which Edward VIII signed his abdication, the duke's golf clubs, and a piece of the couple's petrified wedding cake.

Chirac was so pleased with the results that in 1989 he awarded Al Fayed with the Grande Plaque du Bimillénaire de Paris, an honor extended to individuals who have rendered exceptional service to the city. In bestowing that honor, Chirac referred in a speech to his "dear friend Mr. Al Fayed" as "a man of feeling and a man of taste . . . to whom Paris owes so much." "What you have done in our city," said Chirac, "places you among our most eminent fellow citizens." Al Fayed returned the compliment by dedicating the 1991 book *The Paris Ritz* to "M. Jacques Chirac, the Mayor of Paris, without whose encouragement and counsel I would have been unable to revive the glory of the Ritz." And in 1995, the Egyptian contributed a hefty sum to Chirac's successful presidential campaign.

In May 1997, Al Fayed suddenly announced that he would clear out the Windsor belongings and turn the home over to his family's private use. The 40,000 items, valued at more than $7 million, had been set to go on sale at Sotheby's New York auction house on September 11. Following the tragedy of August 31, however, Al Fayed postponed the sale. It was eventually held in February 1998, and raised $23 million for a charity set up in Dodi's name.

During the summer of 1997, the news of the impending Windsor auction became intertwined with reports of the budding romance between Dodi and Diana, prompting speculation that the villa was being prepared for another outcast British royal exile to take up residence in France. In fact, Al Fayed had decided to clear out the mansion long before the first spark had ever flown between his son and the Princess of Wales. But plans can change.

Harrods, the elegant neo-Renaissance palace in London's fashionable Knightsbridge, is the world's most famous department store. Small wonder, then, that the world's most famous woman was one of its best customers. Princess Diana liked to shop in women's fashion on the first floor. If she brought her sons, they might visit the toy and sporting goods departments, then stop at the ice cream parlor on the fourth floor for a sundae. If she was alone, she would drop by Al Fayed's fifth-floor office to say hello and perhaps share a cup of tea with the man who had been one of her father's friends.

Mohammed and Diana got along so well that she could always ring up after closing hours and do some shopping in privacy. One evening in November 1996, when Cindy Crawford was visiting Kensington Palace, Diana exclaimed, "I know where we can go!" She bundled the American supermodel into her car and headed for Knightsbridge. At Harrods they ran into Dodi, whom Diana introduced, certainly in jest, as "my boyfriend."

It is easy to understand why Diana was so enthralled by the store. Behind its gabled and domed terra cotta edifice are 140 sumptuous galleries, stocked with the finest merchandise that 5,000 suppliers around the world can provide. Each day, £100 million worth of goods is on display, ranging from designer dresses and tailored suits to ruby necklaces and golf tees with *Harrods* imprinted in little green letters on the side. In the food halls, tiled with Art Nouveau ceramics, London's gourmands can find anything they desire: pearls of Caspian Sea caviar from Iran, fresh mozzarella cheese from Italy, bottles of Château d'Yquem from France, Oreo cookies from the United States—even fresh salmon from the proprietor's Balnagown Castle estate in Scotland. From the four corners of the world, the rich flock to Harrods like some fantasy land, making it one of London's top tourist attractions.

Winning control of Harrods in 1985 made Mohammed Al Fayed one of Britain's most powerful—and controversial—businessmen. But the fabled department store is by no means Al Fayed's only concern. The Harrods Group also runs the Kurt Geiger and Carbella shoe lines as well as Harrods International, which licenses the company's famous brand. Al Fayed also owns Metro Business Aviation, the largest handler of executive jets in Europe, and Harrods Helicopters. Mohammed's brother Salah, 67, has no involvement in the family business, but the third brother, Ali, 64, is deputy chairman and owns the Turnbull & Asser store in St. James's. Mohammed has recently raised his profile even further with the purchase of *Punch,* Britain's 157-year-old satirical weekly, Liberty Radio, and the Fulham football club. But it is the world-famous retail palace in Knightsbridge that remains the proudest jewel in his crown.

Founded in 1848 as a wholesale business, Harrods had grown by 1909 into Europe's largest department store. Fifty years later, it had become the fabulously successful flagship of a chain of British retailers—and an undervalued prize for a corporate raider. In 1959, a descendent of the Burbidge family dynasty that had owned Harrods for nearly seven decades hastily sought a merger with Debenhams, another British chain. But Hugh Fraser, a Scot intent on becoming Britain's king of retailers, picked a fight that became known as the "Battle of Knightsbridge." After a clash of merchant titans, Harrods was absorbed into the House of Fraser.

In 1985, history repeated itself. This time the battle was between Mohammed Al Fayed and R.W. "Tiny" Rowland, a pair of tycoons with towering egos who had both earned their fortunes in dealings on the faraway and often murky fringes of Britain's crumbling empire.

Rowland, an imposing man standing six-foot-two with a booming voice and aristocratic affectation, was the swashbuckling head of Lonrho (for London Rhodesian Mining and Land Company), a conglomerate with extensive mining and agricultural interests in Africa. He knew how to play the back-scratching game on a grand scale: as British colonialists receded from the continent, he befriended the tyrants and guerrilla chiefs left behind, financed peace talks and even hired private armies to protect his operations, making a fortune doing business in troubled spots.

Since the 1970s, Lonrho had owned a substantial stake in the House of Fraser. Anxious to establish a stronger United Kingdom base for his far-flung interests, Rowland in 1981 made a bid to acquire the entire company. The Monopolies and Mergers Commission blocked the takeover, in part because of the company's lack of retail experience. Many people considered Lonrho an unfit company due to its dubious dealings with African despots. In 1973 Prime Minister Ted Heath famously branded Lonrho "the unacceptable face of capitalism," for allegedly depositing payments to company directors, including a former government minister, in tax havens.

When Lonrho made a second bid for the House of Fraser in 1984, Rowland believed its chances with the commission would improve if it "cleaned the slate" by selling its 29.9% share in Fraser pending the review of its case. Rowland sold the stake to Al Fayed in November 1984, thinking the Egyptian would sell it back at a tidy profit for himself once the Monopolies and Mergers Commission greenlighted Lonrho's takeover of Fraser.

Rowland knew that Al Fayed was wealthy, but he had no idea he was interested in buying Fraser himself, or had the funds to do so. It was the biggest mistake Rowland ever made. Four months later, Al Fayed and his brothers suddenly produced a cool £615 million in cash and bought up the remaining Fraser shares "in one feverish day," as an associate put it. Most galling of all to Rowland, the purchase sailed through the Department of Trade and Industry in 10 days.

Rowland cried foul and launched a relentless campaign against the man he felt had outrageously betrayed him. He claimed that Al Fayed was acting as something of a front man for the 39-year-old Sultan of Brunei—one of the world's wealthiest rulers, thanks to immense oil riches in his miniature South China Sea nation (population: 260,863), which had only received independence from Britain in 1983.

Certainly Al Fayed and the Sultan were acquainted. The circumstances of their initial association are unclear, but in 1985, Al Fayed represented him in the purchase of the Dorchester Hotel. In January 1985, Al Fayed accompanied the Sultan to tea with Prime Minister Margaret Thatcher. At the time, sterling was in a freefall. Although a Downing Street spokesman insisted that no monetary issues were discussed, the Sultan soon started transferring billions of dollars into sterling, thereby shoring up the pound.

Both Al Fayed and the Sultan denied that any Brunei money was behind the Harrods purchase. Their claim was backed up several months later when Thatcher's Department of Trade and Industry pronounced itself satisfied that the Al Fayeds were the true owners of the House of Fraser. Fraser's board, moreover, which included many distinguished British businessmen, had carefully studied Al Fayed's offer and approved it.

But Rowland refused to give up. No ally of the Establishment, he nonetheless tried to enlist its aid: in the ensuing years, Rowland bombarded virtually everybody in *Burke's Peerage* with leaflets denouncing Al Fayed's acquisition and a 186-page softcover book, *A Hero from Zero,* detailing Al Fayed's background and business rise.

In 1987, thanks to Rowland's intense lobbying, the Department of Trade and Industry appointed two distinguished inspectors to probe the circumstances of the Harrods takeover. Their damning 752-page report, accepting much of what Rowland had alleged, was completed a year later.

The central finding was that the Al Fayeds had lied about "their background, their past business activities and the way in which they came to be in control of enormous funds in the autumn of 1984 and the spring of 1985." The more than £600 million that was at their disposal in British and Swiss banks at the end of October 1984 had only recently come under their control, the report said. The inspectors said they could not uncover the whole truth because of limits on their investigative authority, but they said it appeared likely the funds had been acquired through wide powers of attorney granted by the Sultan of Brunei. In other words, it was probably the Sultan's money, a suggestion that Al Fayed has continuously denied.

In 1988, the DTI report was referred to the Serious Fraud Office. But the government concluded that the "evidence available is insufficient to afford a realistic prospect for conviction of any criminal offense relating to any matter of substance raised in the report." Mohammed himself was nonetheless outraged, not only over the DTI's conclusions, but also over its decision to make the report public so people could "judge for themselves whether they wished to do business with the Fayeds."

Al Fayed filed a case against Britain with the European Commission on Human Rights, arguing that the government had first violated his civil right to defend his honor and reputation and then denied him legal redress. Vowed Al Fayed: "I will not go to my pyramid leaving my children under the shadow."

But the European Court of Human Rights found that the Egyptian's rights had not been violated and opined that he had been given "every reasonable opportunity to respond to the allegations made against [him] and to furnish evidence . . ." Five months later, in February 1995, Al Fayed suffered an even more devastating rebuff: without explanation, the British Home Office rejected his application for citizenship, as well as that of Ali Fayed. (Neither Salah nor Dodi ever requested British nationality.)

The humiliation was too much for such a proud and stubborn man. Furious at the ill-treatment he had received from an Establishment that had once so eagerly accepted his generosity, he now sought to get revenge. In October 1994, he launched a determined campaign to bring down Prime Minister John Major's Tory government. Al Fayed leaked stories to the papers about how he had provided money and free weekends at the Ritz to three government ministers in exchange for political favors. These consisted mainly of raising questions on his behalf in parliamentary debates in his campaign to defend himself against forces supporting Tiny Rowland.

The cash-for-questions scandal was no personal gain for Al Fayed. By exposing his own unsavory role in the affair, he alarmed even some of his closest Egyptian friends, who were concerned the affair would damage the image of Arabs in Britain. "He is extremely generous with those who return his favors," said one associate. "But when they don't respond, he is ready to exact revenge." If revenge was what Al Fayed was after, he was well served: badly tainted by the scandal, the Conservatives suffered one of the worst defeats in British electoral history in May 1997, enabling the Labour party to return to power for the first time since 1979.

In December 1997, Labour Home Secretary Jack Straw announced that he was opposed to the practice of refusing explanations when citizenship was denied, and that he intended to review the applications of Al Fayed and his brother Ali. Nor was the damning DTI report the last word. In a June 1997 speech in the House of Commons, Charles Wardle, a

Conservative MP and former minister, called on Tony Blair's new Labour government to recognize that the report was conceived from "Rowland's malice" and therefore have it stricken from the record. "I have come to the fairly dramatic conclusion that the Al Fayeds were stitched up by a DTI inquiry," said Wardle. "What should be remembered is that they did come up with the cash for the takeover bid and nobody—not even the inspectors—has proved that the money was not theirs to spend." In response to a query from the authors, a DTI spokesman said, in late 1997, that the department had no intention of reconsidering the report.

However bitter he was over his treatment by the British Establishment, Al Fayed had nothing to complain about where business was concerned. In 1994, he had sold off all the House of Fraser holdings except his crown jewel in Knightsbridge. The rest, 56 department stores from Inverness to Plymouth, fetched him and his brothers £410 million. Thanks to its upmarket goods and clientele, Harrods had always just about matched the profits of all the other stores combined.

And Al Fayed ran it brilliantly. In an August 1997 report, *Verdict,* the business analyst publication in London, praised Harrods as the leading department store in the world, setting Britain's standards for merchandise and merchandising. The Al Fayeds' "lengthy bad publicity," *Verdict* observed, had scarcely affected the operation of Harrods. "Anyone looking around the store now cannot argue that the change of ownership was against the company's interests," it said. "Harrods is in superb condition."

Al Fayed's business connections enabled him to maintain cordial relations with the House of Windsor even as the politicians were excoriating him. Partly through his lease of the Windsor villa, he had become fascinated with the monarchy, and as a leading proprietor and philanthropist, he continued to come into contact with royals. When he purchased Harrods in 1985, he discovered that ownership included the tradition of sponsoring the annual royal horse show at Windsor

Castle; Al Fayed would thus receive the honor of joining the Queen in her royal box.

His patronage of various charities helped him develop his particularly friendly relationship with the Princess of Wales. They shared favorite causes such as the Great Ormond Street Hospital, which treated one of Al Fayed's younger sons when he was ill with meningitis, and the Royal Brompton Hospital, where Diana's bon vivant father, the eighth Earl Spencer, was cared for after his stroke in 1979.

Al Fayed and Johnnie, as he called the earl, had become such good friends, according to Al Fayed's account, that when the earl's health was failing before his death in 1992, he asked him to "keep an eye" on the children after he was gone. Thereafter, Al Fayed would send Diana's children presents each Christmas inscribed "with love from Uncle Mohammed."

The earl loved to shop at Harrods—his London flat in Grosvenor Square was a mere five-minute cab ride away—and the store considered him one of its most cherished customers. Harrods likes to brag that Spencer shopped at the store every day when he was in London. That is perhaps typical Al Fayed overstatement. Nonetheless, when Al Fayed published *Harrods: Society's Favourite Store* several years ago, Spencer volunteered to make a gushing speech, which he delivered from handwritten notes, at the book launch in the fourth-floor Terrace Bar.

Once, to mark the reopening of a House of Fraser outlet in Milton Keynes, which had been burned to the ground by animal rights activists protesting the sale of fur coats, the earl invited Al Fayed and his entire board to the Spencer estate, at Althorp, for a celebration lunch. Raine Spencer, Diana's stepmother, was later appointed by Al Fayed to the Harrods International board, a position she still holds.

The friendship between the earl and Al Fayed stemmed from Al Fayed's purchase of the Ritz hotel in 1979. Throughout their marriage, Johnnie and Raine visited Paris often and had been hotel regulars—treasured "old faithfuls," as Ritz managers call them. When Al Fayed established the prestigious *Ritz Escoffier Ecole de Gastronomie Française,* they were among the initial enthusiastic apprentices, and subsequently sent Althorp chefs to the school for training before they were allowed to boil water. (Cost of the 12-week advanced course today: 71,000 francs, or about $13,000.)

Al Fayed savored the relationship with this gregarious English nobleman, who, although wobbly in soul and mind after a massive stroke in the year that Al Fayed purchased the Ritz, shared the Egyptian's passion for the finer material pleasures. In a sumptuously illustrated history of the hotel published in 1991 on Al Fayed's instructions, the earl and his wife were listed very near the top of an appendix recounting the illustrious signatures in the *Livre d'Or.* Others mentioned included the Duke and Duchess of Windsor, assorted continental as well as Arab kings, the Sultan of Brunei, Presidents Nixon and Ford, and royalty from the worlds of art, entertainment, and fashion.

At the time, Al Fayed did not know Johnnie well enough to wrangle an invitation to the royal wedding in 1981. He did not first meet Diana through her father, but rather at a polo match Harrods sponsored in the mid-1980s. According to some of Diana's friends, it was only after her father's death in 1992, and particularly since her divorce from Charles in 1996, that their friendship began to strengthen.

When the Diana and Dodi romance bloomed in the summer of 1997, it was widely suggested that Al Fayed was playing Cupid in hopes of shoring up his family's social standing and wreaking his revenge on the scornful British Establishment. The evidence suggests that he had no specific plan in mind—at least not initially. He knew that Dodi had just purchased a new home in California, a long way from where Diana's children, unquestionably the most important elements in her life, were being raised. He also knew that Dodi had been involved for a year in a relationship with Kelly Fisher. When Mohammed brought Diana and the young princes together with his family that summer, Dodi's inclusion seemed almost an afterthought.

But the Mediterranean charmer had a talent for coaxing

important relationships along. Almost playing the role of a consigliore, he had warmed the once cool relationship between Diana and her stepmother, Countess Spencer. And once the romance of Diana and Dodi took off, how could he not be delighted—both as a father concerned for his son's happiness, and as a proud man stung by British snobbery? How could he fail to encourage and nurture that bond? As one of Dodi's relatives put it: "Mohammed's son was perhaps going to be the stepfather of the future king of England. My God! What a knock to the British Establishment that refused to give him a passport!"

Mohammed Al Fayed bounds suddenly into the boardroom at Harrods. The Egyptian tycoon is dapper in his shirt and glen-plaid trousers. Even before introductions can be made, he thrusts Harrods teddy bears into the arms of his unsuspecting guests and says, "Merry Christmas!"

The festive mood inside the vast department store, which is lavishly decorated in the theme of Tchaikovsky's *Nutcracker,* cannot conceal the profound pain he feels as he sits down to discuss the tragedy in Paris for the first time publicly. Although the 40-day Muslim mourning period is over, he continues to grieve for Dodi and Diana: the tie adorning his Turnbull & Asser shirt is black. It is clear that he feels as if he has lost not only a son, but two children, and at a moment when such happiness for them was in the offing. He notes that he has received condolence messages from Queen Elizabeth II, Prince Edward, the Archbishop of Canterbury, and Prime Minister Tony Blair.

He was, Al Fayed says, as surprised as anybody when Dodi and Diana fell in love. But he could see the attraction. "She had been excited to marry the future king when she was young," Al Fayed explains. "But she had no experience of life. She faced this maze of tradition and bureaucracy and found that this was not the life she was looking for. After her father passed on, she would sometimes come to me for advice. She wanted to live like an ordinary person. She came from the aristocracy, but she was an ordinary girl."

Al Fayed believes that Diana's St. Tropez holiday with him, his wife, and his five children opened her eyes to the possibilities of a happy family life.

"Our family, she never saw anything like it in her life," he says, noting that she had an unhappy childhood amid her parents' bitter divorce. "The freedom she enjoyed, no formalities." With a laugh, he adds, "Dodi had the same sense of humor as me. For the first time, she meets somebody like me, only younger! She enjoyed our family, and Dodi was part of it. Things worked out naturally. If my son is happy, I am happy. It was his choice, his problem. I want to make him completely independent, not relying on me all the time."

The lightheartedness in his manner fades as soon as Al Fayed begins to speak of the crash in the Alma tunnel. While he is keeping an open mind until the French investigation is completed, he is disturbed by the conspiracy theories that have appeared, and will not accept that it was an ordinary accident until all the facts are in.

What he can't get out of his mind is the horrible thought that his bitter battle with Britain's Establishment somehow played a part in the tragedy.

"You can't believe what I am fighting here," he says with a visible wince that wrinkles his brow. "They can't get over the fact that I own Harrods. It's an Egyptian, not a Briton, who built this store, this fantasy. How can a bloody Egyptian come from another planet and do this?"

This brings Al Fayed to the "sleaze" scandal, and he makes no apologies for his role in bringing down a Tory government that had insulted him, failed to appreciate what he gave to the country, and denied him citizenship. "I brought down part of them," he explains, his lip suddenly trembling, tears filling his eyes. "I won't stop until I bring down the rest of them. I won't stop until I reveal the true extent of the political conspiracy that I have been the victim of, how they set up a government inquiry to please my business rival, Tiny Rowland, who lost out when he sold me the shares so that I could acquire Harrods. There was no reason for that." He gets up and walks across the room to get a box of Kleenex from a small table in the corner.

"I am a taxpayer in this country," he continues. "I have devoted thirty years of my life employing people, bringing in business, paying hundreds of millions of pounds in taxes. This is my country. You don't want to end, after you sacrifice for all this, to be humiliated in a report commissioned by a corrupt Tory government. I am fighting a crusade for the masses, for the ordinary people."

It was precisely these influential forces, Al Fayed believes, who were appalled and alarmed by the news that Princess Diana had fallen in love with his son Dodi.

"It was a very serious matter," he says. "Maybe the future king is going to have a half-brother who is a 'nigger,' and Mohammed Al Fayed is going to be the stepgrandfather of the future king. This is how they think, this Establishment. They are a completely different type of human being."

The meeting has been a difficult one for the Harrods chief. By the end, the tension in his body has become palpable, his quest for answers to his tragedy intense. But before excusing himself to attend another appointment, he makes a vow: "I am not going to rest until I know what happened. It is not only my son. It's the mother of two boys."*

---

*In a subsequent interview with the *Mirror* published February 12, 1998, Al Fayed said, "I believe in my heart 99.9 percent that it was not an accident. There was a conspiracy." He said that he believed that Dodi and Diana were deliberately driven off the road, but provided no concrete evidence that supported this theory. Al Fayed's comments about a conspiracy provoked controversy in Britian, where commentators sharply criticized him for needlessly causing renewed distress over Diana's death.

7

St. Tropez

THE *EVENING STANDARD* CALLED IT AN "ASTONISHING AND exhilarating spectacle." Indeed, the English National Ballet benefit performance on June 3 was one of the biggest productions of *Swan Lake* that Britain had ever seen—and one of the most successful, raising tens of thousands of pounds in support of the company's 46th season. But for the Princess of Wales, the ballet's patron for the past eight years, that evening at the Royal Albert Hall would have a special, and fateful, significance.

Wearing an elegant and revealing powder blue Jacques Azagury evening dress, Princess Diana was viewing the performance from the royal box of the semicircular Victorian auditorium. Seated near her, owing to his position as a sponsor of the company's seasonal production of *The Nutcracker*, was the bow-tied Mohammed Al Fayed. After the performance, Diana and the chairman of Harrods wound up next to each other at a gala dinner at the Churchill Intercontinental Hotel.

Al Fayed had often invited Diana to join his family on holiday, and now she leaned over her roasted lamb and lentils supper and asked, "Where are you going this summer?"

"St. Tropez," Al Fayed replied. "If you want to come, you are most welcome."

"So you are sticking to your invitation?" Diana laughed.

"Of course," said Al Fayed. "Make up your mind."

As fate would have it, this invitation propelled Diana into

a thunderbolt romance and a summer of unexpected bliss. And it was this invitation that set in motion the seemingly random chain of events that ultimately sent Diana and Al Fayed's son to their deaths at the 13th pillar of the Alma tunnel.

By offering Diana his hospitality, Al Fayed unwittingly led a princess who felt hunted by photographers to a place where she could hardly escape them. And he took her into the bosom of a family so controversial that her visit was certain to produce distressing tabloid headlines for weeks to come. Trying to shield Diana from the intense scrutiny that resulted, probably the greatest since her separation from Prince Charles in 1992, Al Fayed, and later Dodi, brought her under the protection of his private security apparatus, with planes, helicopters, and limousines at her disposal. It was all this, ultimately, that put Diana and Dodi in harm's way that fateful night in Paris.

As a man who loved playing the host, who was intrigued by royalty and embittered by the slights of British snobs, and who considered himself "almost a brother" of Diana's late father, Al Fayed had every reason to reiterate his long-standing invitation that night. Ever since her marriage fell apart, Al Fayed had been trying to lure the Princess and her young sons to come on holiday at one of his family estates. "Why don't you come to Scotland?" he would ask Diana when they bumped into each other at one gala or another. "Why don't you come to Gstaad?" he would ask as a winter holiday season approached.

Al Fayed hoped that one day Diana would finally accept his hospitality, and 1997 was a good bet to be the year. It would be the first full summer since her divorce had become final. She had made it clear that her personal life would no longer be as constrained by royal decorum. Al Fayed was undoubtedly aware that, being a divorced royal with two school-aged boys, her holiday options were minimal. "She could no longer go to the royal estates," explains a friend of the Princess. "She couldn't go to Balmoral, she couldn't go to Highgrove, she couldn't go to Sandringham. And she has two strapping sons. How can she keep them in a palace during the summer?''

Diana, it turns out, did get another offer. A few days after *Swan Lake,* Diana and Gulu Lalvani, a 58-year-old Karachi-born businessman, had gone to dinner at Harry's Bar in Mayfair, and then dancing at Annabel's until well past midnight. It was the first time, royal watchers said, that Diana had been out to a nightclub openly with a man since her divorce. Lalvani, said to be worth $100 million, had offered Diana a holiday at his luxury beach house on the white-sanded shores of Thailand.

But now Diana rang Michael Cole at his new South Kensington mews house to inquire about St. Tropez and what sort of holiday might be in store. She had decided: not Thailand, but France. Although she had no particular attachment to the south of France, Thailand seemed too far away. There was a more important reason for her choice: Al Fayed's four children were roughly the same age as Wills and Harry. And her paramount concern was to enable her sons to have a great time.

On June 11, Diana wrote an affectionate ''Dear Mohammed'' note in black felt pen on her personal red-bordered salmon stationery. She formally thanked him for his invitation to St. Tropez—friends regarded her as the best thank-you–letter writer they knew—and asked if Wills could bring along a friend. He had already invited the boy to come along on the family holiday with his mother and brother. (Al Fayed readily assented, but the boy was taken ill at the last minute and missed the trip.)

Michael Cole followed up with a note on July 2 to Diana that succinctly outlined the many facilities available for her children at Al Fayed's Côte d'Azur estate and provided a timetable for the travel arrangements. It had everything one could possibly want for a lovely holiday, he said, including privacy: the family's compound was situated high on a cliffside and was not overlooked by other properties. ''Mr. Al Fayed will send a helicopter for you,'' Cole informed Diana. Presuming the Princess' desire for discretion, he added: ''If we handle this thing properly, nobody will ever even know that you've gone. The idea is that you have a quiet, private, family holiday."

Privacy was an almost obsessive concern for Diana. This was especially so when it came to Wills and Harry, since she was determined to provide them with as normal a childhood as possible—complete with hamburgers at McDonald's, ice cream at Harrods, and fun-filled holidays. All this, of course, within the limitations due to their status as second and third in line to the British throne.

Problem was, St. Tropez was probably the worst place in the world to go for privacy. Notorious as one of the trendiest spots on the Côte d'Azur, it is packed bikini to bikini in the summer months with millionaire yachtsmen, playboys, gigolos, gamblers, bronze-breasted bimbos, and celebrity-stalking paparazzi. Already in the 1920s the French novelist Colette complained that St. Tropez was overcrowded. A London newspaper cartoon lampooning Diana's choice of vacation spots depicted her on a desert island throwing bottles out to sea stuffed with SOS notes that read: "I want to be alone."

Diana was anxious for the sojourn to begin. The boys had finished school, but Al Fayed himself had to sandwich his time in St. Tropez between the famous semiannual sale at Harrods, on July 9, and a regular summer visit to his wife's family in Finland. When the holiday finally began on the morning of Friday, July 11, Dodi Fayed was nowhere in the photographers' viewfinders. Nor was he yet in Diana's sights.

Diana's day began at Kensington Palace with a final check on security arrangements. She had ceased using British detectives for protection after her divorce, feeling that they were intruding on her privacy and spying on her. But the necessary arrangements for the boys were made with Charles' chief of security, Colin Trimming, the intrepid bodyguard who once wrestled down a crazed Australian who rushed the Prince of Wales firing a cap gun in Sydney.

An Al Fayed limousine came by Kensington Palace to

collect Diana's luggage, which was then transported to Stansted Airport northeast of London. At 11:30 A.M., with flight clearance from the lord chamberlain's office at Buckingham Palace, a cream, green, and gold Sikorsky S-76 belonging to Harrods Helicopters touched down lightly outside Kensington Palace. It was apparently the same chopper that Prime Minister Tony Blair had used in hopscotching around Britain in the last few days of an election campaign that had ended with Labour's crushing return to power three months earlier. This time, it carried Diana, Wills, Harry, and a Scotland Yard detective (a second detective had flown ahead to St. Tropez) to Barrow Green Court, Al Fayed's Elizabethan manor at Oxted, Surrey.

At 3:20 P.M., following a light lunch, Diana, Wills, 15, and Harry, 12, accompanied by Al Fayed, his wife Heini, and four young children (two boys aged 14 and 10 and two girls aged 17 and 12), took off for Stansted. There they boarded Al Fayed's executive jet, a Gulfstream IV, for the 2½ flight to Nice. The party was driven a few minutes away to the small harbor of St.-Laurent-du-Var, where they boarded Al Fayed's yacht, the *Jonikal*.

The long cruise westward to St. Tropez gave Diana and the boys a chance to admire the striking panorama of the Côte d'Azur, its ocher buildings and red-tiled rooftops nestled against the steep, pine-covered foothills of the Alps. Pinkish clouds drifted through the early-evening sky, white sails and twinkling lights dotted the darkening seascape, and rows of palm trees marked a seashore lined by sandy beaches and marinas. None of Britain's royal holiday estates in rainy England and Scotland could compare with Al Fayed's sun-drenched compound in St. Tropez's Le Parc, an enclave embracing 170 wealthy mansions.

Castel Ste. Hélène, Al Fayed's 10-acre estate high on the cliffs above the sea, is anchored by a 10-bedroom cream-colored, century-old villa that once belonged to Suez Canal builder Ferdinand de Lesseps. When the party finally arrived at 8:20 P.M., Mohammed's wife Heini led Diana, Wills, and Harry to the Fisherman's Cottage, the eight-bedroom quarters for guests, set just down the hill from the main villa and boasting its own butler, cook, swimming pool, tanning deck, and garden view of the sea.

A mile-long row of steps leads down to a private beach, pier, and the sea. From there, a launch shuttles guests out to the *Jonikal*, a 140-foot motor yacht with 12 sleeping cabins and a crew of 16, an impressive Italian vessel purchased only a month earlier from a Milanese textile magnate. Anchored near the *Jonikal* was the two-masted schooner *Sakara*, a sailing enthusiast's dream featuring varnished timberwork, hand-washed sails, polished brass fittings, and davits set with British pennies marking the year of the vessel's manufacture.

That night the holidaymakers had a light supper at the villa followed by a stroll through the village of St. Tropez. Over the next 10 days, the Al Fayeds and their guests abandoned themselves to the pleasures and privileges of wealthy seaside vacationers, who included the next-door neighbor, Bernard Arnault, chief of the Moët-Hennessy Louis Vuitton (LVMH) luxury goods conglomerate. Delighting in horseplay with Al Fayed's security men, among them former Royal Navy Seals, the young princes went sailing, jet-skiing, and scuba diving, or splashed in the water at the villa's private beach and swimming pools. An excellent athlete, Wills took to performing 30-foot swan dives from the *Jonikal*'s top deck. On several evenings, Diana and the boys walked into St. Tropez for dinner.

They were not always alone. As it turned out, Diana had scarcely awakened from her first night in Castel Ste. Hélène when reporters from British tabloids began streaming toward St. Tropez. The big-lens paparazzi were among the first to show up, but photographers also poured into town from international news agencies like Agence France-Presse and local papers on the Côte d'Azur. By the end of the first afternoon, fuzzy pictures were already being wired back to London newspapers of a man who looked like Mohammed Al Fayed and a young woman who looked like Diana sailing aboard, as one Fleet Street editor could best make out, a vessel called the *Sax-ara*.

The initial press coverage made much of Diana's choice of holiday companions. Britain's *News of the World* set the tone with a front-page photo of Diana and Al Fayed having a midday drink on the deck of the *Sakara* under the bold headline: "Di and Sleaze Row Tycoon: Harrods boss sails off with princess." "Di's Freebie" was the *Sunday Mirror*'s opening volley; the story inside quoted Harold Brookes-Baker, editor of *Burke's Peerage,* saying: "This is totally irresponsible of the princess."

Indeed, Diana's close friend Rosa Monckton, the president of Tiffany & Co. in London, who had asked the Princess to be godmother to her daughter, had "strongly advised her not to go on holiday with the Al Fayeds." Her opinion may not be surprising, given how Mohammed Al Fayed helped bring down the last Tory government with his "sleaze" allegations. Monckton was the wife of *Sunday Telegraph* editor Dominic Lawson, himself the son of a former chancellor of the exchequer under Margaret Thatcher. But Diana heard the same advice from less politically connected friends. Their concerns were based on simple logic: whatever the truth about Al Fayed, he was so controversial a figure in England that a holiday with him and his family was bound to create unpleasantness for the Princess.

Diana told friends that she didn't see Mohammed that way at all. She did not look on him as a businessman who had been damned by a government inquiry. The Princess could be surprisingly naive about current affairs, and strongly loyal to those who treated her well. If she knew anything at all about the DTI findings, said a friend, "she simply drew a veil over it."

On Monday, with the Sunday tabloid barbs still stinging her ears, she made her first and only attempt to get the photographers to go away. Wills and Harry came down that morning to go jet-skiing under the cloudless sky and dazzling sun. When Diana joined them on the pier about 11 A.M., looking fetching in a leopard pattern one-piece, she might as well have been on a fashion show ramp for the volley of shutters she unleashed. The Princess said nothing to the paparazzi but let them get their pictures and retreated to the beach in front of the Al Fayed villa.

Suddenly, Diana got into a launch with a bodyguard and churned straight towards a motor boat called the *Fancy* bearing three British reporters and three British cameramen 150 yards offshore. Pulling alongside the craft, she asked them how long they intended to maintain their watch. She was embarrassed by the press attention, says James Whitaker of the *Daily Mirror,* clearly worried that it might disturb her sons' holiday. According to the reporters present, she then launched into a remarkable monologue, hinting that because of the constant scrutiny she was under, she might one day quit Britain and reside in a foreign country. (She had said something similar to Annick Cojean of the respected French daily *Le Monde* in an interview conducted on June 13 and published on August 27.)

It was Whitaker who engaged her in the conversation and heard her profess moments after arriving that: "My sons are always urging me to live abroad to be less in the public eye, and maybe that's what I should do—go and live abroad." When asked why she didn't speak to the French reporters, she said, "I can't, I don't speak the language, so I have to speak with you." She complained that "people follow me around everywhere I go in London. We've been watched every minute since we've been here. There is an obsessive interest in me and the children." She said that William got "freaked out" by all the attention. Then the Princess made an enigmatic remark whose significance will forever remain a source of speculation: "You will have a big surprise coming soon, with the next thing I do." (Whitaker, as chief witness, has given this comment much thought and concludes that the remark was meant simply to confound the press who were tormenting her.) Diana held on to the side of the boat and chatted for a good ten minutes before turning around and heading back to the villa.

The next day, Diana had Kensington Palace issue a statement saying that she had been "misquoted," leaving the press to wonder whether the Queen had pressured her into reversing her comments about living abroad. Whitaker says that Diana was furious with him. She had thought the conversation was off the record, though Whitaker believes that she knew enough about the press to understand that any interview she gave would be invaluable and would never be off the record unless strictly specified.

The impromptu press conference only seemed to whet the reporters' appetites. Later that day, Diana made a few short excursions in the *Jonikal* with a flotilla of press speedboats trailing in its wake and communicating with one another on mobile phones. She made the mistake of visiting a nudist island, where she was snapped in a pose that made her appear to be inspecting the anatomy of a naked male sunbather. The photo ran on the front page of a German tabloid the next day.

Questions arose, however, of how the press found out about Diana's presence in the south of France. Michael Cole adamantly denied that he tipped anybody off, saying any such suggestion was libelous. In fact, the leak could have come from any number of other sources who were informed of Diana's presence in France: French immigration authorities, the St. Tropez prefecture, the British consulate in Nice, British intelligence, the staff at Kensington Palace—even Diana herself. "This being in France," complained Cole, "these things get out. I won't speculate how much money passes hands. But there was no point in denying it. By Saturday afternoon, 20 hours after they arrived, the cat was out of the bag, which was a very great shame."

Diana's complaints about the St. Tropez press gang—not to mention the hysterical denunciations of the paparazzi after her death—obscured a fact that was well established in British press circles: Diana was only too willing to cooperate with photographers when they made her look good. Doubtless, she loathed the guttersnake paparazzi who stalked her on London shopping sprees or trips to the gym. Yet, as most London editors knew, she regularly leaked information to favored reporters and tipped off certain photographers about when and where they might get a good picture.

It could also depend upon her mood, says *Daily Mirror* correspondent James Whitaker. When reporters first arrived in St. Tropez on Saturday, July 12, Diana did her best to avoid the press. She hid herself on the villa's deck "with a great big pink towel on her head," says Whitaker. As the week progressed, however, the Princess was far from reticent. "She started absolutely parading herself." Whitaker believes this was in direct response to Camilla Parker Bowles' impending 50th birthday party, hosted by her ex-husband. She hoped, said Whitaker, to push her old nemesis as far out of the press as possible. "The more she did, the more photographers loved it, the more it drove Camilla to the back of the paper."

In her August 27 *Le Monde* interview, Diana acknowledged that she used her image to benefit social causes, which cynics saw as a manipulative effort to style herself as Saint Diana. "Being in the public eye all the time," she told French reporter Annick Cojean, "imparts a particular responsibility. Photographs, for instance, send a message to the world about an important cause and emphasize the message." Clearly, Diana had a complex relationship with the media.

The truth is that, as the summer of 1997 wore on, Diana herself encouraged selected photographers, which led to those sensational photos for the tabloid press. In the end, it was a publicity stunt gone wrong. The publication of the photos prompted the increasingly aggressive hunt, which ended with paparazzi on motorcycles chasing her Mercedes from the Ritz to the Place de l'Alma on the last day of August.

It is doubtful that Diana herself tipped off anybody about her trip to St. Tropez: she would not have wanted her children's fun to be spoiled by a pack of paparazzi. But the fact is that, for the most part, the photographers in St. Tropez did not hound the Princess and her sons, and that she did not feel unduly bothered by the attention. Diana enjoyed almost total privacy inside the cliffside compound, barring a few times when she ventured too far out into the garden of the Fisherman's Cottage and into telephoto range. She largely escaped the cameras while on board the *Jonikal,* nor were she and her sons followed when they went into St. Tropez with the Al Fayeds in the evenings. The photographers, for their part, had an unwritten rule that they should not harass the Princess at night as long as they got good photos during the day. And at those times when she was in the presence of her unwanted audience, Diana almost always appeared friendly and relaxed with them.

Diana had said at one point that she hoped to keep her holiday "all covered up and quiet." That statement was either naive or disingenuous. Even the respectable mainstream press regarded the personal life of the mother of England's future king as worthy of legitimate news coverage. It was thus to be expected that the press would show up in St. Tropez. And when they did, the openness of the seascape and the range of outdoor activities pursued by the Al Fayed party made it inevitable that photos would be taken of the Princess and her sons. In the beginning French photographers, acting in all legality, set themselves up on a jetty about 20 meters from the one used by Al Fayed's deckhands. From there they were able to snap shots of the Princess swimming on the private beach, diving off the jetty, or embarking on a launch.

Photographers from British and international agencies, in contrast, forked out large sums for rented speed boats and moored offshore for a vantage point on both the beach and the Al Fayed vessels anchored a little further out. If the Princess had desired 100 percent privacy, she had three options: remain inside the Al Fayed compound, ask Mohammed to take her on a cruise further out to sea, or choose a more out-of-the-way destination for her vacation. From that standpoint, Thailand might have been the better option.

Jean-Louis Macault, who grew up in St. Tropez and took some of the widely published photos of Diana for his MaxPPP agency (which wags say stands for Maximum Price

Per Pixel), says Diana's cooperation made it impossible to take a bad picture. He is a general assignment photographer who covers everything from state dinners to crime scenes, but spends his summers at home on the Côte d'Azur. When he got the call that Diana was in town, he figured she wouldn't spend much time in public places so as to avoid being photographed. He was completely wrong: for the entire week, she did little to hide herself, says Macault, letting out a typically French exclamation of delight somewhere between a sigh and an "Ooo, la-la!"

Diana would appear like clockwork at 11 A.M. each morning, diving and swimming with her sons and usually at a beach that was closer to the photographers than one that would have afforded somewhat more privacy. Macault, who had never photographed the Princess before, believed that at times she was actively courting pictures. She would flash a complicitous smile toward the photographers whenever she arrived or departed from their view.

Macault denies that the photographers did anything to agitate her deliberately. The published photos of her St. Tropez holiday seem to bear him out: not one shows the Princess in a defensive pose, a hand held up to block an unwanted photograph. She never appeared distressed, scolding photographers, running away from them, or otherwise looking annoyed. According to Macault, the pictures he was getting were so wonderful that there was no reason to risk upsetting Diana. That might have brought heavy action by the police and ended the daily photo sessions.

On the whole, the St. Tropez photos tended to convey the image of a beautiful woman having an enjoyable time being a good mother to her children—precisely the sort of impression that Diana told friends she wanted the world to have of her. For his part, her host encouraged her to pose for the photographers and not to be too hard on them. After all, he said, it was their job. They had wives and kids, too. On the last day of the holiday, the *Mail on Sunday*'s Brian Vine rang up Al Fayed, who told him that Diana had not been particularly bothered by the photographers. "She was never going to hide from them and wanted to be natural with them,'' he said. ''She was helpful, so long as they wanted to take happy pictures.''

Not that there weren't some tense moments. Later that week, the British press boat, *The Fancy,* set out after the *Jonikal.* They were unsure whether Diana and her sons were on board, but after arriving at Ile de Port-Cros, about 60 miles from St. Tropez, they caught up with the *Jonikal* and established that the royal family was on board with the Al Fayeds. What ensued was an extraordinary scene. The *Jonikal* was flanked by the *Cujo,* a former U.S. Coast Goard cutter which sometimes operated as a kind of guard boat. This boat, much sturdier than the *Fancy,* began to play a game of cat and mouse with the British press boat as it approached. The two boats were sparring, not so much for access to the Princess, who was not visible, but because the British journalists had begun to get bored in the hot summer game of waiting. After a few moments, both boats left.

At this point, Mohammed descended the *Jonikal*'s staircase for a swim. The *Fancy* made a beeline for a better photographic vantage point, drawing the *Cujo* in quickly as well. The combined wake of both motor boats buffeted Mohammed against the side of his own boat. As the *Fancy* renegotiated for position—and attempted to see whether all the ruckus had roused the Princess—the *Cujo* shot near, missing the British press boat by a foot.

Following these maneuvers, the Al Fayeds apparently summoned the French coast guard, who appeared to check the passports of those aboard both the *Fancy* and the *Cujo.* No initial warnings were issued, but about 20 minutes later, the *Fancy* received an order via telephone requesting that they leave the area.

After they had pulled away, Whitaker would learn later, Diana appeared in a swimsuit for a boat of French journalists and put on an amazing show. The French, who had not engaged in the manuevers with the *Cujo,* had been allowed to stay close to the *Jonikal.* They witnessed Diana descend to the water, catch hold of a dangling rope and swing ''like

Jane out of Tarzan'' into the water. Later, the grateful French press pitched in and sent Diana a huge bouquet of 100 red roses.

Although Mohammed Al Fayed was not pleased with the sniping coverage of Diana's holiday with his family, it hardly came as a surprise. But when he felt the intrusions were violating the law, he called in hired muscle and brains to handle the matter. He began by beefing up his security contingent to 20 guards. Meanwhile, Al Fayed sought to learn the identities of the paparazzi who flew a helicopter over Castel Ste. Hélène in order to have his lawyers sue them. Before the holiday was over, his legal representative in Paris, Bernard Dartevelle, had laid the groundwork for an invasion of privacy writ against *Paris-Match, France-Dimanche,* and the Sygma photo agency. "There is only one thing that will make a man in designer clothes crawl through undergrowth in the middle of the night with a Nikon around his neck," Michael Cole later complained, "and that's money." The mobilization of Al Fayed's security apparatus to shield Diana from the paparazzi was certainly well intended. In hindsight, however, it may have begun a pattern of overly elaborate protection that went seriously wrong in Paris at the end of August.

The remarkable thing about St. Tropez, in retrospect, was that nobody suspected that romance was in the air. *Paris-Match* put a resplendent Diana on its cover with a photo showing her jumping from a pier into a launch boat, and titillated readers with headlines that suggested Diana and Mohammed were about to become a nineties version of Jackie Kennedy and Ari Onassis. "Diana: A free woman in St. Tropez," the cover line began. "A year after her divorce, her first happy vacation. The tender gesture of a millionaire: the photo that scandalized Britain." The hazy picture in question caught Mohammed and Diana from behind on the *Jonikal,* with the tycoon firmly gripping Diana around her waist, and Diana affectionately resting her hand on Mohammed's shoulder. The photo didn't particularly scandalize Britain, though, since most British editors and their readers would have been aware that Heini Al Fayed was along on the holiday.

Dodi, for his part, was already involved in a one-year-old relationship with Kentucky-born Wilhelmina model Kelly Fisher. The couple had planned to spend their summer holiday together in the Côte d'Azur starting July 15. In Paris they spent Bastille Day watching the morning parade down the Champs-Elysées from the balcony of Dodi's Rue Arsène-Houssaye apartment.

In mid-afternoon, the phone rang and Dodi told Kelly that his father was asking him to attend to a business matter in London. Dodi flew off in a private plane, and then annoyed Kelly by not phoning her for the rest of the day. Dodi, it turned out, had flown from Paris to Nice, and then had joined his father's party in Cannes for the resort's Bastille Day fireworks display. It was during this night of spectacular pyrotechnics that Dodi and Diana made their fateful reacquaintance.

At 2 A.M. the next morning, Kelly finally reached Dodi on his cellular phone, but Dodi admitted that he had gone ahead to the Côte d'Azur without her. She angrily threatened to return to Los Angeles, but Dodi soothed her feelings by sending a plane to fetch her the next day.

Kelly met Dodi on the *Sakara* in the port of St. Tropez on the afternoon of July 16, and after sailing around for a while, she transferred to the *Cujo* where she and Dodi were to sleep for the next two nights. But Dodi repeatedly slipped off to Castel Ste. Hélène, leaving her behind on the excuse that the Princess did not want to meet new people. He would annoy Kelly by announcing that he was going over for a quick lunch, only to return six hours later. She also recalls that it was strange how the sailing crew kept moving her from boat to boat. "I didn't think anything was going on," she says. "I knew his father was important to him, and he had to do what he said. But I was livid. I thought I was part of the family. His family was there and I wanted to spend time with them. Apparently, the wheels had already been put in motion and they basically kept me hidden."

By chance, Kelly had a modeling assignment in Nice from July 18 to 20, and Dodi let her take the *Cujo* and its crew for the entire three days. By the time she returned late Sunday, Diana and her children had left for London. After a few more days of sailing, the couple took the *Cujo* to Nice on July 23 and boarded a private plane to Paris. The next day, Kelly returned as scheduled to Los Angeles. Dodi, it seemed, had other plans now.

The press was none the wiser about any of Dodi's comings and goings. One day Macault managed to get a scoop but he didn't even realize it at the time. He snapped a series of photos of Diana and Dodi beaming at each other in the *Jonikal*'s launch. He had no idea that he had just taken photos of a couple whose hot romance was about to scorch front pages around the world. "We thought he was a sailor," said Macault.

Diana fell in love with Dodi at St. Tropez. And it happened so naturally. Diana had accepted Al Fayed's invitation in the first place because she wanted to give Wills and Harry a holiday. They were having a fine time with Al Fayed's kids. And amid the happy spirit of the holiday, she found herself as an unattached woman in the company of her host's charming bachelor son.

Dodi caught her at a vulnerable moment. The day after his arrival, news came that Diana's friend, extravagant Italian fashion designer Gianni Versace, had been murdered by a gunman stalking him outside his Miami Beach palazzo. Another death that would have dismayed her which occurred on the last full day of the holiday was that of Sir James Goldsmith, whose daughter Jemima was a close friend of Diana's. Moreover, Diana continued to simmer over Charles' increasingly public relationship with his mistress Camilla Parker Bowles, for whom the Prince of Wales threw a gala 50th birthday party at his Highgrove country estate. It seemed to everybody in Britain that Charles was preparing the country for his eventual wedding to the woman Diana blamed for ruining her marriage.

What largely drew Diana to the Al Fayeds was the warm

atmosphere that surrounded the family. A week at Castel Ste. Hélène only confirmed Diana's view of Mohammed as an affectionate paterfamilias. In this setting, despite Dodi's playboy image, she was able to see another side of him: the warm-blooded Mediterranean soul, strongly attached to the traditions of family, completely at ease with children—including hers. In short, the holiday had an easygoing ambiance that was lacking in Balmoral or Sandringham.

Diana declared as much the day after returning to London when she penned a lots-of-love thank you note to "Dearest Mohammed." Her words indicated strong affection and thus belie the notion that Al Fayed enticed Diana to St. Tropez as part of a cynical public relations ploy. "I miss you all enormously," Diana started out in girlish handwriting, going on to thank Al Fayed for giving her and the boys a magical holiday, and a "great deal of happiness." Diana did not mention Dodi by name, but seemed to make an oblique reference when she referred to his "entire flock" as "hugely special."

Mohammed and Heini received touching hand-written thank yous from Diana's sons as well. Wills was grateful for the "superb holiday" and noted that Al Fayed's boat was "an amazing piece of kit" and he "loved sailing on it." Harry said he liked the villa and the delicious meals, too. He thanked him for their extreme generosity to "Mummy, William and I," adding that "we really appreciated it."

"She told me afterwards that it was the best holiday of her life," says a friend. "She saw a close, happy family, telling jokes and enjoying being together. Okay, they are very rich people, but they give the impression they would be having just as good a time if they were not. Dodi was gentle, kind, patient, and unthreatening. He is not the sort of person who is going to ask you, 'How many A levels did you get at school?' "

It is unknown whether Diana or Dodi ever confided to anyone the precise moment when the sparks started flying, but the Al Fayeds did notice that they were getting along well in St. Tropez. Heini, as a Finn married to an Egyptian for some 20 years, was keenly aware of the different worlds

Diana and Dodi came from. "But when they were together, they were *so* together," she would remark later. "They had a shared sense of having fun. They loved talking about films, and loved the same sort of films." Once when somebody recommended they see *Art*, a hit West End play, they simultaneously made faces and agreed they would see any film before going to a play.

Diana and the boys were due to head back to London on Friday, July 18. But when Wills and Harry implored their mother to stay for another weekend, they easily prevailed. The Princess, her sons, and their hosts finally packed up and left Castel Ste. Hélène at sunset on Sunday evening. "It was laughter from early in the morning until we went to bed each night," Heini would say later. "But, in Finland, we have a saying: 'After too much laughter, tears.'"

8

The Kiss

BACK HOME, DIANA FOUND BOUQUETS OF PINK ROSES DE-
livered to Kensington Palace. They were from her new admirer. Although no one outside the Ritz management may
have been aware of it, the first sign that Diana and Dodi
were smitten with each other came four days later on Friday,
July 25, when they showed up at the hotel for a discreet
weekend together. The trip was so secret that even Al
Fayed's security team was unaware of it. Dodi had picked
up Diana at Kensington Palace, then flown her to Paris in a
Harrods helicopter. For a romantic thrill, he did not tell her
the destination in advance. They arrived in the afternoon and
checked into the $10,000 a night Imperial Suite. Not a whis-
per about the cozy weekend leaked out at the time, and not
a single photo was taken.

The night of their arrival they dined at a corner table at
Lucas Carton, Alain Senderens' three-star restaurant a few
blocks away on the Place de la Madeleine. They also drove
to the Windsor villa, in the Bois de Boulogne, so Dodi could
show Diana the handsome three-story mansion that his father
had leased from the city of Paris since 1986 and lovingly
restored. When the secret weekend later became known, the
tabloids, remembering her St. Tropez musings about living
abroad, would speculate that Diana was contemplating going
into exile and even living in the same house as the late Duke
and Duchess of Windsor. As improbable as that might have
seemed at the time, one thing was very true: Diana and Dodi

were fast becoming an "item," as his L.A. publicist would later put it.

They returned to London on Sunday, July 27. The following Thursday, Diana left again for a six-day vacation with the man who was now her lover and almost constant companion. The couple choppered to Stansted airport and took the Gulfstream IV to Nice. There they boarded the *Jonikal* and headed south, first to Corsica, then to Sardinia, the two mountainous, thickly forested Mediterranean islands belonging to France and Italy respectively.

Off Calle di Volpe in Sardinia, the *Jonikal* rendezvoused with the *Ramses,* another family yacht, where they visited Mohammed Al Fayed's brothers Salah and Ali. Next, the couple stopped in Monaco, then cruised back into Nice just before dawn on August 6. According to a New Zealander stewardess who served them, their nights were filled with champagne and caviar, Frank Sinatra, George Michael, and *The English Patient* soundtrack on the stereo and passionate embraces under an inky star-filled sky. "It was as close to paradise as you can get," the stewardess would later tell the *News of the World.* When they flew back to London, and Dodi dropped off Diana by helicopter at Kensington Palace, their affair was still a secret. The couple was already back on British soil before anybody knew that they had been in the Mediterranean together. Anyone, that is, except for a pair of photographers named Mario Brenna and Jason Fraser.

Brenna had just come up with one of the royal scoops of the century: a set of photographs showing Diana in the arms of a man for the first time since her separation from Charles a full five years earlier. The pictures would sell for well over $2 million, earning a record sum for Brenna, who shot them, and Fraser, the British photojournalist who brokered their publication in the United Kingdom, the U.S., and Australia.

Brenna, a fortysomething Italian based in Monaco, had already made a name for himself as a celebrity photographer with good connections—especially in the jet-setting playgrounds along the Côte d'Azur and the Italian Riviera. Well known to the catwalk models in Milan, he had worked as

Gianni Versace's personal photographer. He was thus in the enviable position of being allowed to shoot photos at the late designer's parties and syndicate them to fashion and gossip magazines around the world.

Sometime in late July, Brenna received a tip, apparently from someone very close to Diana or Dodi, that the couple would be cruising on the *Jonikal* off the coast of Italy the first week of August. The implication was that they were ready for their still-secret love affair to come out in the open. Brenna located the *Jonikal* on August 2, but for the next two days he simply shadowed the yacht and took no photos. On the morning of August 4, however, he spotted the elusive couple again, and moved into action. He managed to talk his way onto a small private yacht in the harbor and got into a position to take photographs. Around 11 A.M., the couple took a launch from the *Jonikal*, which was moored about a mile out at sea, and puttered into the shallow waters around Porto Cervo. As they sunbathed on the boat and frolicked in the surf, Brenna snapped photos of them at times from as close as 10 yards away. They could hardly have failed to see him.

At about midday, Diana and Dodi went back to the *Jonikal.* Brenna shadowed the vessel for the rest of the afternoon. Shortly before 5 P.M., he found the couple standing conveniently on the deck of the *Jonikal.* As they embraced, Brenna readied his Canon 800-mm lens, which became a 1,600-mm when he attached an optic called a doubler. The late afternoon light was wonderfully soft. He took eight photos although he was a good 300 yards away. The most important frames turned out to be pretty fuzzy. But they clearly showed Diana, her blond, neck-length hair, the same red floral print tank suit she had displayed in St. Tropez, with her arms around a bare-chested Dodi Al Fayed. Brenna caught the first flight to Paris the next morning and headed straight for the offices of *Paris-Match* on Rue Anatole France.

The problem was that *Match*'s weekly deadline had just passed, and it would not be able to publish Brenna's photos for another 12 days. In any case, the hottest market for them was Britain. And if the pictures first appeared in a foreign market, British newspapers would simply "rag it out"—that is, publish a photo of the pages of the foreign publication containing the exclusive pictures. A legal and journalistically acceptable practice, it would make it unnecessary to purchase the original photo itself.

From Paris, Brenna phoned Jason Fraser, a 30-year-old hustling London photographer and the broker with a reputation for winning the highest prices for other photographers in the competitive British market. Fraser, who was attending a barbecue with his wife and toddler, immediately thought of the notorious toe-sucking photos of the Duchess of York a few years back: some tabloids crucified the photographer for invading her privacy, and John Bryan, Fergie's financial advisor and friend, went to court seeking an injunction against publication and wound up suing him. Fraser needed to be sure that the pictures were not a violation of privacy that might cause him professional and financial headaches.

At that point, only Dodi's closest family and associates knew that he and Diana had fallen in love. Off Sardinia, Dodi had phoned his press agent Pat Kingsley in Los Angeles and mentioned who he was with. "You and Diana are an item?" she asked incredulously. To which he replied, "It's more than that." "O-kaaaay," said a delighted Kingsley. He told Kingsley that he suspected he and Diana might have been followed and photographed. "I can't be sure, but they couldn't have seen too much," Dodi said. "We tried to be very careful not to be visible on the deck when we were near land or another boat."

On Wednesday August 6, Fraser quietly informed picture editors on Fleet Street that he had kiss photos to sell. It didn't stay quiet for long. A furious bidding war erupted, and word of the pictures reached Harrods just about the time that Dodi walked into his father's office that afternoon after his return from Sardinia. According to Michael Cole, Dodi became concerned. Even though he had lived in celebrity-crazy Los Angeles, he now seemed taken aback by the intensity of interest in his new romance. "What can we do?" he asked.

Cole replied that they would just have to wait until they saw what the photos revealed. "We don't know where we are," he told Dodi. "We are in uncharted waters."

Cole believes that Dodi was trying to keep the cruise with Diana as secret as possible. At first, he even denied that he and Diana had kissed, saying that they had merely embraced. It almost seemed to Cole as if Dodi was cupping hands around a flame so that it would not be blown out by the winds now swirling around it. But Cole, himself a former BBC royal correspondent accredited to Buckingham Palace, knew the pace of the hunt would now step up.

"How can you buy pictures taken by a photographer who was stalking them?" Cole demanded after ringing an editor whose paper had acquired publication rights. When the journalist replied that the pictures had been a "lucky hit," Cole jumped down his throat. "These paparazzi do talk this way," says Cole. "I know, I was a royal correspondent. These yobs say, 'I *hit* Diana, I *whacked* Diana, I *smacked* Diana.' It's always men, not women. It's almost like a physical assault, it has those almost sexual connotations. Certainly, there is a defilement involved." Not everyone around Dodi was upset, however: Raine Spencer told a reporter: "I love the whole [Al Fayed] family. I've known them all for fifteen years." Dodi, she remarked, had "immaculate manners."

Diana, for her part, told friends she was not the slightest bit bothered. To them, this was the first sign that she was serious about Dodi. "Ordinarily, she did care if her private life was going to be splashed all over the newspapers," says a friend. "She went to enormous lengths to protect herself. People would say to her that Dodi was a controversial figure because of his father. She said she didn't care. She wasn't interested in his father's business, but his father's son." When the Princess had disembarked from the *Jonikal*, Dodi's butler René had remarked, "Madame, I hope you had a pleasant time. I hope to see you again." Diana's eyes had lit up. "You will!" she replied.

From the day after their return to London, it seems, she could not bear to be without him. On August 7, Dodi sent a dark blue Toyota sedan to collect her from Kensington Palace. Natalie Symonds, her hairdresser for five years, later recounted in the *Sunday Mirror*, "When I was doing her hair she kept shouting, 'Give it plenty of bounce. I need lots of bounce!' Dodi made her feel beautiful." Diana told her other hairdresser, Tess Rock, "I love his exotic accent, the way he says 'Di-yana, you're so naughty.' "

When Diana arrived at the driveway of the Al Fayed apartments at 60 Park Lane, she stepped out wearing a clingy blue dress as if they were going to a nightclub. In fact they stayed home and Dodi had supper sent over, on silver platters, from the kitchen of the Dorchester Hotel next door.

Word of the affair was now all over Fleet Street. When Diana left Dodi's apartment to return home at 11 P.M., 50 photographers were waiting in the drive. As an Al Fayed driver whisked her away, the car ran over the foot of one of the photographers.

For the two lovers, the supper marked a temporary farewell: Diana left for Bosnia the next day. By the time she arrived there, the first stories about her and Dodi were making the front pages. The timing couldn't have been worse, for the media circus that would inevitably follow was sure to overshadow whatever she said about the inhumanity of land mines. Once again she was confronted by the conundrum that had bedeviled her all her adult life: how to perform duties commensurate with her role as a British princess while avoiding the press frenzy that feasted on the quirks of her personality.

This time, though, Diana remained unperturbed. No doubt, a friend believes, because she had grown comfortable in her new role as a dating divorcée, and in her relationship with Dodi. When she showed up for a small dinner in her honor at the Vezir's Elephant Hotel in Travnik, recalls *Daily Express* royal correspondent Robert Jobson, "she seemed to be more relaxed than on any other royal trip. She looked like a woman in love, to me." Polish journalist Anna Husarska, who was among the dozen or so dinner guests, recalls that Diana was "extremely, extremely happy"—laughing, joking, and relaxed in the midst of the international speculation about her love life.

Dodi's name came up obliquely when someone at the table asked if she had enjoyed any privacy this summer. "Only once, when we sailed at night," Diana replied. Her charm worked on Husarska, a crusading reporter who generally frowns on royalty for stealing headlines "from far more important matters." By the end of Diana's trip, Husarska was impressed by how cleverly she had "used the flame of her affair to illuminate the fate of land mine victims."

As she moved around the country with Jerry White and Ken Rutherford, co-founders of the Washington-based Landmines Survivors Network, cheering on a volleyball match played by mine victims, attending a Muslim amputee's birthday party, visiting hospitals and rehabilitation clinics, Diana simply brushed off questions about Dodi from the British reporters following her around. When one of them shouted, "What is it like to be in love again?" he was rebuked by a bodyguard, who humbled the questioner by calling him "a silly boy."

The Princess arrived back in London August 10 just as 2.8 million Britons were picking up their copies of the *Sunday Mirror,* which had increased its print run by 300,000. In 1¾-inch white letters against a royal blue background was the simple headline: "THE KISS." Alongside the six-by-seven-inch color picture was the subhead: "Locked in her lover's arms, the princess finds happiness at last." Inside, the *Sunday Mirror* published another 10 pages of photos from Brenna's shoot. One of them has Diana and Dodi sunbathing on the deck, with the straps of Diana's blue and white tank suit dangling down provocatively around her elbows. In another, Diana seems to be bending over to kiss Dodi, who is out of the frame; in another, Dodi appears to be rubbing oil on Diana's body, again out of view.

The technical quality wasn't great, but the scoop was all that mattered. The *Sunday Mirror* paid £250,000 for the first rights; The *Sun* and the *Daily Mail* paid £100,000 each for the second rights, available the next day.* But the Sunday papers that lost out didn't give up. The *News of the World* ran a front-page story headlined: "MY LOVE FOR DI," with a photo that showed a barechested Dodi cuddling a blond woman in a swimsuit. The woman in the picture, though, was his ex-wife Suzanne Gregard. On page three, the *News* ran a large computer-simulated image of The Kiss photo it had lost to the *Sunday Mirror.*

If Dodi had any apprehensions over The Kiss photo, they proved to be well founded: it immediately turned him into a target for the Fleet Street mudslingers. While the *Sunday Mirror,* enjoying its world exclusive, filled its pages with fluffy stories about Diana's happiness, its competitors wasted no time digging up scandal about the new man in her life. It was just as Diana had predicted: Who would want me? she had once asked, noting that any man who went out with her would have his rubbish bins turned over by nosy reporters.

The *News of the World* followed its computer simulation of The Kiss with a two-page spread on "stunning actress" Denice Lewis, pictured nude in a bed, who revealed how Dodi didn't like making love with the lights on during their 1983 affair in London. Even more aggressive was the *Mail on Sunday.* Its front-page story revealed how Dodi and Diana had spent their secret weekend in Paris, but then the paper went on to run a two-page exposé about Dodi's debts entitled "Dodi, Daddy and All Those Bills." The tabloid even printed copies of Dodi's confidential American Express receipts from the Giorgio Armani boutique in Beverly Hills, Nieman Marcus, and Victoria's Secret, the lingerie retailer. And on it went.

The cascade of gossip did nothing to dampen Diana's interest in her new man. Only a few hours after her return from Bosnia, Dodi picked her up in the helicopter again and flew

---

*Paris Match, which had acquired French rights to the photo, was successfully sued by Mohammed Al Fayed for invasion of privacy and was ordered in April 1998 to pay 100,000 francs ($18,000) in fines and damages.

her to Oxted for a romantic interlude at his father's country house while the Al Fayeds were away in Finland. They spent the next day relaxing together on the 500-acre estate.

On August 12, Diana invited Dodi to come along to visit her clairvoyant near Chesterfield in Derbyshire. It was an important gesture, since Rita Rogers, who had been recommended by Diana's ex–sister-in-law Sarah Ferguson, had become a pivotal figure in her life. As usual, Diana and Dodi traveled by Harrods helicopter.

Dodi was by now beginning to take greater precautions against the press pack. According to a relative, he shared his father's spy-novel mentality when it came to secrecy and security. When he and Diana lifted off for Derbyshire, the pilot was not even told their destination. "He didn't trust anybody," says a friend of Dodi's. When the helicopter arrived, it had difficulty finding the right dwelling, and attracted the attention of townspeople as it hovered overhead. By the time it landed in a field next to Rita Rogers' home, a crowd of children had gathered. One of them snapped a photo of Dodi and Diana climbing out of the chopper. All the secrecy precautions had only attracted more attention. The kid's picture wound up in the *Mirror* the next day.

When word of their visit to the fortune-teller reached Fleet Street, news editors dispatched teams of photographers to capture their arrival back in London. A TV team cleverly staked out the South Downs overlooking the Al Fayed estate, and managed to film the helicopter as it landed at Oxted late that afternoon. Although the footage did not show much of the couple, Dodi was extremely annoyed. "How did they find out?" he asked Michael Cole at Harrods. "You are the world's number-one story," Cole replied. "People are going to invest a lot of money and waste no effort to get pictures. You've got to understand that."

The day after consulting Rita Rogers, Diana left Oxted for Kensington Palace. The clairvoyant must have seen something in the stars: now Diana's romance with Dodi was beginning to smolder. On August 13, they arranged a night on the town. She went to 60 Park Lane at 8:30 P.M., they caught a film screening in Soho at 11:30 P.M., and Diana did not go home until 2 A.M. The next evening, it was the same routine. Diana got to Dodi's at 7:43 P.M. and didn't get back to Kensington Palace until the wee hours the next day.

On August 15, Diana and Dodi were briefly separated when she left for a long-planned vacation in Greece with Rosa Monckton. Although the two women had been booked to fly on Olympic Airways, they took the Al Fayed Challenger IV at Dodi's insistence because, as Monckton later recounted, he thought "we would have more chance of escaping the paparazzi."

On the third night of their cruise, the two women saw a TV report describing how 250 journalists were combing the Greek islands in pursuit of the Princess, and saying that a Greek newspaper had offered 280 million drachmas for a picture of her. The report said that the women had been using five boats and four helicopters, and had been spotted on Khios, Oinouses, Mykonos, and Naxos. The truth, in fact, was that they were hundreds of miles away on Hydra.

Instead of prompting satisfaction over how they had eluded the media, the report only fed Diana's sense of melodrama. "It's a hunt, Rosa, it's a hunt," Diana exclaimed. "Will you really tell people what it is like?" She made Monckton promise she would write a story about "the hunt," as she persisted in calling it. Her sense of being besieged, even when she was not, was infectious. "She had talked often to me about the intrusion of the press, about what it is like to be hounded by the paparazzi and to have to fight for every second of her privacy," Monckton later wrote in her husband's paper, the *Sunday Telegraph.* "But this was the first time I had been caught on the other side of the lens with her, and I was horrified."

Monckton later described how "the lengths to which we went to avoid the paparazzi became more complicated every day." The captain of their small cruiser would call his friends around Greece to learn the whereabouts of paparazzi, and then he would motor in the opposite direction. But the truth is, despite all Diana's dramatizing about the hunt, no paparazzi ever came within miles of them. On Hydra when they were strolling back to their boat, a tourist spotted Diana, leapt out of a cafe, and snapped her photo. "That's it," Diana said. "All over the front pages tomorrow." Sure enough, Monckton said, it turned up on the front page of *The Sun*.

Diana's paparazzi phobia was getting to Dodi as well. Photographers started staking out 60 Park Lane, and he would stay home—even missing a dinner with a friend— rather than face the pack. He worried that the Princess would think badly of him because of the negative press he was getting. The U.S. weekly magazine *People,* with its circulation of 3.2 million, put the key question on the cover for its "A Guy for Di" story: "Is he a dreamboat or deadbeat?" Harrods executives even began tracking down the alleged debts to rectify any misunderstandings and clear Dodi's name. Using the store's close relationship with American Express, one executive inquired discreetly about Dodi's Amex bill and was told there was no overdue balance. The owner of the 21 Club in New York also denied a report that Dodi owed him $7,000 for a dinner tab. Harrods was still looking into the alleged debts the day Dodi died.

Dodi's ex-girlfriends were a potentially bigger public relations problem. In particular, Dodi was growing alarmed by the prospect of some nastiness from Kelly Fisher. According to Kelly, she knew nothing of the budding romance until it hit the British tabloids on August 7 and a girlfriend phoned her from London with the news. "They are seeing each other!" her friend said. It was the middle of the night in California.

Kelly was already furious with Dodi for another reason: he was supposed to have flown to Los Angeles on August 4 to help celebrate the 20th wedding anniversary of her mother and stepfather, who were visiting from Chicago for the occasion. On August 5, Kelly had spoken to Dodi, who explained that he was on the *Jonikal* with Princess Diana and entertainers George Michael and Elton John and that there would probably be some "pictures coming out." Dodi said he would get to Los Angeles as soon as he could.

Now, with evidence that Dodi was romancing Diana, Kelly tried to reach him on his cellular phone. When that didn't work, she called his family's apartment house at 60 Park Lane and demanded to speak to someone. Mohammed, who had always treated Kelly caringly, got on the line. "He told me not to ever call back," Kelly recalls. "If you knew what he said, you would be floored. I will never repeat it."

Kelly says she then tried reaching Dodi through the Park Lane operator, who informed her that her calls were no longer to be put through. Finally, she reached Dodi on his portable. "He asked me what I was so mad about," she says. "It was unbelievable. He just kept saying, 'I'll talk to you in L.A.' " She tried to phone him again, but this time got another man, who told her not to call Dodi back.

Hell hath no fury like a woman scorned. Dodi told Michael Cole, "There may be a bit of a problem with a girl called Kelly Fisher." As Cole recalled it, "He told me that he was never engaged to her, would never have been engaged to her, but that they had spent the previous Christmas together."

On the eve of Diana's departure for Greece, Kelly and her celebrity attorney, Gloria Allred, held a press conference in Los Angeles to announce that she was suing Dodi for breach of contract. According to Allred, Dodi had asked Kelly's parents for her hand in marriage in November, and had later given her a $100,000 engagement ring. Kelly's claim was that she was entitled to money because she had curtailed her modeling career at Dodi's request and on the strength of his promises to compensate her with a $200,000 check, which later bounced. Dodi made good on a later check for $60,000.

"We are going public with this," said Allred, "because we care about Princess Diana and her future. We would like the Princess, who has suffered greatly in her past, to know of Miss Fisher's experiences with Mr. Fayed so she can make an informed decision regarding her future and that of her children." Kelly, she added, was ready to meet privately with Diana "anywhere in the world" to share "a great deal of

information which is not being made public at this time."
Dodi quickly hopped on the Concorde to New York, then
took a private jet to California to see what could be done
about the Kelly Fisher problem. Neither he nor Harrods had
issued any statements about her lawsuit. Now her press conference and his arrival in Los Angeles fed the tabloid feeding
frenzy. Unscrupulous "journalists" tried to break into Dodi's
Allied Stars office on the Sony lot in Culver City, and they
besieged the driveway of his $8 million mansion in Malibu's
Paradise Cove. Whenever he left the house, a volley of electronic flashes would go off and photographers would leap
into their cars and chase him.

It wasn't what you'd call a successful trip. Dodi went to
Los Angeles to see the legal firm of Burt Fields, evidently
with the time-tested Al Fayed philosophy: "You can't beat
them in the press, so beat them in the courts." When Dodi
came out of the Century City offices, he was not in a good
mood. A press pack was there, and one of Dodi's bodyguards
shoved a TV cameraman out of the way.

But the damage had already been done: Kelly, fuming over
suggestions by Harrods that Dodi hardly knew her, had sold
her story, and a salacious one it was, to Britain's *News of
the World* and its sister daily, *The Sun*. The first installment
of a four-day serialization was being splashed on the front
page of the *News of the World* even as Dodi was flying to
Los Angeles.

By now, three days after her press conference, Kelly was
becoming a household name in Britain. The *News of the
World* series kicked off with a modeling photo of a nude
Kelly crossing her arms across her breasts, accompanied by
a headline on the other half of the front page proclaiming:
"Dodi wanted to bed me AND Diana." The story went on
to quote her telling, among other things, how Dodi had made
love to her on a yacht without a condom at night before he
joined his father and Diana across the bay on the *Jonikal* in
the daytime. "Wow, that was a risk," Kelly said. "I could
be pregnant now." She said Dodi had told her: "I love you
so much, and I want you to have my baby."

* * *

Subsequent front pages of *The Sun* touting Kelly's story featured banner headlines like "Dodi is a dud in bed," complete with quotes from Kelly explaining how "he doesn't know how to pleasure a woman . . . After we made love, Dodi would say, 'My God, that was so great.' I would be thinking, 'Is that it?' " In *The Sun*'s last installment, the paper published a full-page photo spread picturing 11 expensive jewelry items that Dodi had presented to her, including two Cartier watches, necklaces and rings, two of which he said had belonged to his late mother. With a set of Bulgari fish earrings, he enclosed a card that read, "I do adore you. I know as nothing can be sweeter as you [sic]. Love you so much. Dodi."

After his death, Kelly deeply regretted selling her story to the tabloids, although she continued to feel justified in seeking the money that she said Dodi had promised to her in lieu of her modeling work. (In any case, Kelly did drop the suit following the tragedy.)

"He happened to fall in love with her," says Kelly. "She was an incredible woman. I might have dumped me for her, too. But he shouldn't have let me find out in the newspaper. If it makes the fairy tale of Dodi so much greater to say that I wasn't engaged to him, fine.

"I'd like to tell you something. While I was with Dodi, he was a really wonderful caring man. I really loved him. I wish I could tell him how happy he made me. Maybe I did make some mistakes. Maybe I shouldn't have talked to the tabloids. The only thing I feel horrible about is that I threw daggers. I took revenge in that way. I wanted to hurt him, you see, because I was hurt. I didn't know that this was the last thing he would hear. I wish I could tell him how happy he made me."

Adds Kelly's mother, Judith Dunaway, "He was nothing but a gentleman until he turned his back and walked away. What I learned about Dodi is that when a situation becomes problematic, he just walks away."

Just 36 hours after arriving in Los Angeles, Dodi rushed

back to London so that he would be there when Diana returned from Greece. As his lavish gifts to Kelly illustrated, he loved giving presents, and he thought of one for Diana as he was driven to Van Nuys airport. Like many lonely people, Dodi adored animals. He was devoted to his dogs, Bear, a German shepherd; Shoe, a miniature schnauzer; and Romeo, a giant schnauzer. During their Paris weekend together a few weeks earlier, Diana had come to Dodi's apartment on Rue Arsène-Houssaye and become enchanted with Romeo.

As it happened, earlier in the year Dodi had ordered a female giant schnauzer from a breeder in Oregon, and where a bitch was due to have puppies in October. "I think it would make a lovely gift," he told Melissa Henning, Allied Stars' vice president, as she accompanied him to Van Nuys airport early on Tuesday, August 19. "Well, why don't you name the puppy Juliet?" Melissa joked. Dodi laughed.

Confronted by all the stories of the playboy, the debts, and Kelly Fisher, the Princess could well have called it quits. She did not. The day after returning to London with Rosa Monckton, she dashed into Dodi's arms for one last summer dalliance.

The Princess arrived back from Greece at midday. By 9:00 P.M. that night she was back at 60 Park Lane for another tête-à-tête dinner with Dodi, staying until 1:15 A.M. The next evening at 6:40 P.M., they took off for a final Mediterranean cruise. Following the usual pattern, Dodi and Diana jetted off to the south of France for the third time in six weeks aboard the Al Fayed Gulfstream IV and boarded the *Jonikal* in Nice.

Publicist Pat Kingsley called Dodi on the *Jonikal* periodically to keep him apprised of the Kelly Fisher affair, and she would often hear laughing in the background. Recounts Kingsley: "I would ask, 'How are things going?' and he would respond, 'Everything is great!' 'She still there?' 'Oh, yes. Couldn't be going better. It just gets better and better.' " Kingsley began to worry that Kelly Fisher's story might taint Dodi's deepening relationship with the Princess. At one point, Kingsley asked Dodi how all the negative publicity was affecting Diana. "She feels sorry for me," Dodi said. "She knows what I'm going through."

Though the negative press articles were unpleasant, it is not clear whether the couple was really that upset over the photographs of them together. Diana's posing in St. Tropez, like Mohammed Al Fayed's comments to the press about "happy pictures," suggest that she did not object to the photos per se—as long as she could exert some direct or indirect control over what pictures were taken. Images of her looking tanned, healthy, relaxed, and happy didn't seem to trouble her. What she detested was being constantly hunted by any yob with a camera and a motorbike who fancied her as easy prey for a quick quid. Diana clearly adored the results when she agreed to photo shoots with glamor photographers like Snowden, Terrence Donovan, Patrick Demarchelier, and, most recently, Mario Testino (whose pictures appeared inside and on the cover of the July 1997 *Vanity Fair*). It was the wolf pack she hated, not the pictures.

"Hiding away has a thrill to it," says Dodi's friend film director Roland Joffé. "You are hiding from these people, who at one point you loathe, but in a strange way you have come to need, because they have become the way in which you measure yourself. A kind of dependence grows up." This could explain not only Mario Brenna's photos of The Kiss, but also a remarkable set of shots taken during this last cruise by Brenna's London broker, Jason Fraser, who had covered conflicts in the Middle East and Northern Ireland before switching to softer (and more lucrative) subjects, was waiting on the pier at St. Laurent-du-Var when Diana and Dodi arrived at 9:50 P.M. August 21. Since the couple had only left London a few hours earlier, it would have been a miracle for Fraser to have caught them the minute of their arrival unless he had been tipped off.

What happened next indicates that Fraser's source was not some Kensington Palace gardener, but perhaps someone aboard the *Jonikal*. How, otherwise, could Fraser have managed to take photos throughout the week in the Mediterranean, evidently off Portofino and Sardinia, that were published on the front page of London tabloids until the day before they departed for Paris? Scores of other photographers were hunting the couple; only Fraser and a colleague he was working with seemed to find them. Fraser refuses to say how he managed to get his scoops. But he does acknowledge: "I was receiving information. I knew exactly when and where they were going. But under no circumstances will I ever reveal my sources."

Dodi is known to have suspected that Mario Brenna, who snapped The Kiss photos earlier, had been tipped off by somebody working with his father at Harrods in London. But it is possible that Diana herself was Fraser's, if not Brenna's, source. A photographer with movie-actor charm, he was described by the conservative *Daily Telegraph* as being "known to have the favor of certain young royals and is a regular attender at upmarket black tie functions."

Fraser does not mind being described as a photographer who goes after sensational pictures but avoids doing anything aggressive or offensive. While he is not on the payroll of the celebrities he shoots, his work is not altogether different from that of Versace photographer Mario Brenna: photos professionally done but with the consent of the subject. Fraser says that when he does paparazzi work, 75 percent of the time the photos are done with a green light.

The summer was drawing to a close and Dodi, as usual, wanted to give his lover tokens of his affection. When they were apart, he had a habit of phoning Diana and telling her about things he had just purchased for her. According to Rosa Monckton, this was something about Dodi that made Diana truly angry. "I don't want to be bought, Rosa," she would say.

But on their last cruise of the summer, Dodi was ready to open his heart as well as his wallet. He presented her with something very special: a silver plaque from a London jeweler (cost: $1,300) inscribed with a poem he had written for her. During their times together Diana gave Dodi a silver cigar clipper, inscribed "From Diana with love," and a pair of gold cufflinks with the family crest which were the last gift she had received from her late father. "I know it would give my father great joy," she said, "to know that they were now in such safe and special hands."

Then there was the ring.

During their cruise, Dodi pulled the *Jonikal* into the harbor at Monte Carlo on the evening of August 22. The couple went ashore and walked together to the boutique of jeweler Alberto Repossi in the Hermitage hotel near the principality's famous casino. They had previously been to the shop on August 5, looked at some rings, and took a catalogue away with them. Now they seemed to know exactly what they wanted.

The Princess had chosen an item from Repossi's new line of engagement rings called "Dis-Moi Oui!" (Tell Me Yes!). Cost: $200,000. Customized specially for Diana, it was a band of yellow and white gold, with triangles of diamond clusters surrounding a stunning emerald jewel. "We tried to show them other things," said Repossi, "but they had decided on this ring." It was agreed that Mr. Repossi himself would bring the ring to Paris on August 30.

Some people close to Diana and Dodi believe that the main reason for their one-day stopover in Paris on August 30 was to allow Dodi to pick up Diana's engagement ring at Repossi's shop in the Place Vendôme. Since the couple had already enjoyed a three-day weekend in Paris the previous month, there would have been little point going back just to have dinner. Diana was due in London by midday Sunday to see her children, who were coming down from a vacation with their father in Scotland, so the visit to Paris would have lasted less than 24 hours in any case. The fact is that Dodi's only fixed appointment in Paris that Saturday was his 6:30 P.M. meeting with Alberto Repossi.

Not even Mohammed Al Fayed, who now has possession of it, knows whether Dodi actually presented Diana with the Tell Me Yes ring that day. Nor is there any evidence that Diana and Dodi had become formally engaged. That they intended to marry seems likely. But Diana, friends believe, wanted to inform her children before making the news public. Possibly she meant to do just that when she saw Wills and Harry back in London on Sunday.

For his part, Dodi told two men who were closest to him that he and Diana had decided to get married. On Friday, August 29, Mohammed Al Fayed phoned the *Jonikal* and spoke to Diana. They chatted about shopping, as she wanted to pick up some birthday presents for Harry, who was turning 13 on September 15. She didn't mention wedding bells at that time, but Dodi spoke to Mohammed later that day. "We have decided to get married, Moomoo," he said, using the affectionate nickname by which he always called his father. "I'm going to Paris and I am going to buy her the ring."

Al Fayed was pleased, but reacted cautiously. "Easy, easy," he told Dodi. "Don't rush into anything. I think this is too fast. Make up your mind. Just be sure you are doing the right thing." But Dodi had already begun mapping out his future with the Princess. He told his father that he wanted to take Diana back around to the Windsor villa during their Paris stopover. "If I get married, do you think you can give me the house?" Dodi asked. Mohammed replied: "No problem."

After Diana and Dodi arrived in Paris, Dodi called his maternal stepuncle, Hassaan Yasseen, who by coincidence was staying at the Ritz that weekend. Yasseen, a Saudi businessman who once served as a press counselor at the Saudi Arabian embassy in Washington, had heard from Dodi during his latest cruise. "He was very joyful and very happy, and his words percolated with excitement," he recalls.

At 8:45 P.M. on Saturday, August 30, Yasseen and Dodi spoke for five minutes on the phone. "He called me and told me that he and Diana were going to go to dinner, and would I join them afterwards. And then we got to talking." It was then, Yasseen says, that Dodi dropped the bombshell. "I said, 'The relationship seems to be getting more serious,' and he said, 'Yes, it is.' Then I asked him, 'Are you going to get married?' He said, 'Yes, we are going to get married.' " Yasseen was overjoyed. "I said, 'We are very happy for you, she is a nice girl, she has tremendous character, I'm glad that you have found love between you,' that kind of nice talk.''

During that brief conversation, Dodi did not elaborate on specific details, such as the ring, the formal announcement, and the timing of the wedding. But he invited Yasseen to join him and Diana at the restaurant for coffee after their dinner. Yasseen figured he would hear more about the engagement then. But near midnight when Yasseen went looking for them, a hotel concierge informed him that Mr. Dodi had phoned to ask if they could meet for breakfast the next morning instead. "There is too much media," Dodi had told the concierge. Yasseen never spoke to Dodi again.

Dodi also spoke about marriage to two family employees, his butler René and Ritz president Frank Klein. René had worked for Dodi for more than six years and was the only long-serving family employee present during his two Mediterranean cruises with Diana. Dodi had said nothing to René about his intentions, but as the couple prepared to leave the Rue Arsène-Houssaye apartment for dinner, he told him he planned to propose to the Princess when they returned. Earlier that day when Dodi was still on the *Jonikal,* he spoke to Klein about the Windsor Villa and informed him that he and Diana planned to use it once they were married.

Richard Kay, the *Daily Mail*'s royal correspondent, and a close personal friend of Diana's for five years, received a call from the Princess at about 5:30 P.M., 6:30 Paris time, on August 30. She rang on his cell phone just as he was parking his car outside a shoe repair shop in Chelsea. Diana was at the Ritz, marking time while Dodi ran an errand. She told Kay she planned to withdraw from public life after completing scheduled commitments around November. The reason, Kay believes, is that she was in love with Dodi and seemed likely to marry him.

Rosa Monckton, who perhaps knew her recent thinking better than anyone, reported that Diana's telephone conversations with him were "full of laughter" during the trip the two women took to Greece. Once Diana insisted that Rosa listen to a cell phone answering machine message Dodi left to hear "his wonderful voice." Monckton concluded that Diana had apparently achieved "some emotional stability" with Dodi. Rosa and Diana spoke by cell phone three days before Diana's death as the *Jonikal* cruised around Sardinia. "Just tell me, is it bliss?" Rosa asked, and Diana replied, "Yes, bliss. Bye-bye."

Dodi kept his love for Diana very private. Throughout the two Mediterranean cruises with Diana, he constantly rang up friends and relatives on his cell phone. Yet only to a few did he confide his true feelings, and then only guardedly. The word that nearly everybody uses to describe Dodi is discreet. "Knowing Dodi, he would not tell anyone in the world," said a close woman friend in London with whom Dodi spoke during that period. "He was such a private boy. He would never name-drop, or say that he is dating so-and-so." The friend, a young married woman with whom Dodi had a strictly platonic relationship, spoke to Dodi last on Thursday, two days before his death. "He said, 'I am really happy.' Not 'I am really happy with Diana.' He never told me anything else." Saying he was "really" happy, the friend explains, was Dodi's way of saying he was in love.

Dodi spoke several times during the summer to his half sister Jumana. He told her that he wanted to introduce Diana to her, and they planned to rendezvous in Paris on the fateful Sunday, which happened to be Jumana's 32nd birthday.

Pat Kingsley spoke to Dodi 12 hours before his death. "He was discreet, but he gave the distinct impression that the summer romance was blooming wonderfully," says Kingsley. "He never mentioned marriage, but he dropped enough strong hints." In that conversation, Dodi told Kingsley he would be back in L.A. toward the end of September. "I have some great news for you," he said. Professional or personal, she asked. "It is strictly personal," Dodi said. "I'm not going to tell you about it until I get to California, but it is really great and I think you'll be thrilled for me."

Michael Cole recalls that when Dodi made his last trip to L.A. to sort out the Kelly Fisher problem, Cole warned him to stay away from women lest the tabloids write a story that he has dumped Diana for a new girlfriend. "He never raised his voice, but he said, 'Michael, there will never be another girlfriend, ever.' He was so emphatic about it. And he wasn't someone who was usually emphatic."

There was no confirmation from Diana's family that she intended to marry Dodi Fayed. But confirmation of her happiness with Dodi came unexpectedly at her funeral in Westminster Abbey on September 6. Her brother, Earl Spencer, chose to close his moving eulogy to Diana before an abbey congregation including Britain's ruling elite and a global television audience of some 2 billion people by speaking unambiguously about her feelings. "I would like to end," he said, "by thanking God for the small mercies He has shown us at this dreadful time, for taking Diana at her most beautiful and radiant, and when she had joy in her private life."

When she had joy in her private life. That brief phrase, a reference to a man that the Princess of Wales had been close to for scarcely six weeks, seemed to speak volumes about his sister's love for Dodi.

Five months after Diana's death, Monckton and another of Diana's friends stepped forward to dispute the fresh evidence that Diana planned to marry Dodi. In a *Sunday Telegraph* article on February 15, 1998, Monckton wrote that "while it is absolutely true that she found happiness" with Dodi, "as for marriage, there was no question of it." She said Diana had joked to her that if Dodi presented her with a ring, "that's going firmly on the fourth finger of my right hand." Monckton also reported that on August 30 Diana had told another friend, Annabel Goldsmith, that she needed another marriage "like a bad rash on my face." Such accounts, while worth noting, prove little. For one thing, Diana's friends may have an interest in preserving her memory and image in a way they deem fitting. For another, Diana's plans were apparently quite recent and she knew many of her friends did not approve of her relationship with Dodi. Thus it seems entirely plausible that she would have waited to return to England before breaking the news to her friends and family.

9

The Last Day

ON THE MORNING OF SATURDAY, AUGUST 30, DODI AND Diana sat on the top deck of the *Jonikal* and admired the sparkling waters of Sardinia's Emerald Coast. Relaxed, tanned and blissfully happy, as Diana had told Rosa Monckton, they chatted and basked in the sun, enjoying the last moments of their magical Mediterranean cruise.

Butler René Delorm, who had been with the couple on both trips, arrived on deck at 9:30 with their breakfast: coffee, croissants and jam, a basket of bananas, apples, grapes, oranges, and kiwis. Diana, as usual, took a large glass of fresh orange juice and poured milk in her coffee. Dodi skipped the juice and drank his coffee black.

"It was a quiet morning. They were in a good mood," René recalls. "They never stopped talking the whole cruise. It was amazing, they never ran out of things to talk about. They were always laughing, holding hands."

While the couple was lingering over their breakfast, Dodi's cell phone rang. It was Frank Klein in Antibes, returning Fayed's call from the previous night. Dodi had an urgent need to talk to Klein, who in addition to running the Ritz was also responsible for overseeing the Windsor Villa, which Mohammed Al Fayed had leased from the City of Paris since 1986. The elder Fayed had ordered the Duke and Duchess' effects cleared out and auctioned off in order to turn the property over to his family's personal use. Dodi had a plan for the stately mansion.

"Frank," he said. "Where do we stand on the Windsor Villa?"

Klein informed him that the Windsor artifacts had been removed as of the end of July and were to go on auction at Sotheby's in less than two weeks. The house now stood empty.

"Good," said Dodi. "I've spoken to my father about moving in. My friend"—he didn't want to mention Diana's name for fear of electronic eavesdroppers—"doesn't want to stay in England."

Klein quickly guessed who he was talking about.

Then Dodi broke some startling news: "We want to move into the villa, Frank, because we are getting married in October or November."

"That's wonderful, Dodi!" said Klein. "Really wonderful. I'll be back in Paris on Monday and we'll talk about it."

Dodi called his father at about 11:00 A.M. It was an upbeat chat, full of excited plans. Then he passed the phone over to Diana, who told Mohammed what a wonderful cruise it had been and said she was looking forward to doing some shopping in Paris for Harry's upcoming birthday.

At about 11:30, René piled the couple's baggage into the *Jonikal*'s launch and headed for shore, accompanied by a masseuse Dodi had brought from L.A. to work on his bad back. Shortly after noon, along with two bodyguards and a housekeeper, Diana and Dodi boarded the launch and motored to a jetty behind the Cala di Volpe hotel. The couple was met there by Tomas Muzzu, a veteran VIP taxi driver, who helped load their baggage into the trunk of his white Mercedes as Diana and Dodi settled into the backseat. A second car, a black Mercedes, carried the other members of their party. There were no paparazzi in sight.

After a 30-minute drive through winding roads that overlooked the rugged Sardinian coastline, the two vehicles arrived at Olbia airport. Waiting on the tarmac was the Gulfstream IV emblazoned in Harrods' green and gold. By the time the baggage was loaded and the passengers on board, the plane had lost its 1:04 P.M. takeoff slot and had to idle nearly half an hour before it roared down the runway and lifted off into clear blue skies.

The sleek craft touched down at Le Bourget airport, 10 miles north of Paris, at precisely 3:20. Alerted by their Italian and British colleagues, a dozen or so journalists were already waiting for the couple upon their arrival from Sardinia. Among them: Chassery, Oderkerken, Guizard, and Rat with his motorcycle driver Darmon. The telephoto lenses were trained on the craft as it taxied and stopped at the Transair terminal, which handles VIP arrivals for the Ritz hotel.

Dodi, who could see the paparazzi from his window, was visibly annoyed and asked the Transair personnel who came on board if they could help them avoid the cameras. He and the Princess only had one night to spend together in Paris before she returned to London to greet her sons and prepare to send them back to school. Dodi did not want this special occasion ruined by a bunch of shutter-happy cowboys trying to corral them on motorcycles and shoving lenses in their faces.

There was not much anyone could do about it. As soon as the door opened, the cameras started clicking. The resulting photos record every detail of their arrival in a series of stroboscopic images. First down the ramp is Trevor Rees-Jones, 29, the former British paratrooper and rugby player who served as Fayed's personal bodyguard and proudly wore the nickname "Dodi's shadow." He is followed by the Princess of Wales, wearing tan pants with a matching jacket, a dark top, and designer sunglasses. She smiles and shakes hands with the ground personnel. Next is Kes Wingfield, 32, the other Fayed bodyguard. Then comes Dodi, wearing a black shirt, vest, and dark jeans.

He is greeted on the tarmac by burly, balding Henri Paul, dressed in a gray suit and sporting dark glasses. Dodi shakes Paul's hand and leans in close to him as if to hear his voice over the drone of the idling jet engines. Paul is talking, gesturing, apparently explaining the logistics of their drive back to Paris. The two men know each other well. Theirs is clearly a relationship of shared confidence.

Parked on the tarmac next to the plane is a black Mercedes 600, license number 405 JVJ 75, a powerful, fully equipped luxury car with black leather seats and tinted windows. Di and Dodi slip into the back. Rees-Jones sits in the front passenger seat. At the wheel is Philippe Dourneau, 35, a former Ritz driver now hired permanently by Dodi to drive him around whenever he's in Paris. It was Dourneau who had chauffeured Diana and Dodi during their secret July 25–27 weekend in Paris, when they had managed to enjoy dinner at Lucas Carton, a well-known three-star restaurant, without the paparazzi ever getting wind of it. The couple had managed that exploit by entering and leaving the Ritz via the rear exit, a trick that had greatly impressed Dodi by its efficacy.

Dourneau was proud of Dodi's confidence in him. As he would later explain, Dodi had hired him because he appreciated his "professional qualities": discretion, punctuality, intimate knowledge of the Paris region, and, not least, his way of driving "gently" even when they were in a hurry. "Even if Dodi was pressed for time," said Dourneau, "he never asked me or incited me to break the law." If Dodi was late for an airplane, perhaps, Dourneau would sometimes surpass the speed limit—"but always in total security and never with the slightest accident." Clearly, a good man to have at the wheel.

As the Mercedes pulled away from the plane, it was followed by a black Range Rover with British plates. This was Dodi's personal vehicle, kept permanently in Paris. Its driver on this occasion was Henri Paul, a man who did not normally serve as a chauffeur but who, as acting security chief of the Ritz, had been sent to greet the couple personally at the airport and ensure their safety. Next to him sat Kes Wingfield. In the back were Dodi's butler, housekeeper, and masseur. Paul's mission, in addition to transporting the couple's baggage, was to act as a screen to keep the paparazzi at bay.

Dodi and Diana had not sought an escort by France's Service de Protection des Hautes Personalités (SPHP), a special branch of the interior ministry that guards visiting dignitaries. French officials say that Diana, as a former member of the

British royal family, would have been entitled to such protection had she requested it via the British embassy. But the SPHP received no official notice of the couple's presence in France; the interior ministry was simply apprised of their arrival for a "private visit."

The Princess was also entitled to round-the-clock security by Britain's Royal Protection Squad, but had chosen to give up that constant surveillance following her divorce. The main reason, says a friend, is that she believed British security agents were "spying on her and reporting back to the palace. She didn't want her ex-husband to know where she was going and whom she was seeing." But even without such close surveillance, MI-6, Britain's overseas intelligence arm, was able to keep tabs on her movements.

As the two-car convoy left Le Bourget, a policeman attached to the customs service escorted them as far as the A1 autoroute. After that, they were on their own. The paparazzi picked them up at the entrance to the autoroute. Rees-Jones later recalled that Dodi asked the driver to speed up and "lose the journalists." Dourneau remembers being followed by several vehicles, including a couple of motorcycles and a black Peugeot 205. He kept to the center lane at a constant speed of 75 to 80 mph. At one point, he later claimed to police, the motorcycles pulled up alongside to take photos and their electronic flashes almost blinded him.

Wingfield, riding shotgun in the Range Rover, noticed that the paparazzi following them were constantly making calls on their cell phones as they drove, apparently alerting other photographers to the couple's arrival. Wingfield recalls a black Peugeot 205 passing the Mercedes on the right, pulling in front of it, and suddenly braking in order to slow it down. (Fabrice Chassery, owner of an anthracite gray Peugeot 205, later admitted he was following the convoy but adamantly denied that he had passed the two cars or performed such a dangerous maneuver.) According to Wingfield, the Princess later told him that she had feared for the safety of some of the motorcyclists, whose reckless driving, she said, could have caused them to fall or collide with another vehicle. As for Henri Paul's performance at the wheel, said Wingfield, "He drove well. He was a good driver, a good guy."

At the Porte de la Chapelle, the procession joined the Boulevard Périphérique, the ring road around Paris, and headed west. Dourneau managed to lose the paparazzi with a brusque turn into the Porte Maillot exit, winning Diana's compliments for his deft move. Henri Paul continued into Paris and delivered the couple's baggage to Dodi's apartment near the Arc de Triomphe, where they were to spend the night together. Paul and Wingfield then rendezvoused with the Mercedes at the couple's first stop: the Windsor Villa, in the Bois de Boulogne. Diana and Dodi, who had visited the mansion together on July 25, stayed only about 40 minutes on this occasion—just time for a quick tour of the residence and the surrounding gardens.

Next stop was the Ritz, where the couple arrived at 4:35, and were personally greeted by Claude Roulet, 46, the hotel's dapper and attentive number two, who later remarked that they seemed happy "and very much in love." They immediately headed up the carpeted staircase to the second-floor Imperial Suite, a palatial $10,000-a-night apartment.

With a view overlooking the Place Vendôme, the suite is decorated with Empire furniture upholstered in red satin, richly colored Persian carpets, crystal chandeliers, and brass candelabra. It includes a salon, dining area, oak bathroom, and double bedroom. It was in this luxurious haven (whose previous occupants have included Hermann Goering, Winston Churchill, Richard Nixon, Woody Allen, and Madonna) that the couple rested up after their trip.

Diana's hopes of doing some shopping in Paris appear to have been compromised by the crush of the paparazzi. Press reports claimed that at one point the couple tried to get out of the Mercedes 600 and enter some boutiques along the Champs-Elysées, but gave up in disgust after being mobbed by photographers. In their detailed accounts of the day's events, neither chauffeur Dourneau nor the two bodyguards made any mention of an aborted shopping excursion. Nonetheless, Diana did manage to get some presents for Harry's birthday, as well as some other items, probably by sending someone from the Ritz to shop for her in the chic boutiques along the nearby Rue du Faubourg–St. Honoré. The packages, beautifully wrapped by the stores, were later found unopened in Dodi's apartment; a maid from the Ritz packed them into Diana's luggage on Sunday and Mohammed Al Fayed had them returned to Diana's sister Lady Sarah McCorquodale in Lincolnshire. Some time after their arrival at the hotel, the Princess went to get her hair done in the hotel's *salon de coiffure* near the basement and pool health spa. Dodi took this moment to run an important errand. He had an appointment with the jeweler Alberto Repossi, who had brought the Tell Me Yes ring up from Monte Carlo after resizing and other modifications that Dodi had requested eight days earlier.

A little before 6:30 P.M., Dodi sent Claude Roulet and Wingfield on foot to Repossi's boutique, just across the Place Vendôme. True to his security fetish, Dodi insisted on being driven to Repossi's in the Mercedes 600, though it was less than 100 meters from the Ritz. Rees-Jones accompanied him and waited in the car while Dodi went inside.

Dodi took delivery of the Tell Me Yes ring, but also examined another that had caught his fancy. He asked Repossi if he could take both rings to see which one the Princess preferred. The jewels were handed over to Roulet, with details about price and payment left to be worked out later between the shop and the Ritz management.

Diana had returned from having her hair done when Dodi got back to the room. Shortly afterward, Roulet knocked on the door and delivered the rings to Dodi, who took them and disappeared into the next room of the suite. Dodi later returned the second ring to Roulet. It was thus the Tell Me Yes ring that Fayed had selected and probably intended to slip on Diana's finger that night. Whatever Dodi may have planned, he never had time to carry it out. The ring was later found in his apartment, still in its unopened box. (It now lies in a safety-deposit box in a Swiss bank, along with several love letters from Diana to Dodi.)

Princess Diana on vacation in St. Tropez in July, on the yacht of Mohammed Al Fayed. (*James Andanson/ Sygma*)

Princess Diana vacationing in St. Tropez. (*Gamma Liaison*)

Mohammed Al Fayed, Princess Diana, and Dodi on Mohammed's yacht, *Jonikal*.

Princess Diana in St. Tropez with Mohammed Al Fayed's daughter. (*Sygma*)

Princess Diana and Dodi Al Fayed aboard *Jonikal* on August 22. (*Gamma Liaison*)

Princess Diana and Dodi Al Fayed enjoy a quiet moment of intimacy aboard *Jonikal*, August 24, 1997. (*James Andanson/ Sygma*)

Princess Diana visits the Northwick Park Hospital to lay the foundation for the new children's wing. July 21, 1997. (*Andrew Shaw/FSP/Gamma Liaison*)

Princess Diana and Prince Harry enjoying a quiet moment in the sun.

Princess Diana arrives at the Ritz Hotel in Paris. Saturday, August 30, 1997. (*AP/Wide World Photos*)

Dodi Al Fayed, left, arrives at the Ritz Hotel in Paris, Saturday, August 30, 1997. Princess Diana's body-guard, Trevor Rees-Jones, is following Al Fayed. (*AP/Wide World Photos*)

Above: Henri Paul arrives at the Ritz Hotel in Paris. Saturday, August 30, 1997. (*AP/Wide World Photos*) *Below:* Dodi Al Fayed puts his arm around Princess Diana as they talk to driver Henri Paul at the Ritz Hotel early Sunday morning, August 31, 1997. Bodyguard Trevor Rees-Jones is in the background. (*AP/Wide World Photos*)

Above: This image taken from video shows seven photographers detained in connection with the high-speed motorcycle chase through the streets of Paris. August 31, 1997. (*AP/Wide World Photos*) *Left:* Police services take away the car in which Princess Diana was killed. August 31, 1997. (*AP/Wide World Photos*)

Flowers in front of Kensington Palace in memory of Princess Diana. (*Andrew Murray/Sygma*)

The funeral of Princess Diana. (*FSP/ Gamma Liaison*)

Queen Elizabeth II and Queen Elizabeth, the Queen Mother, at the funeral of Princess Diana. (*FSP/ Gamma Liaison*)

Bodyguard Trevor Rees-Jones, wearing cap, arrives at the Issy-les-Moulineaux heliport near Paris—after leaving the Pitié-Salpêtrière hospital more than one month after the car crash that killed Princess Diana. October 3, 1997. (*AP/Wide World Photos*)

Diana made several phone calls from the Imperial Suite, including one to her friend and confidant in London, Richard Kay, the royal correspondent of the *Daily Mail*. "She told me she had decided to radically change her life," he wrote in the paper's September 1 edition. "She was going to complete her obligations to her charities and to the antipersonnel land mines cause and then, around November, would completely withdraw from her formal public life."

Kay believed that her relationship with Dodi was a "significant factor" behind her decision. "She was in love with him and, perhaps more important, she believed that he was in love with her and that he believed in her. They were, to use an old but priceless cliché, blissfully happy. I cannot say for certain that they would have married but in my view it was likely." She did not dwell on Dodi during their long conversation, but she did ask Kay why the press seemed so hostile to her Egyptian boyfriend. "Is it because he's a millionaire?" she suggested naïvely, seemingly missing the point about why many Britons found the divorced Muslim playboy an unsuitable match for the mother of England's future king. Summing up her mood at that moment, Kay wrote: "On that Saturday evening, Diana was as happy as I have ever known her. For the first time in years, all was well with her world."

At 7:00 P.M., the couple exited from the rear of the Ritz and got into the Mercedes 600. The Range Rover behind them was now being driven by Jean-François Musa, 39, manager of the Etoile Limousine company that maintains a car-lease contract with the Ritz. Henri Paul had called Musa the night before and asked him to meet him at the hotel at 5:00 P.M. Saturday to drive the Range Rover as a backup car. Thus Paul handed over the keys to Musa, who took off behind the Mercedes 600 with Rees-Jones and Wingfield as his passengers. Destination: Dodi's apartment near the Arc de Triomphe. As soon as he had seen the convoy off, Henri Paul considered his workday over and left the hotel. Time: 7:05.

The Mercedes and Range Rover pulled into the Rue Arsène-Houssaye 10 minutes later to find a band of photographers lying in wait. "The paparazzi literally mobbed the couple," said Wingfield. "That really disturbed and frightened the Princess, even though she was used to paparazzi. These paparazzi were shouting, which made them even more frightening. I had to push them back physically."

When the photographers rushed in too close to the couple, a Ritz security agent assigned to guard the apartment put his hand on the lens of a camera and gave it a hard shove. The photographer, identified by several witnesses as Romuald Rat, bellowed in protest. Another photographer threatened to call in the English paparazzi—reputed to be even more rapacious than their French counterparts—and still another reportedly said, "It will be too bad for the Fayeds if you don't let us work, we'll tell everybody they're scum." Shortly afterwards Rees-Jones and Wingfield came back out of the apartment and tried to cool the overheated tempers, telling Rat and the others that they would let them do their work if they would only keep a respectable distance. By this time, says Wingfield, "Dodi was very angry over the behavior of the paparazzi."

Meanwhile, up in his third-floor apartment, Dodi was making plans for a special evening. While Diana was preparing herself in the green living room, just off the marble foyer, Dodi crept discreetly into the kitchen. "René," he told his butler, "make sure we have champagne on ice." A few moments later, he came back. "René, I'm going to propose to her tonight," he whispered, with a big smile on his face.

The butler was not surprised that Dodi had wanted to share that good news with him. "He had come to know me, and knew I was concerned about his happiness," he says. "I would sometimes tell him, 'Why don't you get married, settle down, have kids?' Dodi would always say, 'Never!' He had never found the right girl until the Princess came along. The only thing missing in his life was the right person."

The couple left the apartment at 9:30 and headed down the Champs-Elysées in the direction of the Concorde. Their initial destination was Chez Benoît, a trendy restaurant boasting one Michelin star located near the Georges Pompidou center. But the photographers were crowding so closely around the cars that Dodi finally got fed up. "This is too much," fumed Fayed. "These guys are crazy!" He told Dourneau to call and cancel the reservation and to tell the Ritz that he and the Princess would dine at the hotel instead. Time: 9:45.

Claude Roulet, the Ritz's second-in-command, was standing on the sidewalk in front of Chez Benoît when he got Dourneau's call on his cell phone. The ever-solicitous Roulet had made the reservation in his own name and was waiting to escort the couple inside and make sure everything was *comme il faut*. Roulet did not want any mishaps tonight. His boss, Ritz president Frank Klein, was in Antibes for the weekend and Roulet was in charge in his absence. He was alarmed at the idea that Fayed and the Princess were now headed back to the Ritz and that no one was prepared to receive them. Roulet phoned the hotel to warn the staff of the couple's imminent arrival. Too late! The cars were just pulling up as his call was answered. Time: 9:51.

A throng of paparazzi and what the French call *badauds*—passersby, groupies, and curiosity-seekers—were waiting in front of the hotel when the couple arrived. The crowd was so thick that Dodi and the Princess could not open the car door at first. Dodi was furious and began shouting at Wingfield and Rees-Jones for not calling ahead to the Ritz so the hotel's security people could clear the entrance for them in advance. Wingfield, who had been riding in the Range Rover with Rees-Jones and Musa, respectfully pointed out that Dodi had never told them he was headed for the Ritz.

Diana got out first, with Wingfield hovering close by her side. "I had to protect her physically from the paparazzi, who were coming really too close to her," he says. "Their cameras were right next to her face . . . Once inside, she sat on a chair and looked rather demoralized, as if she were about to cry." Dodi sat in the car stewing for several moments before he finally got out. His stony face and clenched jaw, clearly visible in the paparazzi photos and the Ritz security video, betray his cold rage.

The couple headed down the main corridor, past two rather vulgar statues of black Nubian slaves brandishing gold candelabra, and entered the hotel's two-star restaurant, L'Espadon. Diana ordered scrambled eggs with mushrooms and asparagus for a starter, sole with vegetables tempura as a main dish. Dodi chose a grilled turbot with Taittinger champagne. No sooner had they ordered, however, than they began to feel the indiscreet stares of other diners. Not only was Di's celebrity status attracting attention; their casual clothes seemed out of place. He was clad in blue jeans, a light gray shirt hanging over his belt, a light brown suede jacket and matching cowboy boots. Diana wore a simple black top, black jacket, white pants, gold earrings and black Versace high heels. All designer stuff, but ill-suited to these posh surroundings. So they decided to retire to the Imperial Suite and have their meal brought up. Another abrupt change in plans—and not the last.

Meanwhile, following the couple's chaotic entrance, night security officer François Tendil had called Henri Paul on his cell phone to apprise him of the situation: Fayed and the Princess were back at the hotel, a hundred paparazzi and *badauds* were jamming the entrance, and the boss' son was mad as hell. Paul, fearing a security screwup that might be blamed on him, apparently decided on his own to come back to the hotel and take the situation in hand. Time: 9:55.

No one knows where Paul was when he got the call. Nor is it clear exactly what he did when he quit work. Even the elite criminal brigade, after weeks of investigating, was unable to piece together his precise movements after his departure at 7:05. One senior Ritz official told detectives that he had seen him at 7:30 in the Bourgogne, a bar near Paul's apartment in the Rue des Petits-Champs. Interrogated by police, however, the manager said she hadn't seen Paul all evening. "We've owned this cafe for eight months, and I saw him in here maybe a dozen times," said the woman, Myriam Lemaire, in an interview. "When he'd come in, he'd have one drink, read his paper, and then leave. I never saw him come in with anyone else, and never take more than one drink.''

There were similarly conflicting accounts that came from Harry's New York bar, just around the corner from the Ritz. The manager insists Paul wasn't there that night, two bartenders say he was, and one of them says he drank two whiskies. To complicate matters, Paul's friends say he never drank whisky. Did he or didn't he?

The mystery continues: at a bar in the Rue du Quatre Septembre that Paul was known to frequent, staffers say not only that he was not there that night but that they had never even heard of him. One begins to suspect that certain bar owners, fearing possible legal problems, would rather not be linked with Henri Paul's alcohol consumption on the night of August 30, 1997.

It seems likely that at some point that evening, Paul went home to his apartment at 33 Rue des Petits-Champs. He was a man with a heavy beard and a tendency to show a five o'clock shadow, yet he was freshly shaven when he showed up at the Ritz and had changed his shirt and tie. Did he drink at home? Quite possible. Detectives later discovered a bottle of Martini aperitif in his refrigerator, three-fourths empty. If he drank all that after leaving work—on an empty stomach— the picture starts to come into focus. Martini contains 16 percent alcohol, almost half as much again as ordinary wine.

One thing is known: Paul did stop in at a bar called the Champmeslé, a lesbian joint in the Rue Chabanais, just before returning to the hotel. Despite his gender, Paul was a regular patron. The girls like him. He would stop in to chat and bring them flowers, but never hit on them. ''I've known him for 20 years,'' says the bar's owner, Josy Champmeslé, fiftyish, blond, tough-looking, and self-acknowledged lesbian. Leaning on the bar under a garish mural depicting nude women, she adds: ''He was a nice guy, gentle. He'd drink Coke, Perrier, maybe a beer.'' Josy insists that Paul appeared normal that Saturday night. ''If he'd been a drunk, we'd have known about it,'' she says.

Paul popped into the Champmeslé around 10:00, but

didn't drink anything. He'd come by to pick up his black Austin Mini, which was parked across the street. Apparently, he had just been called by Tendil and was on his way back to the Ritz. He only had time to stick his head in the door and announce, "See you later, girls. Gotta go to work."

Whether he drank at home or in a bar that night changes little. The fact is his drinking was in no way irresponsible at that point: here was a bachelor, off duty on a Saturday night after a hard day's work; why shouldn't he have a few pops? Henri Paul had no way to know he would be called back that night, much less that he would be asked to drive the Princess and her beau. The irresponsibility came later—and it was not all his.

The Ritz security camera videotape shows Paul driving up to the Ritz entrance at 10:08. Though there was enough room in front of the hotel to park a moving van, the black Mini executes several unnecessary back-and-forth maneuvers before coming to a stop. The edited video shows him walking into the hotel, then talking with various people at different times and places over the next two hours or so. He seems to be conducting himself normally enough, though it is difficult to tell because of the time-lapse images.

Both bodyguards later insisted that Paul seemed "perfectly normal" to them all evening. "He didn't seem nervous," Rees-Jones recalled. "He was always the way I knew him." Wingfield, for his part, told investigators, "Henri Paul drank no alcoholic beverage in my presence. He did not smell at all of alcohol, and he was less than a yard away from me. Furthermore, if he had seemed the slightest bit drunk, Trevor and I would have refused to let him drive the couple. It would have been inconceivable. Dodi would have noticed his drunkenness and fired him on the spot." But Dodi had been drinking champagne himself, and may not have smelled the alcohol on Paul's breath.

In fact, Paul was drinking right under the noses of the bodyguards. While Diana and Dodi were eating, the two Englishmen got a quick bite at the hotel's Vendôme bar; Paul joined them, but did not eat. Instead, Wingfield told police, he ordered a "pineapple juice, which he cut with water from a carafe, because he found it too strong." Rees-Jones later told police that Paul had drunk a "yellow liquid."

Investigators have determined that the "yellow liquid" was in fact pastis, an anisette-based aperitif that is about as strong as whisky. The two Englishmen can be excused for not knowing that, in France, pastis is generally served with a carafe of water on the side and diluted before drinking (recommended dose: five parts water to one part pastis). If you added two shots of pastis to the three-quarters of a bottle of Martini that Paul may have drunk at home, you would get approximately the amount of alcohol that was later found in Paul's blood.

What the Englishmen did not know was apparently evident to a number of Ritz employees. One of them, speaking anonymously, gave this account to the French daily *Libération*: "He was waiting at the Vendôme bar, in the hotel, with the two English bodyguards at a table near the counter. There were a lot of people in the room. The bodyguards did not consume alcohol. But the security chief [Paul] drank aperitifs. I saw him drink two Ricards [a popular brand of pastis]. At one point, the three of them got up suddenly. M. Paul bumped into a waiter, then staggered out. Just before taking the wheel of the Mercedes."

Other Ritz staffers also noticed Paul's condition. An unnamed employee, speaking with his voice disguised on Europe 1 Radio, said that "Paul had been called back in a hurry by the Ritz because Al Fayed was coming. He had been boozing a bit and we all knew it. Everyone knew that he drank when he wasn't working . . . At the Ritz, as soon as the Fayeds are here, it's panic on deck." One lawyer involved in the case says he received anonymous calls from two employees saying they couldn't speak publicly out of fear for their jobs, but that it was obvious to everyone that Paul was drunk that night. "Everyone here knows what really happened but we're afraid to talk," says a longtime Ritz employee. "Monsieur Paul was not responsible. He just took orders."

From whom?

All the evidence points to the fact that Dodi himself asked Paul to drive that night. Both the bodyguards have told investigators that Dodi gave the order—despite their own reservations about the plan. Wingfield, who had returned upstairs with Rees-Jones after eating, reported that Dodi opened the door of the Imperial Suite at 11:15 and asked him how many paparazzi were outside. About 30, plus a 100 or so hangers-on, replied the bodyguard. "Mr. Dodi then told me," reported Wingfield, "that we would leave the hotel in a few minutes according to a plan that he had worked out, consisting of using another Mercedes and another chauffeur. I thought he meant François [Musa], but . . . Mr. Dodi told me it would be Henri Paul. Since I didn't know Henri Paul before that day, I was not surprised that Mr. Dodi had chosen him." Rees-Jones, however, did point out that it would be more prudent to use two cars and said he was "not happy" over Dodi's decision to separate the two bodyguards. Wingfield also thought it better if both bodyguards accompanied the couple. But Dodi overruled them. "The car is too small," he said.

Shortly afterward, Dodi called his father and told him that he and the Princess would soon leave for the apartment. Mohammed Al Fayed didn't like his plan at all. "Don't go," he warned. "There's a lot of press out there, a lot of people. Why don't you just stay in the hotel?"

"We can't, Moo-Moo," said Dodi. "We have all our things back at the apartment, and we have to leave from there in the morning."

"Just be careful," said his father. "Don't step on it. There's no hurry. Wait until you see the atmosphere is perfect, get in your car, and go away. Don't hide, it is unnecessary. You have security with you. If they want to shoot you, fine, then at least we know they shot you. But to go out the back, change the driver . . ."

But Dodi had already made up his mind. During these final moments, he seemed to get more and more excited about his plan. Diana, worn out from the long and harrowing day, waited passively. The Ritz security video shows the couple standing in the rear hall just minutes before their departure. Dodi has his left arm draped protectively around Diana. Henri Paul is facing them, talking animatedly. As Wingfield described the moment: "[Dodi] was happy, so was the Princess. They joked and laughed. It might seem ironic but I had never seen the couple of Dodi and the Princess as happy as at the moment that they were about to leave calmly from the rear of the hotel."

10

The Driver

HENRI PAUL'S BODY STILL LAY ON A SLAB IN THE PARIS morgue, but he knew no peace. His blood, hair, eye fluid, and organ tissues were being examined under microscopes, shaken up in test tubes and centrifuges, and combined with chemical reagents to see what they contained. The first results, announced on the afternoon of September 1, showed that the alcohol level in his blood was nearly three times the legal driving limit of 0.5 g/l. One analysis, done by the police lab, showed 1.87 g/l; the other, given out to a private firm as a control, revealed 1.74 g/l. The news had the effect of a bombshell.

"This changes everything!" declared Gilbert Collard, a lawyer for photographer Christian Martinez. "We are now told that [Paul] was driving extremely fast, in a vehicle he did not master, in a state of drunkenness punished by criminal law. He was endangering people's lives." William Bourdon, attorney for the Sipa agency's Nikola Arsov, chimed in that the photographers had been made "sacrificial lambs" in a frenzy of "showbiz justice" and demanded that the case against them be dropped.

Sensing that the tide had suddenly shifted against them, Ritz lawyers and representatives of the Fayed family launched a vigorous counterattack. First, they flatly rejected the validity of the test results. Fayed spokesman Michael Cole, at a September 5 press conference in London, called Paul an "exemplary employee" and edited portions of a Ritz security camera video to prove that he had been behaving normally on the night of the accident.* "We have as much as possible identified Henri Paul's movements for the two hours or so that he was actually at the hotel and we are satisfied we can account for all of them both with videotape and people giving very detailed statements of his movements and actions that night," said Cole sanctimoniously. "We are satisfied and happy that their accounts of his demeanor are accurate, and those accounts are that he was sober, he didn't smell of alcohol, his gait was steady, and no suggestion or indication that he was anything other than completely sober. We're just trying to demonstrate that this man didn't have 175 ml of alcohol in his blood or he would have been lurching about."

To back up his skepticism about the test results, Cole trotted out an expert witness, Dr. Peter Vanezis, Regis Professor of Forensic Medicine at the University of Glasgow. Vanezis said he had gone to Paris at the request of the Fayeds in order to verify the test results. He was not given access to Paul's body, he said, but was allowed to see the test results. He questioned the handling of the blood samples, saying the parallel tests were actually performed on one blood batch that had been divided into two parts, thus both results would be compromised in the event of a contamination. Though he had absolutely no concrete grounds to indicate that this had been the case, Vanezis stated that, given the "violent" nature of the death, "the possibility of contamination of the blood is real and must be seriously considered." He conjectured that perhaps "stomach contents" could have spilled into the blood. He added that tests on urine or eye fluid samples would have given more reliable results.

Professor Vanezis may not have realized that French pathologists systematically drew blood samples directly from the heart; that five separate samples were collected; that urine,

---

*What Cole screened for the press on that occasion was a heavily edited 26-minute video taken from the six VHS cassettes that Ritz officials turned over to police on September 3.

eye fluid, and bile had in fact also been collected. As for stomach contents, Paul's stomach was intact, as were the other major organs. But before he could answer any journalists' questions, Vanezis excused himself and said he had to rush and catch a plane. His weak performance was just one indication that the Fayed-Ritz side was now clutching at straws to keep the attention focused on the role of the photographers and away from their employee.

Their hastily erected barricades were soon swept away by a torrent of new lab results. On September 10 a communiqué from the prosecutor's office announced that tests on a separate blood sample, drawn on September 4 at the request of Paul's family, put his alcohol level at 1.75 g/l; an analysis of his eye fluid showed a level of 1.73 g/l. In addition, further blood tests revealed "therapeutic levels" of fluoxetine (Prozac) and "infra-therapeutic" levels of tiapride (Tiapridal), two antidepressants that would multiply the effects of alcohol. Tests on Paul's hair permitted analysts to determine that he had been taking Prozac regularly since May and Tiapridal since July.*

Finally, on September 17, the private lab that had been mandated to do more sophisticated blood analysis reported to Judge Stephan that Henri Paul had been in a state of "moderate chronic alcoholism for a minimum of one week [the limit of the test's reliability]." In other words, Paul's high level of blood alcohol on August 31 was not the result of a one-night binge, but was part of a pattern of regular, sustained alcohol consumption. The autopsy results, however, had revealed that Paul's liver suffered no damage related to long-term alcoholism. This is one of the reasons that investigators long hesitated to credit the thesis that he was a full-blown alcoholic.

---

*The report from the private analyst, Dr. Gilbert Pépin, further indicated that, based on tests of spinal tissue, "the fixation in the nerve tissue of the active principles of these molecules [fluoxetine and tiapride] clearly indicates that Mr. Henri Paul was under the influence of these medicines at the time of the events [of August 31]." After performing 12 different analyses, Pépin reported that there were no traces of other drugs or toxic substances in Paul's body.

The evidence was now irrefutable: Henri Paul had been driving under the double-whammy of alcohol and powerful prescription medicines. The Fayed side quickly changed tactics. Spokesman Michael Cole told CNN on September 11 that "Mohammed is shocked. He's appalled. He's outraged that a man in that condition could get into a car and present himself to work that way . . . We condemn in the strongest possible terms anybody who would drink and drive or take these cocktails of drugs, as you say. I don't know [Paul] . . . I am absolutely convinced knowing Mohammed, that if he'd known of any suggestion of inebriation, or a drink problem, if you will, I know he would have been fired—sacked on the spot, because he did often drive Dodi around and he drove other VIPs."

Suddenly depicted as a monster, madman, and de facto murderer, the late Henri Paul had now become the epicenter of the investigation—and a much-vilified target of public opinion. It was an ironic fate for this intensely private man who had already paid the ultimate price for his mistakes. A man who, despite his sudden worldwide notoriety, remains a little-known and poorly understood figure. Irresponsible killer or convenient scapegoat? The jury is still out.

Born on July 3, 1956, into a modest working-class family in Lorient, in southern Brittany, Henri Paul is described by friends as a loyal, hardworking, ambitious, and intellectually curious man who was proud to have risen from his humble origins to a position of high responsibility at one of the world's most prestigious hotels. His father, Jean Paul, 65, was a municipal worker; his mother, Gisèle, 67, a housewife. Henri grew up with his four brothers in a modest two-story house on the Rue Louis Blériot, on the outskirts of this port city of 100,000.

Though he wasn't the eldest son, he was Gisèle's favorite, the one who had gone the furthest in the world, the one she tenderly called *"mon grand"* when he would come home from Paris on weekends. When the scandal broke about his drunken state on the night of the accident, Gisèle stood up for her boy in the face of the widespread opprobrium he was subjected to in the press. "My son was not an alcoholic," she told the daily *Figaro* on September 11. "He's now paying for the personalities that he was driving. Can one imagine the Princess of Wales and Dodi Al Fayed would have agreed to get into a car driven by a drunk? . . . I don't need to defend him. I wish every mother could have a son like him."*

In many ways, Henri Paul *was* an ideal son. He took his baccalaureat degree in mathematics and science at the Lycée St. Louis and won prizes from the local music conservatory as a classical pianist. His real passion, though, was flying. A licensed pilot since the age of 19, he worked for a time as a flying instructor and was qualified to fly by instruments after passing a rigorous certification process. (His first pilot's license, dated June 27, 1976, bears a picture of the young man with hippie-style long hair and a full beard.) Paul spent his year's compulsory military service at the French airbase at Rochefort in 1979, but his poor eyesight prevented him from achieving his dream of becoming a fighter pilot. Instead, he was assigned to the base's security detail, an experience that would later serve him well at the Ritz. He left the service with the rank of lieutenant in the air force reserves.

After his military service, Paul moved to Paris in 1980 and began a six-year stint selling boating equipment at Emeraude Marine, a shop in the Rue des Petits-Champs specializing in catamarans. His big break came in 1982, when a friend, Jacques Pocher, a detective with the Paris judicial police, put him in touch with Claude Roulet at the Ritz. Hotel president Frank Klein had asked Roulet, his number two, to find someone who could help organize a security force for the Ritz. On Pocher's recommendation, Paul was first brought in on contract as a security adviser to the architect who was overseeing a refurbishing of the hotel.

---

*Jean and Gisèle Paul's grief was soon compounded by more bad news: their son's insurance company reduced the death benefit to his family from 2 million francs ($360,000) to 360,000 francs ($65,500) because he had been shown to have been inebriated at the wheel.

In 1986, the new security service was finally set up and Paul was hired as its assistant director. When security chief Jean Hocquet resigned on June 30, 1997, Paul became the acting head of the 20-man unit. At the time of the accident, he answered only to Klein, Roulet, and hotel manager Franco Mora. Friends and employees say he got on well with Klein and enjoyed his confidence. Klein appreciated his discretion, his can-do spirit, and his absolute loyalty. The assistant security chief was not a man to say "no" to any order from his superiors.

Paul also enjoyed the confidence of police and intelligence services, with whom he had regular dealings in connection with the security of visiting dignitaries. He was even said by some sources to have been an informant, or honorable correspondent, of France's foreign intelligence service, the Direction Générale de la Sécurité Extérieure (DGSE). DGSE officials refuse to deny or confirm his links to that service. But Yves Bonnet, former head of the counterintelligence agency, the Direction de la Surveillance du Territoire (DST), said in an interview that it would be "normal procedure for someone in that position at a major hotel to be approached by the services and asked to provide information on its clientele. That is not at all unlikely." Indeed, Paul's private address books, found in his apartment and office by investigators, contain contact numbers at the DST and the Renseignements Généraux, the intelligence-gathering arm of France's national police. Paul, a lieutenant in the air force reserves until 1992, also carried a badge that allowed him free access to the justice ministry, located next door to the Ritz. Friends say he occasionally alluded to such links, but remained discreet on the details.

Claude Garrec, 40, also from Lorient, was probably Henri Paul's best friend. (As of September 3, 1997, his name was still on the mailbox of Paul's apartment, along with the names of Paul's former girlfriend and the woman's daughter.) Ever since they met in 1976, the two men had been in almost constant contact. Paul would join Garrec and three other buddies for a regular dinner in the Grand Colbert restaurant on the Rue Vivienne nearly every Wednesday. On Saturday nights, Paul, a bachelor, would usually join Garrec's family for dinner at their Paris apartment. Garrec would occasionally meet Paul and other friends for bowling parties, and the two men had a standing tennis date on Saturday mornings.

On the last day of Henri Paul's life, August 30, 1997, Garrec picked him up at his apartment and drove to the municipal tennis courts in the southwestern suburb of Issy-les-Moulineaux. They played from 10:00 until 11:00. "Henri won the first set, I won the second," says Garrec, a printing firm administrator with intense blue eyes and close-cropped graying hair. "He was an average athlete who could play an hour of tennis, that's about it." At 11:00, they left the courts and went to a newsstand in the Place de la Madeleine to buy some newspapers. Paul, as usual, bought the left-center Paris daily *Libération* and *Ouest-France*, a regional daily covering his native Brittany.

From there they went to the Pélican, a brasserie near Paul's apartment, for their regular post-game drink. "Henri would usually have a beer or two on such occasions," says Garrec, "but this time he only took a Coke, because he said he was working that afternoon. He said he had to pick up the Princess and her friend at Le Bourget, but he talked about it as a very routine thing." They parted company at 12:30. That was the last Garrec saw of Henri Paul.

Like most of Paul's friends, Garrec is stunned by the accident and baffled as to how he could have become so inebriated. "It's not good to drink and drive—of course, I can't defend that—but how did it happen?" he wonders. "Maybe on that one evening, he let himself go—or someone pushed him to drink. Maybe he made a mistake, but he was a good guy."

Paul was a bon vivant who enjoyed his food and drink, says Garrec. At meals, he'd usually have a pastis or two before eating, but rarely drank wine at the table. He'd occasionally have a shot of bourbon, but never drank whisky. "Even when he had a lot to drink, he was always straight. I never saw him go beyond the limit. He never stuttered, or staggered, or got silly. He was usually the first one to leave the table. He'd get up at 10:00 P.M. and go home. He was never one to hang around drinking until 3:00 A.M."

Bartenders in the neighborhood of the Ritz and near his own apartment depict Paul as a moderate drinker who was as likely to order a Perrier or an orange juice as the occasional beer or pastis. And rarely more than one, they all insist. Leonard Amico, an American writer, would occasionally run into Paul at the Bourgogne. "On weekdays, he'd sit at the counter, have a beer or two, and read his newspaper," says Amico. "On weekends, he'd have a couple of glasses like the rest of us." Paul was known in a lot of bars. One suspects there may have been a revolving-door syndrome going on here: he would have a beer or two in one place and move on to the next bar, then the next.

Including the posh watering holes of the Ritz hotel. Claude Roulet has flatly told investigators that Paul "never drank while he was working." Some employees, though, do recall his drinking on the premises. "He would come into the Hemingway bar maybe once or twice every three weeks or so for a drink or two," says one. "Occasionally he would have a special cocktail prepared for him, and at staff parties he would drink." (One picture of a grinning Henri Paul at a staff party several years ago, sporting a Pancho Villa mustache and brandishing a glass of what appears to be bourbon or scotch, was splashed across the front page of *The Mirror* on September 3.) Understandably tight-lipped in public, some Ritz staffers privately acknowledge that Paul was well known to have a fondness for the bottle.

By all accounts, Paul was an engaging, entertaining companion. He would play piano for his friends, from jazz to classics. He was widely read, intellectually curious, could discuss almost any subject—including movies he had never seen, just from having read the reviews. "His main subject of conversation was aviation—that was his real passion," says Garrec. But he was well informed about almost everything. He read newspapers, magazines, novels, essays—he especially liked essays. He had a surprising memory, and a great vivacity. He spoke fluent English and some German.

Garrec describes Paul as being a "very prudent" driver. "In a car, he was the first one to buckle his seat belt. He had a small car, an Austin Mini, with an automatic shift. He really didn't care anything about cars or speed. We'd drive to Lorient together every couple of months. He usually didn't want to drive. When he did, he was very rigorous. To take off in a plane at night at 160 mph, you have to be in control of yourself." Paul, in fact, far preferred flying to driving and would sometimes rent a small plane at the private airfield of Toussus-le-Noble, some 20 miles southwest of Paris, and fly to Lorient on weekends. There, he'd visit his parents and hang out with a band of childhood friends with whom he kept in touch.

Jean-André Cahuzac, who gave Paul flying lessons for several years, confirms his exceptional abilities as a pilot. "You have to realize that there's no room for improvisation when you are flying an airplane through the fog," he says. "It's something that demands discipline. Paul was anything but a clown." His 605 hours of flight time, like his fly-by-instruments qualification, attest to his skills and experience in the cockpit. Only two days before his death, Paul had passed the physical exam necessary to renew his license. His reflexes and general health were judged to be good, although the report stipulated: "obligatory use of spectacles for long-distance vision." (He was wearing his glasses on the night of August 30.)

At five foot six and 167 pounds, stocky but not fat, the balding, graying Paul could look like a tough guy or a teddy bear. He had long sported a mustache that gave him a sort of Latin American bandito look, but shaved it off about a year earlier. Greeting Dodi at Le Bourget in his tight-fitting gray suit and dark glasses, he looks in the photos like a plainclothes cop about to make a drug bust. On the Ritz security video just before the last ride, his glasses give him a professorial look, like a high school principal chatting with a favorite pupil. Pictures of him on vacation in Spain in July show him relaxing in a bathing suit and open shirt, his chest and legs deeply tanned, an impish half-smile on his perfectly round face.

"He was impertinent, with a gift for communication," says Garrec's business partner, Robert Prunier, 49, another member of Paul's devoted inner circle of friends. "He was at ease talking to anyone. His game was to say shocking things to people he hardly knew to provoke their reaction, then get them to laugh with him. He could quickly size up any person he met."

Henri Paul could talk of anything and everything, but his conversation often revolved around his work at the Ritz, says Prunier. "He loved his job. He'd tell us anecdotes about amazing or funny things that happened at the Ritz. He would tell us things about Dodi, but he was more interested in the father than in the son."

Dominique Mélo, 40, a former schoolmate and flying buddy of Paul's from Lorient, and now psychology professor in Rennes, recalls that he "always had an openness about him. Everyone was won over by his openness." His reading tastes were wide-ranging. "When we were on vacation in Spain together in July," says Mélo, "he was reading a book on the mysticism of Saint Theresa. When he finished that, he read one on the ethnology of tattoos. The last book he was reading was a dictionary of psychoanalysis. We found it on his night table after he died."

Paul's philosophy, says Mélo, was "not to be stuck in your condition in life. We were all from working-class families, but he taught us to be individuals and not to be trapped by our class." It was for that reason, Mélo believes, that Paul was "fascinated by Princess Diana. He said he admired her way of breaking free of her condition and her class and being herself. He always talked with respect of Diana."

At the mention of August 31, Mélo lets out a long breath. "We don't know what happened." He pauses. Clearly he's thought about this a lot over the past few days. "I think what explains it is this: it's 7:00, he's not supposed to be at work anymore. He's free to drink, meet people, talk about his vacation, hang out in bars. Then he gets a phone call. From whom? Did he get an order to come back or did he seek the job out? Did he say, 'Okay, I'll come and take care of things myself'? That would have been like him. Once he's there, Dodi may have said, 'Ah, M. Paul is here? I want to see him.' Then maybe Dodi says, 'You're the one I want to drive us.' So Henri says to himself, 'Okay, I'll break the law and do what the boss' son asked me to do.' Was that something he thought he should do for a Ritz customer, or was it on a friendly basis? No one knows.'' Though Paul did not show any overt signs of depression, Mélo thinks the medication he took may have been related to ''stress and pressure from his job responsibility.''

But Mélo probably knew more about the subject than he cared to say at the time; his wife, who coincidentally also bears the dual gender name of Dominique, was the doctor who prescribed Prozac and Tiapridel for Paul. In a deposition added to the investigative dossier in late December, Dr. Mélo told investigators that she had provided the medication to help Paul deal with depression caused by the end of a long relationship with a woman. ''This treatment suited him,'' she said. ''He had found a certain energy for his work and enjoyment of life, although he still had moments of depression and a feeling of extreme solitude and loneliness that occasionally led him to drink at home.''

There is no doubt that Paul was hard hit by his breakup with Laurence Pujol, thirty-two, a former secretary in the Ritz personnel department, with whom he had lived for four years. Paul was very attached to Pujol's daughter from an earlier liaison. Samentha, now 11, and was said to have been upset over their departure. Pujol had actually moved out in 1992, but their relationship had continued off and on until April 1995. Paul had not seen Laurence or Samentha since that time. Their last contact was a phone call on Paul's 40th birthday, July 6, 1996.

Pujol, a petite, slightly built blonde with large pale blue eyes and a little bow mouth, cradles a coffee cup in both hands as she talks about her life with Henri Paul. She is fragile, still shaken by his death, wracked with doubts about whether she was right to leave him, but full of admiration for the man she says was "like a light" for her and Samentha. They had met at the Ritz in December 1988; after a rapid courtship, Pujol moved into Paul's apartment in April 1989. A long-time bachelor, he was leery at first of having a child come bounding into his life, but soon "cracked" for the little girl, who was then 2½.

"He adored Samentha," Pujol recalls. "They would play together for hours. Sometimes if I had to work early, he'd give her a bath, make her breakfast, brush her hair, and take her to school, just like a mother." In the evenings when he got home from work, Paul would put the child on his knee and play children's songs on his electric piano. When Samentha got a little older, Paul would teach her computer games, give her music lessons, and even take her flying with him in a rented plane. "I was never afraid for her to fly with Henri," says Pujol. "He was very responsible."

But he also had a daredevil side, mixed with a penchant for practical joking, that would lead him to do unexpected things. "Once when he had me up in his airplane," Pujol recalls, "he just let go of the stick and said, 'I don't control anything. Quick! Take the controls!' I shrieked. He didn't tell me he was on automatic pilot. Another time, we were coming in for a landing and suddenly he said, 'Oh no! I don't feel in control of this landing!' He pulled up just before touching the ground. He looked over to see the panic on my face, then burst out laughing. Then he circled the airfield and landed normally." One senses that his high speed cat-and-mouse chase with the photographers on the night of the tragedy may have been part of this pattern.

Paul was so attentive to both mother and daughter that the relationship finally became suffocating to Pujol. He was "possessive," "moralistic," "dominating"—all out of devotion to them. "He couldn't help himself," says Pujol, looking like a runaway teenager in her tight gray jeans, black sneakers, and a baggy long-sleeved sweatshirt. "For him it was natural to love us that much. He couldn't love us less.'' She pauses to wipe her eye. ''Or maybe it's me who didn't understand.''

Not long after she moved out in 1992, Paul began sending her flowers, little notes, inviting her to dinner. They would get together from time to time. Paul would take Laurence and Samentha on wonderful vacations: Israel, Turkey, Greece, Orlando, where they spent one Christmas at Disney World. Then Laurence decided she needed more space. She sent Samentha to live with her father in Paris and moved to a little town near Rennes, in Brittany, where she knew no one. ''I just wanted to take a break. We always intended to get back together. But time ran out on us.''

''Henri was hurt, but he was sensitive and strong,'' says Pujol. ''He was capable of self-analysis. A setback like that would just give him an incentive to forge ahead.'' She sips her coffee and repeats, ''He was hurt.'' Could that explain his use of antidepressants? ''I nearly fell out of my chair when I heard about the drugs,'' she says. ''I don't understand anything. There are too many things I don't know.''

She is likewise stunned by the claim that Paul was drunk that night. ''I don't care what the journalists say,'' she insists. ''Henri was not an alcoholic. I never saw him put away a whole bottle. He'd accept an aperitif if they offered one at a restaurant. When we came home from work, we'd have a little drink together. He would usually take bourbon with lots of water and no ice. But at the dinner table, we'd drink water.''

When friends came over for dinner, or on special occasions like New Year's Eve, the arrival of the Beaujolais Nouveau, weddings, and birthdays, it was different. ''Sometimes, he would drink more than normal at fêtes,'' says Pujol. ''Those are times when everybody eats, drinks, dances, and laughs together. Henri would play the clown then. He was good at that.'' But he could always handle alcohol, she stresses. ''When Henri took two aperitifs or even three, he was totally conscious. He walked straight, knew exactly what he was doing and when he felt he'd gone too far, he'd stop.''

But drink did change his behavior. *"Il avait le vin gai,"* says Pujol, a tentative smile appearing on her face for the first time. "Wine made him joyful. He'd get very happy and do gags to make people laugh. Sometimes he would make you think he was really drunk when he wasn't. He was a joker. He played around a lot, but he never got incoherent on alcohol." Pujol, of course, never saw Paul when he was mixing antidepressants with his alcohol. Under those conditions, his normal ability to sense his limits was likely blown away by the potent cocktail of chemicals coursing through his bloodstream, producing the sort of effervescent euphoria that makes people feel all-powerful.

That would go a long way towards explaining why the normally reliable and responsible Paul agreed to take the wheel that night. Another reason is what Pujol calls his "respect for hierarchy"—perhaps a result of his military training and his experience in the security field, where orders and chains of command are not to be questioned. "He was devoted to hierarchy, to the management," says Pujol, who as a former Ritz employee has an insider's knowledge of the power relationships inside the hotel. "If Fayed asked Henri to drive, and if Henri said yes, then he must have felt himself capable of doing it. On the other hand, when Fayed asks for something, it may be presented as a request, but it must be done. Fayed was always snapping his fingers and changing his plans."*

Paul probably never got over the loss of Laurence and Samentha. Recently, though, he had been seeing a blond woman in her midtwenties, an artist from his native Brittany. He was very discreet about the liaison and his friends knew

---

* Kelly Fisher made much the same point in her January 30 deposition before Judge Stephan. Fisher, who had previously stayed with Dodi at the Ritz and knew Henri Paul, voiced this opinion of the events of August 31: "More than the problem with the paparazzi, there was overall the behavior of Dodi and his attitude regarding employees, who were obliged to do what he said because otherwise they were fired." She also told the judge that she and Dodi had become engaged on November 1, 1996, and had planned to wed on August 9, 1997.

little about her. "I think he wanted to make sure it was a durable relationship before he introduced her to us," says Mélo. "After all, we're not teenagers anymore. We're all in our forties." The woman would often meet Paul for lunch or a drink on Sundays. On August 31, oblivious to the previous night's tragedy, she waited for him at the Bourgogne. But Paul did not come.

The blonde seems not to have been the only female in his life. On September 2, only 48 hours after the accident, a different young woman knocked on the door of Paul's apartment. Paul's father and mother were there, going though their son's affairs. The woman gave them her copy of the key to Paul's apartment, saying she had no more use for it, then quietly left.

On September 3, at 3:15 P.M., there was another knock on the door. This time it was two police officers armed with a search warrant. Jean Paul let them in and invited them to inspect the premises. Their report describes the apartment in detail: a living room, kitchen, dining room, two bedrooms, and a bathroom. In the fridge, they found the three-fourths empty bottle of Martini as well as an unopened bottle of champagne and a large quantity of nonalcoholic beverages. There was no sign of empty beer or wine bottles, no large stash of booze. But on the coffee table, among a pile of scattered papers and business cards, they found a note that read: "M. Henri Paul, for you we have gotten a bottle, in fact several bottles, of Four Roses." No conclusive proof of alcohol abuse here, but a clear sign that drinking was part of the lifestyle.

It appears that Paul was not universally popular with the people under him, who considered him something of a bully. "He was Klein's eyes and ears and spent his time harassing and firing people," says one employee. On September 3, police searched Paul's office at the Ritz for clues to his lifestyle. In his desk drawer, they found a hand-written note from an obviously disgruntled employee. It began, "On the [staff] committee, you are all rotten," and ended, "you are all a bunch of good-for-nothing crooks, and the Breton is the worst of all.'' As paraphrased by the police inspector, the gist of the letter was that ''an individual nicknamed the Breton rakes in millions and drinks alcohol all day long.'' No individual's name is specified. But natives of Brittany, as Henri Paul was, are known in French as Bretons. Asked by the authors about Paul's problems with other employees, a senior Ritz official later explained, ''Like all people working in the security field, Henri Paul had his enemies.''

Police found another surprise in Paul's desk drawer: two maps detailing homosexual meeting places in Paris, entitled *Paris Plan Gay 1996.* The detectives didn't know what to make of it. The Ritz employee who had accompanied them to the office was also baffled, saying that to his knowledge Paul was not a homosexual. Indeed, apart from his frequenting a lesbian bar near his apartment, nothing indicated that Paul had any inclinations in that direction. His long-time relationship with Pujol and his more recent liaison with the young blond woman attest to his heterosexual tastes. It is possible that he kept such information on hand in order to be of service to gay Ritz clients. In any case, this discovery added yet another layer of mystery to the ever more curious story of Monsieur Paul.

When police interrogated Laurence Pujol one week after the accident, they focused in on two questions: whether Paul was an alcoholic and whether he was a homosexual. Pujol, of course, was unaware of the *Paris Plan Gay* discovery, but offers her own explanation for the investigators' curiosity on that point. ''You know how rumors get started,'' she says. ''At the hotel, people knew he was a bachelor. He was very discreet about his private life, so no one knew that we were living together. Someone started a rumor. That just made him laugh. He was a joker, he loved to put people on. So when someone would say, 'Hey, Henri, I hear you're a homosexual,' he'd say, 'Of course, didn't you know?' He thought that was funny.''

Paul's sexual inclinations, of course, had nothing to do with his performance on the job. Drinking is another matter—particularly for someone occasionally called upon to chauffeur clients around. To be sure, driving was not part of Paul's official job description, even though he had attended special Mercedes driving courses in Stuttgart yearly from 1988 through 1992.*

As described by Roulet, Paul's job was to take care of security matters under the direction of Jean Hocquet, who was in charge of relations with president Frank Klein and overall security decisions. Paul, who was paid some $40,000 a year, did all the hands-on stuff: overseeing security personnel, coordinating relations with various "official services" (presumably including intelligence agencies), recruiting and managing the security staff, and dealing with emergencies. Among the crises Paul had to manage was the fatal stroke suffered by U.S. Ambassador Pamela Harriman in the Ritz pool area on February 3, 1997. (Rushed by ambulance to the American Hospital, Harriman died there two days later.)

After Hocquet's retirement at the end of June, Paul ran the whole security operation on his own pending the naming of a new chief. It was a stressful situation, but he never complained to his bosses. "Monsieur Paul did his work seriously and zealously," Roulet told investigators, "often even working overtime on his own initiative."

It was typical of Henri Paul that he decided to rush back to the Ritz that night. And that he died doing overtime. In his zeal to take care of the problem, he became the problem. In his blind obedience to orders from on high—from the owner's son, no less—he put himself behind the wheel of a car he was in no state to control. In Henri Paul's personal chemistry, it seems, the combination of booze and zeal—

---

*It was widely reported in the press that Paul had attended the Mercedes courses in 1991 and 1992. Pujol, in her November 20 interview with the authors, says that Paul actually started the annual courses in 1988 and continued them at least through her departure in 1992 and possibly longer. He took the courses extremely seriously, she reports. "He would take photos of the comportment of the cars, of the tires, of the test tracks, the slalom courses. He was very good at it. He was always very proud when he returned because he always got excellent marks in his report."

alcoholism plus workaholism—proved to be a disastrous equation. When one factors in the Prozac and Tiapridal, which would produce an effect of euphoria even as they dulled the reflexes, it is clear that Henri Paul was an accident waiting to happen.

The photographers noticed his "bizarre" behavior, teasing them and strutting around like a cock-of-the-walk. Musa found him unusually "chatty." Chauffeur Philippe Dourneau told investigators he seemed "more giddy than usual." A Ritz chauffeur, interviewed anonymously on Europe 1 radio, said it was obvious that Paul had been "boozing," that he seemed "cocky and sure of himself and wanted to do too much because he was driving the boss' son." An anonymous Ritz employee called the offices of the weekly *VSD* at 11:00 A.M. on August 31, more than 24 hours before the first blood test results were announced, and informed a reporter that Paul was "dead drunk" just before taking the wheel.

How could Ritz officials not know that he was clinically drunk that night, or that he had a chronic alcohol problem? It seems unthinkable that they would allow him to drive had they suspected his condition. But should they have suspected it? Not only had he demonstrably consumed considerable quantities of alcohol on August 30, but there were clear signs that he was a habitual, if controlled, drinker.*

When security chief Jean Hocquet resigned on June 30, Ritz officials decided to look outside for a new director rather than promote Paul to the top job. Asked why Paul was not promoted, a Ritz spokeswoman says, "He was just happy doing his job. I don't know if he even wanted it." Perhaps. But that hardly squares with the picture his friend Dominique Mélo paints of an ambitious, hard-driving man determined "not to be stuck in his condition" but to rise as far as his talents could take him. For such a man to be passed over—

---

*According to French weekly *L'Express* (September 18, 1997), Judge Stephan requisitioned Paul's Social Security records; they revealed that he had previously received a prescription for the medicine Aotal, generally used "for the maintenance of abstinence in an alcoholic patient."

for the second time, in fact*—could be less a sign of his lack of interest than of the management's reservations about his capacity for the top job. Did his drinking have something to do with that? And, conversely, did his disappointment over the rebuff have something to do with his drinking—and his resort to antidepressants?

It was partly to determine how much Ritz officials knew about Paul's drinking, and when they knew it, that investigators began interrogating hotel employees on September 4. In addition to questioning hotel officials, including Klein, Roulet, and manager Franco Mora, about the events of that fateful Saturday, police inspectors grilled the staffers of the Vendôme bar for several hours at the headquarters of the criminal brigade.†

The results of those interrogations were contained in 3,500 pages of depositions and documents that were added to the investigative dossier on December 26. The new material contained proof, based on a Ritz cash register's electronic memory, that Paul had indeed consumed two shots of pastis at the hotel. Testimony from one employee of the Vendôme bar confirmed what several staff members had anonymously told reporters about Paul's drinking. "I have seen Henri Paul drunk at the hotel on several occasions," said the barman. "It was known that Henri Paul had a tendency to drink." On the night of the accident, said this witness, Paul "was inebriated, his eyes were shining, he was excited. Henri Paul staggered to the exit." The witness added that hotel officials had asked him not to tell police that Paul had been drinking in the bar so as not to embarrass "the Royal Family." In another deposition Paul's former boss, Jean Hocquet, told investigators that the security officer should never have taken

---

*The first director of the Ritz security service was Joseph Goeddet, who took over in 1986. When Goeddet was replaced on January 1, 1993, the job did not go to Henri Paul, his number two, but to Jean Hocquet.

†In the wake of the accident, the Ritz became virtually off limits to journalists, and it became almost impossible to obtain the most basic information from the normally helpful public relations office. A spokeswoman, usually eager to tout the hotel and its staff, had "no information" on President Frank Klein and no photo of him.

the wheel that night, but that he was incapable of refusing orders from Dodi Fayed.

It is not yet clear what consequences such testimony may have. But when they started the process, police could not rule out the possibility that Ritz officials might become a formal target of the investigation at some point. Even if no criminal responsibility is imputed to its management, the hotel could be the object of civil suits by Rees-Jones or the families of Princess Diana and Henri Paul. In addition to any legal liabilities it might incur, moreover, the Ritz risked seeing its cherished reputation for perfection tarnished in the eyes of its demanding clientele.

No one could deny that the whole affair has been a scandal as big as the Ritz. "It's been a huge blow to the hotel," says a source close to management. "It's a nightmare from their point of view." Whatever the ultimate legal consequences, it is clear at least according to Etoile Limousine's Musa, that Claude Roulet, the hotel's number two, helped carry out the Rube Goldberg rear getaway plan that Dodi had cooked up. The Ritz management would be more likely culpable if it were shown that they were aware Paul was drinking on the premises before taking the wheel.

That he was in fact drinking at the hotel is no longer contested. "He had two Ricards in the Vendôme bar while he was sitting with the bodyguards, that is true," admits a senior Ritz official. "It is absolutely against the rules for employees to drink in the bars. He should not have done that." What about the antidepressants and the "chronic" drinking indicated by the postmortem tests? "I had no idea about that," says this official. "For me, he was never depressive. There was no hint of alcoholism. When I learned the test results, I was shocked, surprised. I said, how is this possible?"

Lawyers for the photographers, understandably anxious to point the finger of guilt away from their clients, assert that the Ritz bears potential responsibility for the accident. "He was so drunk it had to be visible, people saw it," says William Bourdon, attorney for the photographer Nikola Arsov. "The real question is why wasn't he stopped? The responsibility of the Ritz is complete. French law says that anyone believing that a person—because of the state he's in—puts someone else in danger, must do everything possible to prevent that risk. If he got into the car staggering and no one did anything to stop him, or warn the passengers, that raises serious questions." To Jean-Marc Coblence, lawyer for Rat, Darmon, and Arnal, the issue is clear: "Of course the Ritz bears responsibility . . . The Ritz and the Fayeds could face criminal charges for manslaughter."

Nor are such opinions limited to the paparazzi's lawyers. Aram J. Kevorkian, an American lawyer practicing in Paris, also foresees potential legal action against the Ritz. "The driver is dead, and so under French law he can't be charged with being criminally responsible for their deaths," he told *The New York Times* on September 14. "But the investigating judges are free to interrogate people at the Ritz about why they allowed him to drive a car the hotel had hired from a rental agency that night, and name them as suspects in an investigation if they see fit." Any civil action against the hotel, lawyers say, would be aimed at the French-based Ritz corporation, headed by Frank Klein, rather than the owner Mohammed Al Fayed.

Lawyers for the Fayeds, after initially heaping all the blame on the photographers, and denying the validity of the first test results, finally conceded that Paul's drunken state contributed to the accident. But they still insisted that the paparazzi remained the prime cause. "If the latest blood tests are accurate, I can't deny there is responsibility of Henri Paul, who shouldn't have taken the wheel with such a level of alcohol," said Fayed lawyer Bernard Dartevelle, in a September 11 interview with the Associated Press. But, he added, "I would say it's almost a secondary responsibility. There is an initial responsibility of the paparazzi who led the aggressive chase of the Mercedes."

The photographers, Dartevelle insisted, were the "fundamental and determining" factor in the accident. Asserting that "Paul took the initiative to take the wheel"—the bodyguards later said it was Dodi's idea—the attorney declared:

"We condemn in the strongest possible terms anybody who would drink and drive or take these [sic] cocktail of drugs ... Obviously, Mr. Paul should not have been at the wheel. But he was probably the only one to be aware of his real condition."

Dartevelle's partner Georges Kiejman, for his part, told Reuters on September 3: "The drunkenness of the driver is a point but it is not the only point. In French case law, it's enough that you can prove that the chase played a part in the accident." Kiejman elaborated on that argument in an interview published by the *Figaro* the same day. "If they had not had to try to shake off their pursuers, Princess Diana and Dodi Al Fayed would have taken another route, because they were headed for [Fayed's] domicile near the Champs-Elysées, in the neighborhood of the Etoile. The pursuit by the photographers certainly remains the initial and determining cause of the accident."

Those statements had a whistling-in-the-graveyard air about them. The Fayed lawyers were now thrown on the defensive. What had seemed at first as such a clearcut case against the photographers had suddenly become more complex—and would become even more so when investigators later revealed that another major factor had contributed to the crash.

For the moment, the spotlight had shifted from the paparazzi to Henri Paul. And behind Paul stood the Ritz. And behind the Ritz stood Mohammed Al Fayed, whose dream of seeing his son marry the Princess of Wales had vanished in the smoke of the Alma tunnel. The bitter irony was that Mohammed Al Fayed, having lost his eldest son, might now find himself, as owner of the Ritz, potentially saddled with at least some responsibility for the accident.* "If there is responsi-

---

*On September 2, Attorney Georges Kiejman filed to make Mohammed Al Fayed a civil party to the investigation. This gave Fayed's lawyer access to the investigative dossier and the right to collect damages in the event of a criminal prosecution and conviction. The same step was taken on behalf of the Spencer family (September 3), Mr. and Mrs. Jean Paul (September 2), and Dodi's bodyguard Trevor Rees-Jones (October 16).

bility to bear,'' says Al Fayed spokesman Michael Cole, ''Mohammed will bear it with the same dignity and courage as he's borne his own grief.''

Meanwhile, Henri Paul finally got his brief moment of dignity. His burial had been repeatedly delayed while lawyers wrangled over the validity of the toxicological examinations and demanded new tests. On September 12 Judge Hervé Stephan at last issued a burial permit, but he instructed Paul's family not to have the body cremated, as they had planned, in case it would prove necessary to exhume it for future tests.

On Saturday, September 20, three weeks after the accident, Henri Paul was buried in his hometown of Lorient. Before entering Sainte-Thérèse church, Paul's family stood in a semicircle around a polished blond wood coffin covered with sprays of lilies. Jean Paul, an exceptionally tall man with thinning gray hair swept straight back and a large pair of dark glasses covering his eyes, towered like an oak tree over the others. He clutched the hand of his wife, Gisèle, who was clad in black, her black hair gathered in a tight bun. There was no sound but the whirring and clicking of cameras. After a minute of silence, they entered the church and took their seats on the front row. Garrec, Mélo, all Paul's old friends and neighbors were there, along with about 15 employees of the Ritz, who had made the four-hour trip from Paris in a chartered bus to bid their ex-colleague adieu. Laurence Pujol and Samentha stayed away for fear of being mobbed by journalists.

''Since the drama in the Alma tunnel, important questions are being raised about the race towards sensationalism,'' intoned the parish priest Léon Théraud. ''We must all think about this, for each of us has a role in it . . . Jesus denounces all the judgments, rumors, and lies that we repeat about others without verifying them, without taking into account the complexity of the facts.'' Henri Paul, he said, ''was very human, generous, welcoming and faithful . . . His laughter will continue to echo in the hearts of his friends and family.''

Seated in the flower-bedecked church, and perhaps pondering the priest's words, were Frank Klein, Claude Roulet, and Jean Hocquet. It was the least the senior Ritz management could do. But Monsieur Henri, the "exemplary" employee of yore, had by then become an embarrassment and a liability to them. It was a cruel destiny for a man who had lived for his job.

11

The Paparazzi

IF THE NEWS OF HENRI PAUL'S DRUNKEN STATE SEEMED TO diminish the responsibility of the photographers, the police continued to treat them as criminal suspects. Six photojournalists, plus an agency motorcycle driver, had been corralled in the tunnel at about 1:30 A.M. and hauled into the eighth arrondissement police station in the Boulevard de Courcelles for booking.* At Courcelles, they were placed into separate police cars and called into the station one by one. A desk officer announced to each man brought before him, "You are under arrest on suspicion of involuntary homicide and nonassistance to persons in danger." Each man was then asked to sign the arrest papers.

Nikola Arsov was stunned. He hadn't even pursued the Mercedes, and was the last to arrive in the tunnel, long after the ambulances were at the scene. "Involuntary homicide? Nonassistance?" he protested. "I won't sign that!" Others also grumbled, but in the end every man signed. There are no Miranda rights in France, and no access to a lawyer for the first 20 hours of detention. For the time being, the paparazzi were in the hands, and at the mercy, of the police. And French police can be tough.

"They took our shoes, glasses, watches, wallets, every-

*The arrested men were Serge Arnal, 35 (Stills); Nikola Arsov, 38 (Sipa), Stéphane Darman, 32 (Gamma); Jacques Langevin, 44 (Sygma); Christian Martinez, 41 (Angeli); Romuald Rat, 24 (Gamma); and Laszlo Veres, 50 (indépendent).

thing," says Langevin. "We were strip-searched, made to get down on all fours while they looked up our rear ends for hidden film. It was humiliating. We're not criminals. But to them, we were the guilty parties, designated in advance."

The photographers were taken across the river to the Hôpital du Val de Grâce, near the Luxembourg Gardens, for the obligatory blood test. Then the cortège of police vehicles headed north along the Boulevard Saint-Michel and over the bridge to the Ile de la Cité, the large island in the middle of the Seine. The Cité is best known to tourists as the site of Notre-Dame cathedral. Its other prominent landmark is the Palais de Justice, Paris' main court complex. On the south wing of the Palais, along the banks of the river, sits 36 Quai des Orfèvres, headquarters of the judiciary police.

"When I saw where we were headed, I said to myself, 'They're really pulling out all the stops,' " recounts Langevin. "We were put in isolated cells with no right to communicate with one another. They told us nothing. At 4:00 A.M. Sunday morning, they came to get us one after the other, took our mug shots, then posed us in a lineup behind a one-way mirror for witnesses to identify."

After the lineup, the prisoners were brought into the offices of the criminal brigade for interrogation. There were only a handful of inspectors on duty that night. They immediately dropped whatever cases they were working on to jump on what had already become a homicide investigation— although the photographers were not told of Diana's death until much later that day.

The first interrogations took place in a large, open room containing several desks. The businesslike detectives treated the photographers with respect, asking for their accounts of the events of August 30–31 and typing the responses on desktop computers. Then they printed them up and read them over with their interviewees, who were asked to sign them and attest to their accuracy.

Langevin's initial session took an hour and a half. It left him woozy. "By that time it was late morning," he says. "I had hardly slept. There was no coffee. The cell only had a wooden plank for a bed, with no covers. A neon light was on all the time. There was a glass door from floor to ceiling, so we were watched day and night. Poor Martinez was in a cell so small he couldn't even stretch out. The toilets were outside the cells, so we had to knock on the walls when we wanted to piss. I asked for water once and a cop said, 'Drink water from the toilet if you're thirsty.' For food, we were given little plastic bags containing two hardboiled eggs, plastic-like bread, a Vache-qui-Rit processed cheese, and an apple. One of my eggs was rotten.'' To a Frenchman, such a meal must qualify as cruel and inhuman punishment.

The photographers were allowed to see their attorneys after 20 hours of detention, but it was little more than a getting-to-know-you session, since the lawyers at that time had no access to the dossier and formal charges had not yet been lodged. After 24 hours, the prosecutor prolonged the detentions for another 24, the legal limit for holding suspects without charging them.

There were more interrogations, as investigators started to compare testimony, zero in on contradictions, clarify essential points. With the 20 confiscated rolls of film now developed, they could see which photographer was where and what kind of shots he was taking. The photos also showed the positions and actions of other photographers caught in the frames. Not least, they showed the exact position the wrecked car and victims were in before and after the rear door was opened.

With the photos in hand, detectives could sit down with each photographer, confront him with contradictions, pump him for explanations, ask the identity of this or that paparazzo who may have slipped the net. To one photographer, for example, they said, ''You claim you arrived some time after the crash, but your photos show the car still smoking and none of your colleagues is in the frame. Were you the first on the scene after the accident, as your photos indicate?'' Answer: ''Actually, I guess I *was* one of the first there.''

Sometimes, the photos were exculpatory: Romuald Rat,

admittedly the very first on the scene, the one who opened the rear door, and the one who many witnesses said was "groveling" inside the car to take pictures, turned out not to have taken a single photo of the car's interior. Nor did he take any closeups of the victims. Arsov's electronic flash didn't work and his film was blank, so he couldn't be blamed for taking any photos at all. Langevin's photos, taken from some distance away with a telephoto lens, all showed rescue workers in the frame, tending to back his claim that he had arrived some time after the accident.

Most significant of all, perhaps, there is not a single photo on any of the 20 confiscated rolls that was taken during the chase.* The pictures all jump from the scene outside the Ritz to the scene in the tunnel. This was a powerful piece of evidence that appeared to discredit all the eyewitness testimony about motorcycles surrounding the Mercedes, shooting off volleys of pictures like "machine guns," and blinding the driver with their flashes. It is not impossible that some photographer did that, but certainly not one of those arrested that night.

Reflecting the results of the first round of interrogations, both of photographers and eyewitnesses, Commissioner Martine Monteil, head of the criminal brigade, drafted a September 1 report to the prosecutor that was far more tentative about the role of the photographers than the one she had written at 2:00 A.M. on August 31. In her latest report, which took account of Henri Paul's first blood test results, she stated: "The exact circumstances of the origin of M. Paul's loss of control of the vehicle cannot be determined during the period of flagrancy [i.e., the 48-hour time limit for holding the suspects], in spite of numerous interrogations of wit-

---

*Bernard Dartevelle, attorney for the Fayed family, told reporters on September 9 that the investigative dossier contained a photo taken directly in front of the Mercedes, proving that Henri Paul had been "dazzled" by a photographer's flash. The photo, he said, showed Rees-Jones pulling down the front right visor and Diana turning her head away, with the reflection of the flash visible on the windshield. There is indeed such a photo in the dossier: it was taken by Langevin, standing in front of the car before it had ever left the Rue Cambon.

nesses and paparazzi. *None of the testimony heard thus far permits us to establish whether a vehicle could have approached the Mercedes to the point of touching it or making it leave its trajectory.*"* By this time, it was no longer an assumption that a photographer had bumped or interfered with the car.

None of which eased the immediate situation of the seven detainees. They expected to be released Monday night. Instead, guards came for them at midnight, strip-searched them again, then slapped on handcuffs and transferred them to a prison in the bowels of the adjoining Palais de Justice. They were being handed over from the control of the police to that of the justice system.

Their new digs were quite different from the little holding pens they had occupied at the Quai des Orfèvres. "This was an old, cavernous prison, with huge, vaulted stone ceilings, where every voice and footstep echoed like something from Kafka," recounts Langevin. "The cells were dank affairs with wooden floors, wash basins, and open Turkish-style w.c.'s."

Arsov recalls that the whole place "stank of piss—it was not exactly a hotel they'd put us in." Hardly! It is one of the oldest, most primitive prisons in Paris, its stone walls adjoining those of the famous Conciergerie, where Marie Antoinette had languished while awaiting the guillotine in 1793.

On Tuesday morning, the prisoners were fingerprinted and made to pose for new mug shots, then taken to see the judge. "We were marched through infernal tunnels like the sewers of Paris," says Langevin. "The tunnels were signposted with directions to the different courtrooms. They call this labyrinth the *Souricière* [literally, the mouse hole]."

The photographers were paraded one by one before Judge Hervé Stephan, the investigating magistrate who had just been assigned to oversee the case. With the initial police reports and depositions in hand, as well as a report from the prosecutor's office, Stephan decided to place all seven men

---

*Authors' italics.

under formal investigation (roughly the equivalent of charging them) for involuntary homicide and nonassistance to persons in danger.

Involuntary homicide, equivalent to manslaughter in the Anglo-Saxon legal system, is defined by article 221-6 of the French penal code as "causing by clumsiness, imprudence, lack of attention, negligence or by failure to observe legal safety requirements the death of another." Nonassistance, a violation of France's so-called Good Samaritan law (art. 223-6), is defined as deliberate failure to aid a person in danger, or a deliberate failure to summon assistance. Though both are criminal charges, they are considered misdemeanors, not felonies, under French law and are punishable by up to five years in prison and fines of up to $90,000. (In the event of convictions on both counts, the two sentences would run concurrently and the total fine could not exceed the maximum amount of $90,000.)

Based on the first reports from police and eyewitnesses, Gabriel Bestard, the chief Paris prosecution had recommended that Rat and Martinez be kept in prison. The two men had been singled out in several depositions as having been particularly aggressive, quarreling with or pushing police, blocking access to the victims, ravenously snapping pictures instead of trying to help. Though Rat and Martinez strongly contested those accounts, Bestard seemed determined to make an example of them. Stephan rejected the move to keep them behind bars, but demanded $18,000 bail of Rat and Martinez, confiscated their press cards and driver's licenses, and forbade them to leave the country. The others were released on their own recognizance, but also forbidden to leave the country or have any contact with one another. On Friday, September 5, Chassery, Oderkerken, and Benhamou, who had left the tunnel before the others were arrested, turned themselves in and were placed under investigation on the same charges. Police continued to search for others who might have fled the scene.*

---

*On September 18, two unidentified photographers presented themselves voluntarily

* * *

The 10 photographers placed under investigation adamantly denied that they were close enough to the Mercedes to interfere with its trajectory, a claim that investigators eventually came to accept. Nor, they said, could they be blamed for nonassistance. One of them, Arnal, did try to call an emergency number; the rest all claimed that "others" had done so, thus they didn't bother making redundant calls. None but Rat had any first-aid training, and Rat maintains he tried to help by taking Diana's pulse; the others say they refrained from touching victims, which could do more harm than good.

As for the claim that they had interfered with police and rescue workers, it appears that Rat and Martinez did grouse when police tried to push them back. But both men deny reports that they shoved an officer and insisted that they did not get in the way of medical workers. Dr. Mailliez, the first physician on the scene, confirms that the photographers "in no way" hampered his work, even though he considered their incessant picture-taking "inappropriate."

That, in fact, is the main reproach against the paparazzi. The first witnesses on the scene, understandably horrified by the sight of the smashed car and bloody victims, were shocked by the fact that these men dared take pictures of the spectacle. But that's what photographers do. They shoot accidents, bombings, famines, and battlefields all the time. That may be shocking and repugnant to many people, particularly when the victim is a celebrity like Princess Diana, but there is nothing illegal about it. "Public opinion took this totally the wrong way around," says Laszlo Veres. "It's not a photographer who pushed that car up to one hundred mph. It was not a photographer at the wheel. Sure we took pictures afterwards, but I don't know why photographers shouldn't

to police to give testimony about the events of August 30–31. They had not pursued the Mercedes, but had gone directly from the Ritz to Dodi's apartment, where they had learned of the accident on their cell phones and subsequently went to the scene. They were heard as witnesses, but were not charged or designated as suspects in the case.

take pictures of an accident scene. That's our job."

But the photographer's job has changed in recent years. The end of the Cold War and its persistent global frictions has caused editors in the U.S. and Europe to scale back dramatically on what was once almost blanket coverage of hot spots. The growing cult of celebrities, meanwhile, has tended to push many photographers into so-called people journalism, focusing on personalities, glitz, and glitter, in order to make a living. The fact that the famous Dodi-Diana kiss photo by Italian paparazzo Mario Brenna reportedly fetched well over $2 million shows how skewed today's market is towards celebrity journalism.

"They push us to do this kind of show-biz photography and treat the news via people," says Langevin, himself basically a hard-news man who has reported on wars and revolutions around the globe. "Covering the news, as I practiced it, meant photographing the event without adornment, without special effects or mise en scene. But the market for that kind of photojournalism is shrinking like a dried-up raisin. People won't buy a magazine today with war photos on the cover. They want sequins and dreams. It's been like that for ten or twelve years now."

Sipa's Tom Haley, 47, a Paris-based American photographer who had no involvement in the Diana episode, agrees. "I've been told several times to quit the news business, because it just doesn't pay," he says. "In the past few years 'people' journalism has gained steam, and magazines pay incredible money for it. I sometimes get burned by the injustice of it—look at the money paid for this crap compared to what we [hard news photographers] do. We work far from our families, often at the risk of our lives, and still have a tough time breaking even. I just don't understand the money paid for this stuff. If anything good comes of this, it may be that the scale of values will be reset."

Roger Thérond, editor of France's best-known celebrity magazine, *Paris-Match* (weekly circulation 800,000), also wondered if it wasn't necessary to reexamine the priorities of photojournalism in the wake of the accident. "We are all responsible," he said. "The machine is getting out of control. Time has come for the public, photographers, and editors to think about all this."

The editor of a rival celebrity magazine, *Gala* (circulation 320,000), doubts that the business will change much. "The only effect of this tragedy is that Diana won't be there to kick around anymore," says Jean Lesieur.* "It won't change anything because the market is too big. There are more and more paparazzi out there. They're young and hungry, and they're having fun. When you're a real news photographer and you see that hard news is not interesting to publications today, you tend to move into the paparazzi field. It requires no talent other than to be ruthless and cunning. That said, there's no way these guys should have been indicted. It's scandalous to charge them just for doing their job. You can say they're animals, that they have no decency, but what's the difference between shooting a picture of Princess Diana dying and shooting some guy being necklaced in Soweto? What about the Zapruder pictures of Kennedy being shot and the top of his head flying off? It's horrible, but now everybody thinks it's an important document for history. Where do you draw the line?"

Photo-industry watchers say the main factor that sparked the boom for paparazzi photos in France was the success of the weekly *Voici*. Launched in 1987 as a more or less conventional women's magazine, it found its business sluggish until the editors switched into no-holds-barred celebrity journalism. Suddenly circulation skyrocketed, reaching some 750,000 copies weekly by 1996, just behind the long-established *Paris-Match*.

Those sales figures reflected a growing appetite for celebrity news on the part of French readers, who increasingly resemble consumers of popular "Anglo-Saxon"-style publications typified by Britain's Fleet Street tabloids or

---

*A former editor of the weekly newsmagazine *L'Express*, Lesieur stresses that, of the three main French celebrity magazines, *Gala* (launched in 1993) is the least inclined to use paparazzi photos and refuses to enter bidding wars with the other two.

America's *National Enquirer.* According to a poll cited in the weekly *L'Express,* one French person out of two admits to reading, at least occasionally, newspapers and magazines that focus on the lives of celebrities. France is thus becoming an increasingly lucrative market for paparazzi photos even though the country boasts one of the world's strictest privacy legislations. A 1970 law (article 9 of the civil code) states that "Everyone has the right to respect for his private life." Among other things, the law specifies that each individual has a "right to his own image," meaning it is illegal to publish a photo of any person without his or her express consent, even if the picture was taken in a public place. In general, the law is applied loosely, but some celebrities (e.g., Catherine Deneuve and Princess Caroline) regularly sue under article 9 and regularly collect damages from offending publications. Had Diana survived the accident, industry professionals point out, publications like *Voici, Paris-Match,* and scores of tabloids around the globe would probably have been bidding millions for the very same photos that are now locked up in the police files and considered by public opinion as the moral equivalent of child pornography.

Nor are the celebrity glossies and tabloids the only ones to have encouraged the sort of photographic feeding frenzy that took place on that fateful weekend in Paris. As *New York Times* columnist A. M. Rosenthal noted on September 3, in one of the more intelligent comments on the affair, "The paparazzi, as they liked to be called, pursued the couple as a jackal his prey. They knew that a 'good picture' like a kiss or a hug seen through a car window would bring scores of thousands of dollars and that any picture would bring a price handsome enough for their gas and waiting time until the next gathering of the jackals, the next day."

The reason, said Rosenthal, is that "the pictures would be bought by certain newspapers, magazines, and TV networks to attract readers and advertisers: spending money to make money." Though most fingers were pointed at the tabloids, Rosenthal noted, it was wrong "for real journalists not to acknowledge that enough more 'mainstream' newspapers and glossy-paper magazines print that kind of picture, and are publishing more unverified and sadistic gossip of their own creation.''*

Le Monde made much the same point in a September 3 editorial entitled "Hypocrites' Ball." Noting that movie stars, politicians and the international media were demanding the heads of the photographers, the respected French daily commented: "Even part of the press does not hesitate to designate a convenient scapegoat within their own ranks. This is the same press that, under other circumstances, does not refrain from using, with no scruples at all, these same photographers . . . [These photographers] can certainly commit excesses. But the last ones who should be giving them lessons are the media who liberally use their work and the celebrities of all sorts who, at their own convenience, place themselves in front of the camera."

But it was conservative author Jean-François Revel (*Without Marx or Jesus*), one of France's preeminent political philosophers and a member of the prestigious Académie Française, who brought the argument full circle and put the ultimate responsibility at the feet of the individual news consumer. "What are the photographers guilty of?" he wrote in the French newsweekly *Le Point* on September 6. "Of the degeneracy of our information-as-image civilization? Aren't they the symptoms of that civilization and not the cause?" Revel denounced the growing tendency by the press to treat the news as "anecdote" rather than "information." "It is argued that the public prefers subjects close to their own concerns, which are in general a collection of mindless stupidities," he wrote with his characteristic verve. "Given the atrophy of public curiosity about the issues that count, how can we be surprised if people immerse themselves in inept gossip? The scandal is not that [journalists] track down the

---

*Indeed, even such serious newsmagazines as *Time* and *Newsweek*, in their cover stories on Diana's death, published photos by some of the same paparazzi who had been stalking the couple that day. (The photographers were not among those arrested, and the photos did not show the actual accident scene.)

news, it's the insignificance of the news that they track . . .
The source of this ignominy is to be found in the human
heart, not in the objects with which it satisfies its longings.
The ultimate responsibility for an addiction lies neither with
the drug, nor with the little dealer, nor with the cartel: it lies
with the addict.''

Of the 10 photographers targeted by the investigation, only
a few were true paparazzi—the guys with superlong lenses
who lurk behind bushes, buzz their subjects in crop dusters
and helicopters, or disguise themselves as plumbers or mail-
men to gain access.* Hard core paparazzi—or stalkerazzi, as
they are sometimes known in the trade—don't hang around
outside the Ritz waiting for Diana or Madonna to pass by.
They plan their expeditions well in advance, often investing
considerable amounts of money and time and equipment in
the project. It's the guys who are willing to spend whole
days and nights huddled behind palm trees with huge telephoto lenses who produce such famous shots as Mario
Brenna's kiss photo or Fergie's toe-sucking escapade, which
reportedly fetched more than $2 million.

The lure of such extraordinary profits is only part of what
drives legendary French paparazzi like Daniel Angeli, Pascal
Rostain, and Bruno Mouron, all of whom have been in the
business for 30 years. They are big game hunters who live
for the chase. ''Paparazzi are like Mafia killers, no one es-
capes them,'' wrote Rostain and Mouron in their 1988 shoot-
and-tell book, *Paparazzi,* which recounts such adventures as
stalking Princess Stéphanie of Monaco all the way to Maur-
itius to photograph her frolicking bare-breasted in the surf.
Angeli, for his part, still relishes the story of how he hid for
hours behind a rock before he finally snapped Italian indus-
trialist Giovanni Agnelli diving nude into the sea off his

---

*Dodi and Diana had apparently been targeted by true stalkerazzi during their stay
at St. Tropez in July. On September 9, Fayed family lawyer Bernard Dartevelle filed
suits against *Paris-Match* and *France-Dimanche* as well as two photo agencies for
invasion of privacy and reckless endangerment in connection with the buzzing of the
Fayed villa by helicopter-borne photographers.

yacht. For seasoned veterans like these, it's not worthwhile to snap Diana coming out of the Ritz; but their agencies will dispatch hungry, younger photographers to the scene just in case.

The band of photographers following Diana and Dodi around on August 30 included a majority of so-called "people" journalists—those who seek out celebrities and movie stars, but not necessarily via stakeouts, ambushes, and subterfuges. In many cases, in fact, they operate with the tacit cooperation of their subjects. Some French celebrities have even been known to stage pseudopaparazzi shots of themselves.

Jacques Langevin, 44, soft-spoken and studious-looking with round metal-framed glasses and slightly receding brown hair, is a dyed-in-the-wool hard news man. He was sent to the Ritz by the luck of the draw on August 30 because he was Sygma's duty man that weekend. But he defends the right of photographers to do the glittery stuff if that is their choice. "It's two different aspects of the same profession," he says. "There is a way of presenting information that is more or less serious or light, but the two are related. It's not shameful to do photos of people. It's not my choice, but I do consider myself a versatile photographer." His prize-winning work from such far-flung places as Rwanda, Lebanon, China, the Gulf War, and the Atlanta Olympics attests to Langevin's versatility—and courage: he was wounded by a bullet in the leg while covering the Romanian revolution in 1989.

Romuald Rat, 24 suffers from having "a name that is easy to remember in English and French," says a lawyer involved in the case. Along with Martinez, Rat is the one that witnesses single out as having been particularly obnoxious in the wake of the accident. Witnesses, including several other photographers, also point to Rat as the one who was involved in the scuffle with bodyguards outside Dodi's apartment in the afternoon. More than anything else public opinion was horrified at the idea that he had the effrontery to open the rear door and touch the dying Princess. For the rest of his life, perhaps, Romuald Rat will be remembered as the guy who leaned into the wrecked Mercedes and put his hand on Diana's neck to take her pulse.

The very thought of Rat touching Diana and speaking to her, says a source close to the couple, "makes your flesh creep." According to this source, Rat's behavior had "physically frightened" the Princess earlier in the day. "To think that this is the guy she is worried about, and that he allegedly said to her in English, 'Stay calm, help is on the way.' He would not have talked to somebody who was comatose; it has to be clear to you that she was conscious."

For Rat, that was a spontaneous, human gesture, an attempt to bring what help and comfort he could to her. As he explained the moment in an interview with France 2 television, "I ran to the car, I saw that it was a Mercedes, and I said to myself that it must be them. After several seconds, I got ahold of myself and tried to aid them, simply to see if they were still alive . . . I didn't call the emergency unit myself, because I heard someone say 'I called the fire brigade.' So I didn't bother to do that myself, and I opened one of the car doors." At that point, as Rat later told the BBC, "I tried to take her pulse, and when I touched her, she moved and breathed. So I spoke to her in English, saying 'I'm here, be cool, a doctor will arrive.' " It was only after the first emergency medical workers arrived, he said, that he began taking pictures. As for the claim that he or other photographers blocked emergency personnel from reaching the car, Rat said on ABC's "20/20" that the claim was "ridiculous and unthinkable."*

Rat, a powerfully built young man standing nearly six feet tall, seemed particularly menacing and intimidating to witnesses and police that night. By all accounts, he did appear hot-tempered and overexcited. Interestingly, people who

---

*As of this writing, Rat has given no print interviews. Despite repeated attempts to obtain an interview, through his lawyer Jean-Marc Coblence, through intermediaries, and in a direct telephone contact with the photographer himself, the authors were unfortunately not able to conduct a formal interview with Rat.

know and work with him say he is usually calm and soft-spoken. An editor at Pascal Rostain's Sphinx agency where Rat worked before joining Gamma describes him as "a very gentle guy, agreeable, very sensitive. He deserves to be defended. He's a 'people' photographer, but one who captures very beautiful images, like his photos of Jacques Chirac at La Réunion in early August. He does not correspond to the image of an aggressive and mean paparazzi."

"Romuald is a nice guy, there's never a problem with him," says a limousine chauffeur who often drives stars around France. "Whenever he does a star, he will give me copies of the photos." Tailing somebody on a motorcycle and snapping pictures through the car window is not Rat's style, says this source. "He'll come up to me and ask where we're headed next. I don't mind giving tip-offs to guys like him who don't bother us and don't cause us any stress. They never shoot photos when they're moving. They just ask where we're going next, then they leave first so they can position themselves. They have their networks of informants among cops, concierges, bodyguards, and chauffeurs. If I had the least problem with guys like Rat, I wouldn't work with them." Rat is still stunned by what has happened to him, says the chauffeur. "He tells his friends that he just tried to see what he could do to help Diana, and that's why he's having all these problems now."

The Angeli agency's Christian Martinez, 41, a true paparazzo, is described by one admiring colleague as having the "stealth of a sniper." Short, stocky, and broad-shouldered, with close-cropped brown hair, beady eyes, and muscles pumped up by years of weightlifting, Martinez is a 15-year veteran of the business who is known for his hell-bent-for-leather style. "If you do ambush photography," Langevin says of Martinez, "you can't be tender-hearted. You have to be determined. That can lead to excesses." But also to some successful coups, like the photo he snapped of Cindy Crawford and Richard Gere on a carnival ride in the Tuileries Garden.

Though admired for his tenacity, Martinez manages to rub

a lot of colleagues the wrong way. A newspaper editor who formerly worked with him says, "Martinez is a good professional—but sometimes he tries too hard and goes too far." A French reporter who has worked with him on numerous assignments calls him "a truculent, mean-spirited guy always ready to punch it out."

Martinez is proud of his tough-guy image. In his first interrogation, at 10:30 A.M. on August 31, after a sleepless night in a prison cell so small he could not even stretch out, he described himself to investigators as a "nervous guy ready to jump into action at the drop of a hat." Martinez admitted that he had exchanged sharp words with Rat in the Alma tunnel because Rat had tried to prevent him and others from taking close-up pictures of the victims. He also admitted to having told a police officer, "You piss me off! At least in Sarajevo they let us work!" (The remark seems more like a rhetorical flourish than anything else: Martinez had never gone anywhere near Sarajevo.)

But this cocky little paparazzo is not without his human side. He became increasingly emotional under interrogation as the inspector zeroed in relentlessly on the issue of non-assistance.

"Q: Did you do anything to help the wounded?"

"A: I have a vague memory of people who were taking care of the wounded. Besides, I have no notions of first aid. I remember that I started taking pictures inside the car [only] when people [I took for medical workers] started taking care of the individuals in the car . . . *I was completely disarmed in the face of this thing. I think that it would have been the same with any other victim. The fact of being behind a camera is an aid, a sort of screen, it permits you to keep your distance.*"

"Q: Did you help the people who were trying to treat the wounded?"

"A: No, and no other photographer either. How could we have done that? Perhaps [we felt] a certain sense of respect. It would take a lot of boldness to try to treat people we had been following just a few minutes earlier, and also a lot of respect. *I was paralyzed by the rapport between me and the people in that car.*"*

At this point, the transcript notes, Martinez burst into tears.

Serge Benhamou, 44, who works with the well-known celebrity photographer Laszlo Veres, is less a paparazzo than a groupie. "Benhamou is not a bad guy," says Langevin. "He's in admiration before his subjects. He likes movies, glitter, stars. He really admires these people." He is known as a tenacious pursuer, despite the limited horsepower of his 80cc Honda Lada scooter. A veteran celebrity chauffeur recounts that Benhamou "always rides on a scooter and when the cars are going a bit fast, especially outside the city center, on the ring road or the expressway, he has trouble keeping up with the convoy. However, inside Paris, he is always right behind you and very well informed about [people's] movements. That makes me think he has well-placed informants."

Benhamou, a roly-poly, round-faced man known as Ben to his colleagues, had followed the Mercedes from the back of the Ritz on August 31 and was among the first to arrive in the Alma tunnel. As he later told police, he was profoundly disturbed by the sight of the accident and left the scene before the others were arrested. The cynical interpretation of his act is that he had snapped some spectacular photos and wanted to get away while the getting was good. But there is a certain ring of truth to his declarations, after he had turned himself in to police on September 5, that he left early because he "couldn't stand it" anymore. He told police he did not want to see the pictures he had taken "because I took photos and now I know that people are dead. It's a horrible memory." Before leaving the tunnel, Benhamou had called his partner Laszlo Veres, then riding on

---

*Authors' italics. Martinez, like Rat, declined repeated interview requests. On October 16, in a sign that the case against the paparazzi might be softening, Judge Stephan restored Martinez's press card and driver's license and authorized him to go back to work. Stephan had done the same for Rat 10 days earlier.

his motor scooter along the Champs-Elysées, and asked him to come replace him.*

Veres, 50, had been working the Ritz in tandem with Benhamou that night: Veres in front, Benhamou in back. But Veres got left behind. "Someone told us [Diana and Dodi] had left from the back," he said in an interview, "so I headed home. While en route [Benhamou] called me on my portable phone and said, 'Diana's just had an accident.' I thought it was a banal fender bender, but I went to see. I was amazed when I saw the car. I took a few photos of the overall scene from about thirty meters away." Though one of the last to arrive, on his black Piaggio motor scooter, he was soon scooped up in the police dragnet along with the six others.

Veres, a native Hungarian, runs his own independent agency specializing in celebrity and fashion photography. A big bear of a man with a salt-and-pepper beard, he is noted for his "imaginative" methods of snapping subjects like Stéphanie and Caroline of Monaco—usually without their permission. Hot pursuit, however, is not his thing: Veres limps badly from a foot deformity that, legend has it, was aggravated some years ago when Alain Delon's car collided with him during an abortive chase. "He's wily, gruff, and secretive, but basically a good egg," says an American celebrity journalist who has worked with him. Veres is best known, perhaps, for his photos of the late Christina Onassis, a personal friend, who used to ride around on the back of his motor scooter.

Serge Arnal, 35, is another celebrity specialist who hung

---

*On September 4, an anonymous French photographer who said he had left before the arrests, was interviewed on Germany's Pro-7 television network. From the description of him, it seems probable that the photographer was Benhamou. "My job is to take pictures," he said. "But it was so tragic. Then . . . my friend and I said stop! and then we drove away . . . We saw this tragedy with our own eyes. It was like a film. When we saw the wreckage, I said this can't be true . . . [But] we are not guilty because that is part of the game of life. The paparazzo is someone who offers pictures to the world for millions of people who wouldn't have any access. There are millions of people who buy these newspapers to have a small glimpse into the lives of these people. That is our profession."

around the Ritz that night in hopes of capturing a princess on film. "Our photographer was only a 'people' photographer who usually does festivals and parties," says Arnal's boss Bruno Kalin, head of the Stills agency. "He was only doing his job, to wait for a star in front of a hotel. The driver went too fast. They were there to take pictures of a fairy tale, not a horror movie."

Pursuing Di and Dodi in his black Fiat Uno, with Martinez at his side, Arnal claims to have lost sight of the Mercedes after it "brutally accelerated in a straight line" from the Place de la Concorde towards the Alma tunnel. He continued along the express road and, several minutes later, came upon the wreck. Driving slowly past the twisted, smoking hulk, he parked 30 meters down the road. Martinez jumped out and hurried towards the wreck. Arnal, who told investigators he was "afraid of blood," hung back. He dialed the 112 emergency number on his portable phone (the only photographer to make this effort), but said the signal was not clear. "I was panicking," he said. "I remember shouting at the operator that there had been an accident, but I couldn't describe the location very precisely."

Fabrice Chassery, 30, and David Oderkerken, 26, work for an authentic paparazzi agency, LS Presse. Chassery, in particular, is known for his relentless pursuit of his subjects in his Peugeot 205. "When he is there with his car," says a professional chauffeur who frequently deals with celebrity clients, "we have a hard time shaking him off; he is constantly behind us and has a kind of wild way of driving." Chassery and Oderkerken, who arrived in the tunnel in separate vehicles shortly after Rat, Martinez, and Arnal, took several rolls of film and left just at the moment when police started pushing photographers back from the wrecked car. They drove directly to the office of Laurent Sola, the head of the agency, and dropped their film off for processing.

Sola had the pictures developed immediately. He selected five photos of Diana being treated by medics, scanned them into his computer, and transmitted them to his agent in London. Word quickly got around that LS Presse had the Diana accident pictures, and calls began to flood into Sola's office from around the world. A well-known American supermarket tabloid, he said, offered to buy them for $250,000 sight unseen.* Other orders from Britain, Spain, Italy, and Germany totaled more than a million pounds sterling.

Then at 5:44 A.M. Agence France-Presse, the French national wire service, ran its first dispatch on Diana's death. Oderkerken and Chassery immediately phoned Sola and asked him not to sell the pictures. The head of another French photo agency also advised against distributing the shots. Sola finally agreed to cancel the sales, giving up millions in profits. He destroyed all his computer copies of the images and eventually turned the negatives over to police. Starting on Sunday afternoon, detectives began making the rounds of other French photo agencies to inform their directors that the possession or publication of accident photos could be punished by up to three years in prison and fines of up to 300,000 francs ($55,000) for hindering the investigation. The agency directors were also warned against attempting to destroy evidence.

Meanwhile, it appears, British authorities attempted to track down copies of the accident photos that had made their way to England. At about 3:00 A.M. on Monday, September 1, unknown intruders slipped into the northwest London apartment of Sipa photographer Lionel Cherruault, 37. While Cherruault and his wife Christine slept, these surreptitious visitors went to work in the next room, taking credit cards, cash, and keys from Mrs. Cherruault's purse. Then they went downstairs to Cherruault's office and carefully removed two external hard-disk drives and a laptop computer, leaving the photographer's negatives, papers, and other electronic gadgets untouched. "They were obviously looking for computer images," says Cherruault. "They didn't care about the rest." The burglars loaded their stash into Christine's blue Mitsubishi Spacewagon and drove off into the night.

---

*Editors of the *National Enquirer* admit that Sola had offered them the photos for $250,000, but claim they turned him down.

Cherruault discovered the intrusion at about 3:30 and immediately called the police. Two officers showed up within a half hour to take down the details and check for fingerprints. There were none. Next day, a police detective appeared at the apartment. "I must tell you something," he said, clutching a sheaf of papers in his hand. "I've just read this report. I have to confirm to you that you were not burgled."

"You mean they were the gray men?" said Cherruault, using a euphemism for intelligence agents.

"Call them what you like," replied the detective. "You were not burgled."

The car was found 24 hours later near a housing project in north London. The vehicle had been wiped clean of fingerprints. It is not clear who was behind the operation, but the professionalism with which it was carried out and the nature of the target all point to MI-5, the domestic arm of British intelligence. Cherruault reckons that his status as a London-based French photographer led the "gray men" to assume he was a conduit for Diana accident photos. "If they'd just knocked on the door and said who they were, they'd have been most welcome to search the place," he says. "There was no need to cause such distress, frighten my wife and children, and make us all paranoid."

Despite such extraordinary efforts to scotch the traffic in Diana accident photos, some did leak out and a few publications had the audacity to reproduce them. On September 1, the German tabloid *Bild-Zeitung* ran an accident photo on its front page showing faint images of the occupants and rescue workers seen from the rear of the car. The Italian newsweekly *Panaroma* put a crash picture on the cover and ran another one inside in its September 5 edition. The magazine's editor, Giuliano Ferrara, a close advisor to ex–Italian Prime Minister Silvio Berlusconi and a former minister in Berlusconi's government, explained his decision as a protest against the "hypocrisy" surrounding Diana's death. "Yesterday, readers wanted photos of Diana's kiss . . . today they shed crocodile tears." Yet another purported photo of Diana at the crash scene was later posted on the Internet, and immediately reproduced on the front page of the lowbrow French daily *France Soir* on September 19. That image, at least, turned out to be a fake.

Nikola Arsov will never be blamed for selling his Diana photos to a tabloid: he forgot to turn on his electronic flash in the heat of the action and not a single one of his pictures came out. Arsov, 38, a native of Macedonia who immigrated to France 20 years ago, is a former dental assistant who worked as a Sipa motorcycle driver for seven years before taking up the camera himself a year ago. During his brief career as a photographer, he has covered a variety of assignments, ranging from the Cannes Film Festival and Pope John Paul II's visit to France last June, to British prime minister Tony Blair's vacation in France in August.

Looking younger than his years, with a boyish face, unkempt brown hair, and an ingenuous manner, Arsov still bristles at finding himself the target of a criminal investigation. "I don't see why we're treated as criminals," he says. "Any photographer would have done the same thing. TV cameramen would have done it if they'd been there. I'm no paparazzo. I just photographed Tony Blair. What the hell is this all about? Everything is all mixed up!"

Goksin Sipahioglu, 70, founder and head of the Sipa agency, recalls Arsov's release from detention on the afternoon of September 2. "I went to pick him up at the courthouse with his girlfriend," he says, leaning back in his chair in a modernistic office with black furniture. "He broke down and cried. He cried for everything, the strain, the fatigue, the tragedy he had witnessed. Lady Di is someone we all loved. He was shocked."

But Sipahioglu, a former Turkish journalist with a leonine mane of white hair, rejects the notion that photographers and photo agencies are to blame for her death. "I feel no responsibility, legally or morally," he says. "I am saddened, because someone we adored is dead. But when you become Lady Di, you become a public person. She was posing all the time in St. Tropez, in Bosnia. We can't be hypocrites about this.''

But wasn't there something unseemly, even ghoulish, about taking pictures of dead and dying people in the Alma tunnel? Even if the photographers didn't cause the accident, couldn't they have reacted with more dignity and restraint? Sipahioglu slowly shakes his head. ''When Eddie Adams took that famous photo of the guy being shot in the head in Vietnam, did anyone say to him, 'Why didn't you prevent the execution?' No, he won prizes for that picture. You can't prevent a photographer who sees an accident from taking a photo.''

The irony, says Sipa's boss, is that here was the most photographed person in the world risking her life in an insane high-speed dash to avoid having another 20 pictures taken of her. ''The fact is,'' he says, ''that a photo of two people in a moving car in the middle of the night would have had no value at all. Worthless! That's why not one of those photographers took a picture during the chase. They just wanted to find out where they were spending the night.''

Not that Sipahioglu defends the paparazzi industry. He himself started out as a hard news reporter for the Turkish press, covering such events as the Cuban missile crisis and the Soviet invasion of Czechoslovakia in 1968. ''We're the second biggest photo agency in the world,'' he says, ''but paparazzi stuff only accounts for about one percent of our business. After this tragedy, I would like to think the papers will stop pushing the demand for such things. But I am afraid they are just going to buy more and more.'' He adds: ''The only thing that might slow them down is that there are no more personalities like Lady Di.''

12

The Investigators

CALL THEM THE ODD COUPLE. HE IS TALL, SHY, COURTEOUS, and soft-spoken. She is short, blond, brash, and opinionated. He does little socializing and has no hobbies. She takes exotic vacations, rides Arabian horses, collects fine wines, and holds cocktail parties for 100 people at a time. Together, Judge Hervé Stephan, 43, and Judge Marie-Christine Devidal, 44, are heading the investigation into the death of Princess Diana. It is they who oversee all the interrogations, the collection of evidence, the lab work, the expert analyses. It is they who will hand over the completed dossier, now numbering more than 4,000 pages, to the prosecutor. And it is they who will decide, probably in the autumn of 1998, whether or not formally to charge the 10 suspects and send them to trial. Considering the enormous pressures on them—from the French and British governments, the royal family, the civil plaintiffs, and from the raging public passions that the case has engendered—theirs is indeed a weighty task.

Stephan and Devidal are among France's 550 juges d'instruction, or investigating magistrates. It is a job that has no exact equivalent in Anglo-Saxon jurisprudence. Napoleon called the juge d'instruction "the most powerful man in France." Combining the roles of detective, district attorney, judge, and grand jury, these magistrates can order, on their own authority, wiretaps, searches, interrogations, arrests, and preventive detentions. It is they who lead investigations, with the assistance of judiciary police officers, intelligence services, and other specialized agencies, and it is they who decide whether or not there is sufficient evidence to bring suspects to trial.

Considering their extensive powers, France's investigating magistrates command nothing like the respect and social status accorded to judges in the U.S. or Britain. They are mostly in their twenties and thirties, earn between $30,000 and $60,000 a year, and rank fairly low in the hierarchy of the French justice system. Detractors deride them as *les petits juges*, but this hasn't stopped some of them from going after the high and mighty: in recent years French magistrates have investigated, indicted, and in some cases convicted government ministers, party leaders, and prominent businessmen on corruption, malfeasance, and other charges.

A handful of judges have become media stars for their handling of high-profile cases. The most famous of them, pistol-packing Jean-Louis Bruguière (alias "Le Cowboy"), the man who tracked down the international terrorist Carlos, has fingered agents of Libyan leader Muhammar Gadafy in an airplane bombing and implicated senior Iranian government officials in a series of dissident assassinations in France.

Though he is far less visible, Stephan has nonetheless taken on some high-level targets. In September 1997 he did not hesitate to place Justice Minister Elisabeth Guigou under investigation after Paris mayor Jean Tiberi and his wife Xavière filed libel charges against her. It was a courageous act, and typical of a magistrate who is widely respected for his independence and rigor.

Stephan works in room 58 on the third floor of the Palais de Justice, with just one tall window overlooking the tree-lined Boulevard du Palais. (Devidal is just down the hall in room 65.) Stephan's office is small, cramped, and badly lit with overhead neon installations. His desk is piled high with dossiers, and the walls are covered with a dirty yellowish fabric. The drabness is only slightly relieved by a few nondescript pictures. The most distinctive object in the room is a wall-mounted rectangular metal frame with slots holding color-coded cards. The cards identify the suspects in the more than 100 cases that Stephan, like all overworked Parisian magistrates, must handle simultaneously. Red cards are for criminal cases, green for correctional cases, and so on.

Judges like Stephan and Devidal are the lynchpins of France's "inquisitorial" legal system, which is directed by the bench in search of the truth as opposed to the Anglo-Saxon "adversarial" system, in which opposing sides wage a battle of persuasion, with the judge serving as a neutral referee and final arbiter. In this case—officially designated "Fatal Road Accident, 31 August 1997, 00:30"—it is the two investigating magistrates who will largely decide the fate of the suspects. And they are doing so behind a veil of official judicial secrecy that makes it extremely difficult for journalists to follow the course of the investigation. The judges have kept rigorously off-limits to the press.

Stephan is unanimously described by colleagues and lawyers who work with him as serious, discreet, impartial, and professional. Unlike many judges, he had considerable experience as a prosecutor, notably in Versailles from 1991 to 1994, before being named a senior investigating magistrate of the Tribunal de Grande Instance (Correctional Court) in Paris. As a result, he understands the prosecutors' point of view and gets along with them more easily than most judges, with whom they often have a competitive relationship. One prosecutor who has worked with Stephan often in the past (but not on this case) describes him as "calm, courteous, and affable."

Standing five feet eleven inches with an aquiline nose, blue eyes, and longish brown hair, Hervé Stephan has a wife, four children, and, in the words of a friend, "no particular interests apart from his work. He is the prototype of the average Frenchman."

Probably his best-known case is that of Florence Rey, 21, a self-styled anarchist who, with her lover Audry Maupin, then 23, went on a murderous rampage in October 1994 that left three policemen, a taxi driver, and Maupin himself dead. Under intense pressure from police to avenge their fallen comrades by arresting several of the couple's friends for complicity in the murders, Stephan found no evidence of their involvement and steadfastly refused to go on a witch hunt. Faced with the silence of Florence Rey, who did not utter a word during the first interrogations, Stephan won her confidence, cooperation, and finally her expression of remorse. "He investigates in a very humane way," says a judicial colleague who is also a personal friend. "Hervé cares about the dignity of those before him. He creates a climate in which those under investigation speak more easily because he is someone who respects them."

Marie-Christine Devidal is generally described by colleagues as prickly, headstrong, and temperamental. Even friends, who laud her keen intelligence and dogged determination to get to the bottom of her cases, admit that she can be "overly aggressive" at times. "Stephan is quite tall and visible, but he's so shy he tends to hide behind people when he is walking," says a lawyer who knows both judges well. "Marie-Christine is just the opposite. Anyone who buys an Arabian stallion and trains it herself is not timid!"

Devidal has a reputation as a "hanging judge." "She is very provictim and antiperpetrator," says a friend. "She's not what you'd call a 'social' judge." Devidal and her husband, Tunisian businessman Moncef Haddad, were spending the weekend with friends in Normandy at the time of Diana's death. On hearing the first breathless TV reports about the paparazzi's role, Devidal reportedly reacted with characteristic outspokenness. "If that's what those jerks did," she snapped, "I'd lock them all up!"

Devidal thought she would get the chance to do just that when she arrived at the Paris courthouse at 4:00 P.M. on Sunday. As the judge officially on duty that weekend, she would normally have been assigned the case. But the death of Diana, Princess of Wales, was anything but normal. The British government and the royal family were demanding to know exactly what happened; a shocked and enraged public was demanding the heads of the photographers; already hovering around the tragedy were sensational assassination plot theories emanating from the Middle East and rapidly spilling into Web sites on the Internet. In a sense, the integrity of the French justice system—and behind it, the whole French government—was on trial.

If ever an investigation called for a cool-headed, experienced, and noncontroversial judge, the Diana affair was it. So when the assignment was made on September 2 by the court's first vice-president, the job went to Hervé Stephan. "They chose Stephan because he's calm, unflappable, and has his feet on the ground," says a source in the prosecutor's office. "Devidal is less so. She has a difficult, irascible personality."

According to sources in the Palais de Justice, Devidal was allegedly unhappy over Stephan's appointment since she believed that it was her turn and that she had been unfairly passed over. Stephan, who was assailed in the early days of the probe with 50 phone calls a day, decided to solve two problems—an overwhelming workload and a disappointed colleague—by requesting that Devidal, a longtime personal friend, be brought in to assist him on the case. She was officially named on September 5. It was a redoubtable team.

Heading the police side of the investigation, under the direction of the two judges, is Martine Monteil, 47, the commissioner in charge of the elite criminal brigade of the Paris judiciary police. Blond, attractive, elegantly dressed in designer suits, silk scarves, and gold earrings, this daughter and granddaughter of Paris cops is a tough-as-nails professional. Colleagues call her "a fist of iron in a glove of steel," a no-nonsense image that is reinforced by the most conspicuous object in her office on the Quai des Orfèvres: a 7.63 mm Mauser that serves as a lamp base. Despite her anomalous position as a woman in an ultramacho business, Monteil climbed to the top echelons of the Paris police through a combination of intelligence, hard work, and the kind of intuition that has allowed her to crack numerous cases that stumped her male colleagues. After taking her law degree and finishing at the top of her class at the national police academy in 1976, she worked seven years on the narcotics squad before being named, successively, to head the vice squad, the antiracketeering squad and, in February, 1996, the criminal brigade.

The Crim, as it is familiarly called, is the branch of the judicial police that deals with criminal or terrorist affairs and cases involving unexplained deaths. Comprising 110 officers, it is in the words of one prosecutor "the best service for dealing with physical evidence. They are the top of the top in France, the real pros."

Headquartered in a five-story wing of the sprawling Palais de Justice, overlooking the banks of the Seine on the Ile de la Cité, the Crim prides itself on its high success rate: on average, the brigade cracks six out of 10 criminal cases, a better record even than the legendary Scotland Yard. Part of their secret is teamwork. They work in clusters of five to eight detectives. "They live in osmosis," says a judicial source, "and are always doing two or three things at once."

Their headquarters looks like central casting's version of an overworked precinct station in a tough urban neighborhood. The hallways are dirty, paint is peeling from the ceiling. The offices are small and cramped. The walls are lined with filing cabinets. The desks are covered with coffee cups, overflowing ashtrays, stacks of papers, and file folders. The scene differs little, in fact, from the offices of their nineteenth-century predecessors—like the tenacious Inspector Javert in Hugo's *Les Misérables*—except for the computers on which the officers type depositions as they interrogate witnesses. "The Crim headquarters looks like a mess, with papers, files, and photos scattered everywhere," says a Palais de Justice insider. "But they lose nothing. It is a very old, and very methodical service."

The Crim was called into action on August 31 by Maud Coujard, 31, the deputy prosecutor who arrived at the accident scene on her BMW wearing a motorcycle helmet, tight jeans, and a black leather jacket. A former juge d'instruction, Coujard had seen her share of blood and mangled bodies during her two years with the Paris court's 8th division (criminal affairs) and in her current post with the 1st division (public health, traffic accidents, narcotics). As the weekend duty prosecutor, Coujard had been summoned to the tunnel as soon as the first word of the accident was transmitted by the police radios.

After surveying the scene and conferring with police officials—including Paris police chief Massoni, judicial police director Patrick Riou, and criminal brigade chief Monteil—the young prosecutor took the first steps in what would be one of the most closely guarded investigations in French judicial history. Coujard immediately ordered an autopsy on Henri Paul, the interrogation of the first witnesses, the seizure of the Mercedes' registration and inspection records, and the arrest of the seven photographers. She then assigned the case to Monteil's elite corps of detectives.

Hazel-eyed, brown-haired, and well-endowed, Coujard bears a striking resemblance to the Italian actress Ornella Muti. But along with her drop-dead good looks, she has a steely backbone and knows how to stand her ground. On the morning of the photographers' arraignment on September 2, Coujard engaged in a heated two-hour argument with chief Paris prosecutor Gabriel Bestard. Believing that the paparazzi had played a direct role in the accident, Bestard reportedly wanted to take them before the criminal court and charge them with homicide. Coujard, backed by her boss Bernard Pages, head of the 1st division, favored misdemeanor charges of manslaughter and nonassistance. In the end, that was what Judge Stephan decreed.

The investigation had actually begun within minutes of the accident with the arrival of officers Dorzée and Gagliardone, the first two policemen on the scene. Their reports, highly critical of the photographers for hindering their access to the car and behaving aggressively, were augmented by the accounts of the first four witnesses: the professional chauffeurs Olivier P. and Clifford G. and the couple Gaëlle L. and Benoît B.

Lt. Bruno Bouaziz, commander of the night brigade, summarized these initial findings in his report of August 31: "Witnesses indicated to the first policeman on the scene that the Princess' car was moving at high speed, pursued by two-wheeled vehicles. Others saw the Mercedes being slowed down by a Ford Mondeo so that the photographers on motorcycles could take pictures. The Mercedes, apparently seeking to escape these pursuers, swerved to the left at the entrance to the tunnel and its driver lost control of the vehicle and struck a pillar in the middle of the tunnel.''

After carrying out her own preliminary interrogations in the tunnel, criminal brigade chief Monteil drafted a report at 2:00 A.M. stating that the Mercedes had been ''pursued and interfered with'' by journalists, causing it to lose control. The report also described the paparazzi's voracious picture-taking antics while ''ignoring the basic gestures of assistance,'' and noted the arrest of seven of them.

Meanwhile, detectives working under powerful flood lights were photographing the car from every angle, measuring scrapes and skid marks, calculating angles and trajectories, making the first detailed sketch of the crash scene, and assembling physical evidence.

One of their first tasks was to collect the objects left in the car by the occupants or scattered on the ground nearby. The inventory of these artifacts—plucked by anonymous hands from the intimacy of pockets and bodies and thrown into a plastic pouch—tells a poignant story of lives frozen in time.

DIANA'S EFFECTS:

- A Jaeger-Lecoultier gold watch with white stones
- A bracelet with six rows of white pearls and a clasp in the form of a dragon
- A gold ring with white stones
- One gold earring (on October 22, investigators found the other earring under the dashboard of the wrecked car)

- A pair of black Versace high-heeled shoes, size 9
- A black Ralph Lauren woman's belt, size 30

DODI'S EFFECTS:

- 1000 francs ($180) in the form of five 200-franc notes
- A rectangular Cartier watch with a maroon-colored crocodile watchband
- A Breitling chronocraft watch, in working condition, with no watchband
- A white metal watchband with a Breitling trademark
- A Citizen watch, nonworking, with the hour frozen at 12:00
- A fawn-colored leather cigar holder containing one cigar with no band
- A flat metal dog tag with metal chain, inscribed "D. Fayed, type B pos."
- A gold Asprey cigar clipper

HENRI PAUL'S EFFECTS:

- 12,560 francs ($2,280) in cash
- A driver's license dated August 24, 1979
- A magnetic Ritz hotel ID badge with photo
- A justice ministry ID badge with photo
- A Visa credit card
- A savings account passbook
- An American Express card
- A Diner's Club card
- A Casio digital calculator
- Two sets of keys

TREVOR REES-JONES' EFFECTS:

- A Hodgkinson Telecom beeper
- A black leather address book with addresses in the U.K.
- A Visa card receipt in the name of Trevor Rees-Jones
- A blue Bic lighter
- A set of six keys on a Canal-Plus key-ring

Contrary to widespread press reports, the Repossi Tell Me Yes ring was not found in the car: it was back in Dodi's apartment, where he almost certainly intended to slip it on Diana's finger that night. Also not found in the car, despite persistent rumors, was cocaine or any other drug. A mystery surrounds the £250,000 Bulgari ruby necklace that Mohammed Al Fayed's entourage insists was worn by the Princess that night and "stolen" from her body. French police say the jewelry was not found in the car and doubt that any such necklace could have been snatched from her at the scene, given the number of witnesses who were there from the first moments after the accident. The police version is supported by photos of the Princess emerging from the Ritz to get into the Mercedes, which clearly show her to be bare-necked.

More important than these personal effects, from the investigators' point of view, was the physical evidence they found on the roadway. Just inside the tunnel entrance, they observed a single skidmark 19 meters long in the left lane. It started in the middle of the lane, arched towards the central walkway then back towards the right. After a gap of some 10 meters, skidmarks reappeared, first the right tire alone for some three meters, then two parallel traces leading straight to the point of impact with the 13th support pillar. Total length from the first mark to the pillar: 32 meters.

The configuration of the second set of skidmarks is a curve that moves rightward, barely crossing over the dotted lane divider before swerving left and directly into the pillar. Scrapes on the curb of the central walkway and third support pillar suggested that the Mercedes had nicked them before rebounding back towards the center, then suddenly veered leftward toward the final crash point.

Some ten to 12 meters inside the tunnel entrance, in the right-hand lane, investigators found shards of red and white glass. These fragments, noted police major Jean-Claude Mulès in a report drafted at 2:30 A.M., were "grouped together in a way indicating the zone where they fell." Several meters further, police found pieces of glass from the Mercedes' right external rear-view mirror and the mirror's dark gray plastic housing, which bore traces of paint.

All of this debris was located at least 60 meters behind the 13th pillar, far too great a distance (and in the wrong direction) for the fragments to have been projected by the final impact. Police thus hypothesized that there may have been an initial contact with a second vehicle near the tunnel entrance, which made the fast-moving Mercedes lose control. By the time they finished their work and reopened the tunnel to traffic at 5:00 A.M., this supposition seems to have been taken very seriously. The first police drawing of the accident site on August 31 delineated the area around the glass fragments as a "probable collision zone." Police photos of the same area call it the "probable zone of loss of control of the vehicle."

The initial examination of the wrecked car also supported that idea. A September 1 report by an expert from the criminal brigade detailed the "paint traces or marks" found on the Mercedes. He noted "two long grayish scratches," one of 1.26 m and the other 80 cm, going from the front right fender to the front passenger door. On the same door was a vertical red mark 4 cm long and 1 cm wide. A similar, but smaller red mark was on the rear right door just in front of the handle. A red spot also appeared on the rear bumper. The report noted that the speedometer was at zero (contrary to widespread press reports that said it was frozen at 196 k/h).

Testimony from the first four witnesses* interrogated at

---

*Well over 100 witnesses would be interrogated before the probe was completed.

the Quai des Orfèvres that night further reinforced the idea of a collision between the Mercedes and another car. Benoît B. and his girlfriend Gaëlle L. were driving eastbound through the tunnel in their Renault Super 5 when their attention was attracted by the sound of skidding rubber. "I heard the noise of the tires, and then a little impact," said Benoît. "At that moment, I saw, in the opposite lane, two vehicles. The first one, a dark-colored sedan, accelerated brutally at the moment when the Mercedes that was following it in the same lane, that is, the right lane, lost control. I saw it slide, strike a pillar . . . then spin around and hit the wall to wind up facing in the opposite direction. I think that the Mercedes that was driving very fast, struck the saloon and lost control. When we passed at the level of the wrecked car, I saw a motorcycle or a big Vespa . . . pass the Mercedes . . . The motorcycle slowed down, then accelerated and left."

Gaëlle, who was in the front passenger seat, described the same scene from her vantage point. "I saw a dark-colored car, something like a [Renault] Clio or a [Renault] Super 5, that was driving rather slowly. It hindered the Mercedes which was coming behind it at high speed . . . I am not sure if the Mercedes touched the first vehicle. The Mercedes hit the central walkway by the pillar then crashed into the wall."

Olivier P. and Clifford G., two off-duty chauffeurs, saw the two cars approaching the tunnel but not the crash itself. They were standing on the Place de la Reine Astrid, a grassy triangle about 50 yards from the tunnel entrance, with a view to the southeast. "I saw a Mercedes driving very fast, I would say about 90 mph, towards the Alma tunnel, and it was pursued by a motorcycle. The Mercedes was preceded by a car, the type of which I cannot identify. It was dark colored and was trying to slow down the black Mercedes . . . At that moment, I heard the chauffeur of the Mercedes downshift in order to accelerate and pass the car in its way. Then the Mercedes descended into the tunnel and I heard a huge noise."

Clifford described the scene in similar terms: "The Mercedes was behind another vehicle. The vehicle in front of it was going at a normal speed. The consequence is that the Mercedes accelerated strongly in order to swing left and pass this car.'' This witness, too, spoke of a motorcycle following closely behind the Mercedes.

As the world awoke to the news of Princess Diana's death, other witnesses began to come forward. On Sunday morning, Jean-Pascal Peyret was having breakfast in his apartment in Versailles, 9 miles southwest of Paris, when his 13-year-old son dashed in and announced that Diana had been killed in the Alma tunnel. Peyret, 41, president of a communications and marketing company, was startled. The previous night, he and his wife were returning from an anniversary dinner at the Bristol hotel just before 12:30 and had heard a tremendous crash behind them as they drove through the Alma tunnel. Concluding that the noise must have been Diana's accident, he called the local police in Versailles. They took down his name and number. Within five minutes his phone rang.

"Monsieur Peyret?" said the caller. "This is the criminal brigade. Thank you for contacting us. As a matter of fact, we were expecting your call." Peyret found the remark curious, and vaguely worrisome.

Peyret, accompanied by his wife and son, headed into Paris in their dark blue Saab convertible. When they arrived at 36 Quai des Orfèvres, they parked in front of the building and presented themselves to the two policemen manning the Plexiglas guardhouses on either side of the entrance. One of the officers checked their name on a list and ushered them through the heavy wooden doors. They were escorted to the third floor, where Peyret and his wife were interrogated separately. Their son waited on a bench in the hallway.

Peyret's testimony centered more on what he heard than what he saw. He said he had passed through the tunnel and was ascending the ramp when he heard what he thought was an accident on the street level. There were two shocks, he said, one was only of "relative" force, the other a loud "metallic" crash. His account seemed to coincide with the idea of an initial collision followed by the final impact.

In an interview, Peyret later elaborated on what he had told police. "I was driving at about 50 mph," he said. "We must have been at least 50 yards in front of the Mercedes. I heard two impacts. It is totally possible that the first one was the collision with the second car. The first shock sounded like car-against-car. The second was a deeper sound, like a car ramming into a truck."

Peyret added another important observation: seconds after he heard the big crash, his car was passed by a morotcycle mounted by a single driver wearing a white helmet and dark jacket. This corresponds to Benoît B.'s account of seeing a motorcycle pass the wreck just after the accident. "The motorcycle passed us," said Peyret, "but I can't say he was fleeing. Obviously, he was at the scene of an accident and did not stop." But Peyret did not remember being passed by a car after the crash. He assumed his Saab was the last car to go through the tunnel before the Mercedes. "The police told us it was a miracle we weren't hit," he said. "If we had been two seconds later, we would have been smashed."

By the time Peyret finished his deposition at about 1:30 P.M., the corridors of the criminal brigade were abuzz with speculation about a collision between the Mercedes and another vehicle. Sitting in the hallway, Peyret's son had picked up the vibes. "Papa," he whispered. "The cops are talking about a second car involved in the accident. Maybe they think it's you?" In fact, there was nothing to worry about. While Peyret and his wife were giving their testimony, a discreet check of their mint-condition 1997 Saab in the parking lot showed that it was undamaged.

Unbeknownst to Peyret, moreover, there had been another car between his and the Mercedes. Mohammed M. and his girlfriend Souad M. had witnessed the accident and contacted the police the next morning when they learned the identity of the victims. That night, they had been driving home to the western Paris suburbs in Mohammed's light gray Citroën BX when they heard the shriek of the Mercedes' tires behind them.

Souad, in the front passenger seat, wheeled around to look.

"I saw a large Mercedes heading sideways across the road onto the walkway and strike a concrete pillar," she told police. "Our vehicle was about thirty or forty yards in front of the Mercedes at the moment of the shock. My friend Mohammed immediately accelerated in order not to be hit from behind. After this first contact, the vehicle pivoted around and smashed into the other [right] sidewalk. I could clearly see the chauffeur's body slumped over the wheel.

"At this moment," Souad added, "I saw other vehicles come behind the Mercedes, maybe six or seven, and I had the time to notice that they passed around the wreck. I can't say whether any of these vehicles stopped to help." Nor did she remember their BX being passed by any of the cars that came after them.

Taken together with Peyret's testimony, Souad's observation had major implications. If the car that was involved in the accident was among the "six or seven" that she saw driving around the Mercedes after the crash, that car apparently did not continue in the direction that the Saab and the BX were headed in, that is, westward towards the Place du Trocadero. Or if it did, the driver was traveling at a modest speed—hardly consistent with someone fleeing the scene of a fatal accident.

Souad's boyfriend Mohammed, meanwhile, had observed the accident from a very different angle, through his external rearview mirror. "I was driving about 50 to 55 mph," he told the detectives, "when I was alerted by a noise of skidding tires behind me. I was at that moment in the tunnel, on the flat part just before ascending the ramp. The noise was loud, because I could hear it over the sound of my radio. I looked in the left-hand external mirror. I was in the right lane. I saw a big Mercedes in the bottom of the tunnel, moving across the roadway. It was going very fast, I'd say at least 90 mph. The Mercedes was sliding in such a way that it formed a 45-degree angle with the central walkway. I remember that quite clearly, because I saw its headlights illuminate the eastbound lane . . . I continued to look in the mirror and I saw that the Mercedes straightened itself and headed back in the right direction, then immediately I heard a huge noise and saw a piece of the car go flying as the vehicle smashed into the central pillar. It then bounced off this central axis and headed back to the right, but I could no longer see it in my mirror." In other words, Mohammed had no line of vision into the right lane. If there was a "second car" behind him, therefore, he could not see it. He was convinced that there was no other car between him and the Mercedes.

The initial testimony contained intriguing leads, but also many contradictions and imprecisions. What seemed clear from the early depositions was that there was a slower-moving car in front of the Mercedes, that Henri Paul had swerved to the left to pass it, and that he may or may not have collided with the second vehicle before losing control.

At the outset, despite the physical evidence, there was a fair amount of skepticism about the causal role of a second car. The notion that it may have been a photographer intentionally trying to slow down the Mercedes, as some witnesses speculated, was virtually excluded from the beginning. The vehicles of all the arrested photographers were examined and found to be free of any collision damage. Besides, investigators were convinced early on that none of the 10 men under investigation had been close enough to interfere with the Mercedes directly.

Theoretically, the mysterious second car could have been driven by another photographer (or by anyone else for that matter), but investigators saw no way that a pursuing journalist in a small car could have gotten ahead of the speeding Mercedes; nor did it seem credible that a photographer could have been stationed in advance along the Mercedes' itinerary, since Henri Paul had taken an unexpected and indirect route back to Dodi Fayed's apartment. (Paul's aim seems to have been to outdistance the photographers on the expressway, then loop back through western Paris to Dodi's apartment.)

Moreover, investigators did not see how a small car could

receive even a glancing blow from a 1.9-ton Mercedes at high speed without crashing into the right-hand wall or otherwise being incapacitated. And how could it have avoided hitting the crashed Mercedes in front of it? Or if the second car had somehow slipped past the Mercedes before the impact, why hadn't Mohammed M. or Jean-Pascal Peyret or any other witnesses seen it?

The possibility of a rear escape by backing up or making a U-turn was ruled out because the photographers and other witnesses arrived within seconds and would have seen such a maneuver. Photographer Martinez explicitly told police that there was no car between him and the Mercedes when he and Arnal arrived on the scene in Arnal's dark gray Fiat Uno (which was examined by police and showed no collision damage).

In the early stages of the probe, therefore, investigators were divided into those who believed and those who doubted the second car theory—with the doubters initially holding the upper hand. Two weeks after the accident, for example, one police detective said investigators considered "the idea that a motorcycle or car interfered with the Mercedes 98 percent false." For the doubters, the initial alcohol test results on Henri Paul seemed sufficient to explain the accident. "This is the story of a drunk driver going too fast and losing control of his car—end of story," confided one investigator when the results were announced.

Without being that categorical, criminal brigade chief Martine Monteil clearly reflected this line of thinking in her September 1 report. "None of the testimony so far received," she wrote, "permits us to establish whether a vehicle could have been sufficiently close to the Mercedes to the point of touching it or interfering with its trajectory. Among the elements to consider in explaining this accident, we should note the following: the vehicle was moving at excessive speed; the chauffeur did not regularly drive this type of vehicle (powerful and heavy); the vehicle, according to maintenance records, seems to have been in perfect condition (repairs and tests made in June 1997); the two toxicology analyses on the driver showed a blood alcohol level of 1.87 g/l and 1.74 g/l.''

But the legendary thoroughness of the criminal brigade, not to mention the insistence of Judges Stephan and Devidal, required investigators to examine other possible explanations for the accident. The judges, anxious to snuff out all the speculation about terrorist attacks and assassination plots, were determined to pursue every avenue of inquiry.

Indeed, there were other scenarios to be considered. Some investigators at first theorized that a motorcycle might have made contact with the Mercedes, perhaps touching the rear-view mirror with a handlebar. That would account, perhaps, for the bits of broken glass and plastic mirror housing found inside the tunnel entrance. But it did not explain the shards of red glass (actually polycarbonate plastic), the white glass from the Mercedes' right headlight, or the scratches on the right side of the wrecked car. Any collision with a motorcycle that did that much damage, at that speed, would certainly have knocked the two-wheeled vehicle over and probably killed its driver.

But did a motorcycle otherwise interfere with the trajectory of the Mercedes? The most spectacular claim along those lines came from François Lévi, 53, an out-of-work former harbor pilot from Rouen. Lévi (whose name is actually Levistre) claimed that he entered the expressway from the parallel road, the Cours Albert 1er, and then headed into the tunnel. In his rearview mirror, he said, he saw the Mercedes approaching from behind with two motorcycles close by it and a white car in front. As he told Reuters on September 4, essentially repeating his September 1 deposition, ''I saw the car in the middle of the tunnel with a motorcycle on its left, pulling ahead and then swerving to the right directly in front of the car. As the motorcycle swerved and before the car lost control, there was a flash of light. But then I was out of the tunnel and heard, but did not see, the impact. I immediately pulled my car over the curb but my wife said, 'Let's get out of here. It's a terror attack!' '' In the version he gave police, Lévi added that he saw a big motorcycle with two riders emerge from the tunnel immediately after the crash.

The problem with Lévi's story is that he had first contacted Britain's *Sunday Times*, then Ritz president Frank Klein. Klein put him in touch with Mohammed Al Fayed's lawyer Bernard Dartevelle, who immediately trumpeted Lévi's claims to the press as proof that paparazzi had caused the accident. By the time Lévi finally gave his account to the police, at 3:30 P.M. on September 1, it appeared to be more useful in comforting the Fayed-Ritz version of things than in helping investigators get at the facts. His testimony was contradicted by that of other witnesses and did not take note of the presence of the Citroën BX, which would have had to be behind him. Police ultimately concluded that Lévi was an unrealiable witness.

As discredited as his story appeared to be, Lévi was far from the only witness who claimed to see motorcycles speeding close to the Mercedes. California businessman Brian Anderson said he was riding in a taxi on the express road towards the Alma tunnel when he was passed by the Mercedes closely followed by two motorcycles, one of which seemed to be trying to get "in front of the car." Similarly, Thierry H., 49, a Paris-based engineering consultant, reported being passed on the express road by a fast-moving Mercedes with "four to six" motorcycles in hot pursuit. "These motorcycles," he said, "were tailing the vehicle and some tried to pull up alongside it."

Of the four original witnesses, Benoît B., Olivier P., and Clifford G. all spoke of motorcycles close behind the Mercedes. Benoît, it will be recalled, described a motorcycle driving around the car immediately after the crash and continuing on its way. Jean-Pascal Peyret told of being passed by a motorcycle as he exited the tunnel seconds after the impact.

On September 23, another witness stepped forward and gave the most detailed account of all concerning this mysterious motorcycle. Questioned by Judge Stephan, Grigori R., 29, a professional photographer (off-duty and clearly not involved in the chase) described what he saw as he entered the eastbound tunnel in his blue VW Passat just instants before the accident. Grigori, who was apparently not far behind the car bearing Benoît B. and Gaëlle L., initially saw nothing in the westbound lane before the crash because his vision was blocked by the alignment of the central support pillars.

"Just as I was descending into the tunnel, I heard an enormous shock," he told Judge Stephan. "The cars [in front] hit their brakes and I also slowed down and turned on my warning lights. At that moment, I saw, in the opposite lane, a big car that had just been immobilized. I only saw the last split second of its movement."

Grigori went on to describe what he called "the most important point" of what he had witnessed that night. "I saw a motorcycle moving in the same [westerly] direction as the Mercedes," he said. "It was a rather large motorcycle with a round, yellow headlight. I had an impression of something white, but I can't say whether it was a helmet or the gas tank . . . I am practically sure there was only one person on this motorcycle but cannot be totally affirmative.

"This motorcycle," he continued, "took off very rapidly after passing [around the Mercedes] as I described. As I think about it, considering the short lapse of time, it seems improbable that the motorcycle stopped before departing. I think that the driver only had time to slow down or brake sharply . . . In any case, I saw no vehicle pass the Mercedes between the moment when I saw the Mercedes and the moment that the motorcycle went around it."

It seems indisputable, therefore, that at least one motorcycle was very close to the Mercedes at the time of the accident and that it did not stop. Who was on that motorcycle, and whether it did anything to contribute to the wreck, remains a mystery at this point. Nothing proves that it was or was not a photographer. But one thing is certain: it was not one of the ten who were arrested and placed under investigation.

*   *   *

Investigators also had to consider another possible cause of the accident: mechanical problems with the Mercedes itself. As Montreil had noted in her September 1 report, the car's maintenance records and initial inspection indicated that it had been in perfect working order at the time of the accident. The front air bags had functioned properly (certainly saving Rees-Jones's life); the steering and antilock braking system seemed perfectly normal.

There were two worrisome facts, however. A chauffeur who had driven the car earlier in the day told police that a persistent warning light on the dashboard indicated a problem with the brakes. The man said he had informed Jean-François Musa, director of Etoile Limousine, of the problem before Henri Paul took the wheel. Musa later confirmed this to investigators, but said he did not believe the light signalled an actual malfunction. The other possible cause for concern was that the car had been stolen on April 20, 1997 and stripped for parts. When it was found in a Paris suburb on May 6, it was so badly damaged that it required more than $20,000 worth of repairs.

The Mercedes S280, a 1994 model, was purchased by Etoile Limousine in August 1996 for the quasi-exclusive use of Ritz customers. The S280 sells new for about $63,000. It has a six-cylinder, 195 horsepower, 2,799 cc engine, weighs 1.9 metric tons and has a maximum speed of 130 m.p.h. It can accelerate from 0 to 60 m.p.h. in 11 seconds. This particular model had double frontal airbags (lateral airbags only became standard with the 1996 models), automatic transmission, power steering, antilock brakes, air conditioning, and black leather seats. It had 6,250 miles on the odometer when Etoile purchased it, and 26,660 miles when it crashed. Its book value before the accident was about $38,000, though some ghoulish souvenir hunters have offered millions of dollars for the wreck.

On September 1, investigators questioned Etoile Limousine director Jean-François Musa about the theft and repair of the car. Musa showed them more than 40 pages of invoices from the garage Bousquet-Bauer Mercedes, which had repaired the vehicle, and documents certifying that it had passed its police inspection on July 7, 1997, with flying colors. "The car was stolen in front of Taillevent restaurant while on a job for the Ritz," he later explained in an interview. "It was taken by professionals for parts, mainly small electronic motors, switches, and circuits." Among the devices that were ripped out were those that controlled the windows, the power steering, and the antilock braking system. In addition, the thieves ripped out the linings and inner workings of the doors, and stole the wheels and tires.

Contrary to widespread press reports, Musa insists that the car never had an accident and did not have to be "totally rebuilt." "There was absolutely no accident, no shock of any kind," he says. "The body was not touched, nor any mechanical parts of the steering, brakes, or transmission. It stayed a month at Bauer Mercedes and was put back in perfect condition."

Musa confirmed in the interview that the car was registered with the Paris Prefecture as a *grande remise* vehicle, that is, a professional limousine that could only be driven by chauffeurs in possession of a special license. The conditions for receiving such a license are the following: possession of a regular driver's license, a formal letter from an employer stating that the applicant has been hired as a chauffeur, a special medical exam upon applying and a checkup every five years thereafter. "Henri Paul," said Musa, "did not have this license."

The remains of the car was removed from the tunnel and taken on a flatbed truck to a police impound on the Boulevard MacDonald in northern Paris. On September 11, Judges Stephan and Devidal visited the pound to make an inspection. Though the initial expert's report had certified that the Mercedes had been in good mechanical condition, Stephan ordered it to be taken apart piece by piece and every square centimenter studied.

The aim was not only to obtain 100% certainty about the mechanical state of the car, but to calculate its impact speed as accurately as possible by measuring the degree of deformation of its various parts. Examination of the electronic braking system's memory, it was hoped, could indicate precisely when and how the brakes were applied. Stephan also ordered a thorough chemical analysis of the paint fragments found on the right side and right rearview mirror of the Mercedes in an effort to identify the car it was presumed to have collided with.

That was a job for the vehicle department of the Institut de Recherche Criminelle de la Gendarmerie Nationale (IRCGN), a highly specialized 160-man research unit operating under military authority and housed in the Fort of Rosny-sous-Bois, about 6 miles east of Paris. Founded in 1987, the vehicle department is one of the most sophisticated laboratories in the world for the identification of cars by paint, glass, tire tracks, and other forensic data. "With just a few clues, and antlike teamwork, we can track people down a year and a half after they flee an accident scene," says Warrant Officer Gilles Pouilly, founder and head of the vehicle department.

Even before they received the whole Mercedes, the department's experts had been examining key pieces of the wreck and the glass fragments found in the tunnel. They quickly confirmed that the white glass came from the Mercedes' right headlight. The red polycarbonate plastic required more time to analyze. By examining the shards under a microscope then piecing them together like a jigsaw puzzle, they were able to reconstruct almost the entire part, which turned out to be the cover of a left taillight. They then compared it to the hundreds of samples they have in stock and thousands more available in catalogues. By September 12, less than two weeks after the accident, they had positively identified the article: "a taillight manufactured by Seima Italiana and belonging to a Fiat Uno manufactured between May 1983 and September 1989."

Six days later, two new witnesses came forward with a story that seemed to corroborate the idea of a collision with a Fiat Uno. Identified only as Georges and Sabine D., the couple told investigators they had just crossed the Alma bridge from the seventh *arrondissement* at about 12:25 and turned west onto the road that parallels the expressway. As they merged onto the dual carriageway, they said, they were passed by a white Fiat Uno. The driver, described as a brown-haired "European type" about forty years old, was behaving abnormally, zig-zagging, repeatedly looking in his rearview mirror and swerving suddenly to the right to park on the side of the road. Georges and Sabine told police there was a large German Shepherd wearing a muzzle in the back of the car, and that the Fiat made a loud noise and backfired, as if its muffler was damaged in an accident.

Seeking to confirm the thesis of a Mercedes-Fiat collision, Stephan pressed the gendarmes to complete their paint analysis.

That was a far more complicated process, however, and would take more time. The samples collected from scrapes on the right side and right rearview mirror of the Mercedes, as well as chips found on the roadway, had to be subjected to spectrographic analysis then mixed with chemical reagents to determine the precise molecules that composed the paint. Once the pigment's chemical signature was determined, the gendarmes had to compare it with the thousands of samples they have in house or memorized in their computers. That step, if successful, would lead them to the paint's manufacturer, who, in turn, could indicate when and to whom that particular batch paint was sold. In that way, if all went well, it might be possible to identify the precise model and year of the second car and even its place of manufacture. But it would take weeks to get the results, Stephan was told.

By the end of September, the gendarmes were starting to zero in. On October 2, well before they issued their formal report, they communicated their initial findings to the two judges: the paint was white (to be exact, an Italian-manufactured product called *bianco corfu*) and it was used on 10 different models and makes of automobiles, including four kinds of Fiat. Among the four was the Fiat Uno. Further precisions narrowing down the possibilities were expected within two weeks, Stephan was informed.

The discovery that the paint was white raised a few eyebrows. Virtually all the witnesses who had seen a second car in or approaching the tunnel described it as "dark colored." The first expert report on the Mercedes, dated September 1, had described two long "grayish" scrapes and two small red marks. Investigators had earlier described the mystery car as being dark blue, black, or red. But now the gendarmes suddenly declared that the pigment was white.

The dark appearance of the deposits on the Mercedes, it was explained, was due to the undercoats of rust-proofing and primer, which are often blue or blue-green. The fact that everyone saw the car as dark, investigators suggested, could have indicated that the car was "very dirty" or that the lighting in and around the tunnel played tricks with people's color perception. Perhaps. But the sudden claim that "dark" was really "white" had an Orwellian newspeak quality that could not fail to have sinister implications for the conspiracy-minded.

Armed with the gendarmes' preliminary findings, the judges ordered police to begin checking the records of the more than 112,000 Fiat Unos registered in France since the first model rolled off the assembly line in Turin in 1983. By focusing on white cars (plus those of "indeterminate color") registered between May 1983 and September 1989, the dates corresponding to the taillight fragments, they narrowed the choice to some 40,000 cars. They brought that number down to 10,000 by eliminating the vehicles that had been sold abroad, destroyed, or otherwise removed from circulation.

On October 21, the long-awaited paint analysis report arrived on Stephan's cluttered desk. Despite its meticulously documented 100 pages, it added little to the earlier findings: white paint that could come from 10 different vehicles, including the Uno. Stephan was told it would take many more weeks, if not months, for the gendarmes to narrow the choice down further. Given the earlier promises about specifying the exact year and manufacturing plant, the two judges found the results somewhat disappointing.

But the report contained another significant element: the dark gray horizontal line found on the front right fender of the Mercedes had been made by the kind of hard rubber used in the manufacture of Fiat Uno bumpers. The rubber was used on several other makes and models as well, but the height of the marks corresponded to the height of the Fiat Uno's bumper, 18 inches. Moreover, this kind of bumper was no longer manufactured, which allowed the investigators to narrow down the choice of Unos even further.

Based on the latest findings, Stephan launched an intensive car-by-car search. The investigators initially targeted the department of the Hauts-de-Seine, a suburban region just to the west of Paris. The reason for that choice was simple: it seemed logical that any cars driving west on the express road at that hour of the night were likely to be headed for homes in that area. Thus it was decided that the hunt would start there, then move into the western parts of Paris proper and, if necessary, radiate out from the capital.

On November 4, the criminal brigade sent five-man inspection teams to four different police stations scattered through the Hauts-de-Seine. Letters had already started going out to the owners of the 1,800 Fiat Unos in that region that matched the criteria established by the gendarmes. Summoned to appear at a given date and hour with car and registration papers, each owner was made to fill out a form and subjected to an interview dealing, among other things, with his whereabouts on the night of August 30–31. Detectives then gave each vehicle a close inspection, looking inside the trunk to see if the car had been repainted, and paying particular attention to the left rear bumper and taillight for signs of damage or recent repair.

Meanwhile, police contacted hundreds of garage owners in hopes that one of them might denounce a customer who had brought a Fiat Uno in for some suspicious rear-end bodywork. Despite all their rigorous methodology, though, the investigators knew they were looking for a needle in a haystack. "It's like a lottery," said one. "We'll need a lot of luck to hit the jackpot and find the car."

During the first three weeks, investigators singled out a dozen or so suspect cases and, in late November, their search turned up a white Fiat Uno, recently repaired in the rear, repainted red, and owned by a man who regularly transported dogs. Since witnesses Georges and Sabine D. had reported seeing a white Uno with a muzzled German Shepherd in the back, investigators thought that they had their man.

The owner, a dog-handler for a private security company, was arrested and taken in to Criminal Brigade headquarters on the Quai des Orfèvres. He had no criminal record but was previously "known to police", according to the dossier. At the time of the accident, he told investigators, he had been on assignment as a night watchman in the western suburbs of Paris, arriving on the job on the evening of Saturday, August 30, and leaving at 7:00 A.M. If his stated whereabouts were accurate, then he could not have been the driver that Georges and Sabine saw emerging from the Alma tunnel between 12:20 and 12:25 A.M. on Sunday. Furthermore, those witnesses reported seeing a "European type" at the wheel and this man was an Asian.

Although there is no evidence in the investigative dossier to corroborate the owner's alibi, the gendarmes' examination of the car ruled out the possibility that it had been involved in the collision: analysis of the Fiat's white undercoat showed that the paint was chemically different from the samples found on the Mercedes. The man's deposition and documents relating to his car were finally filed in a folder marked "removed from suspicion," an unusual classification according to sources familiar with French investigative procedures.

By the end of December, investigators had questioned nearly 800 Fiat owners and checked more that 3,000 vehicles in the Paris region. Some cars had been sold abroad, making them virtually impossible to trace. One owner said he had abandoned his Uno on a street in Madrid. Many of the registration papers turned out to be inaccurate or not up to date, thus introducing uncertainties that would allow the "guilty" party to slip through the net. Some cars—and owners—had just disappeared. "If I were the guy," said one weary gendarme, "I would have sold the car, destroyed it, or had it stolen."

Police tried to pass the message, via leaks to the press, that the driver would do far better to turn himself in than to wait to be caught in the net. In all probability, they suggested, he would face charges no more serious than leaving the scene of an accident. "The reason the driver has not spoken up," one investigator speculated, "is possibly that he might not have been allowed to drive that car or would not want anyone to know he was in it for family or other reasons."

Among the possible explanations: the driver was with his mistress that night and didn't want his wife to know; he was unlicensed, a fugitive from justice, an illegal immigrant or a minor; he was drunk or on drugs; the car was stolen or uninsured. Or he was at fault. In that case, the driver could be charged with fleeing the scene of an involuntary homicide which carries a maximum penalty of four years in prison and $73,000.

Though virtually none of the investigators now doubted that a Fiat Uno had played a role in the accident, the gendarmes in Rosny-sous-Bois became increasingly skeptical about the chances of finding the car as the weeks wore on. The bloodhounds of the criminal brigade remained somewhat more hopeful, and began to extend their search to other parts of the Paris region even before they had finished with the Hauts-de-Seine. But everyone realized that there was a limit to how far they could go. After all, a car driving on a Paris expressway at the end of the August vacation season could well have come from another country. "We can't verify all the Fiat Unos in Europe," said one source in the prosecutor's office. "The stakes are not high enough to justify deploying all the inspectors in France for the next ten years!" Stephan, for his part, told the investigators to push on.

As this intensive hunt proceeded, some French judges, lawyers, and police started grumbling about the extraordinary time, money, and human resources that were being spent investigating a road accident. "It seems paradoxical that such a staggering amount of research should be done," said Jean-Claude Bouvier, secretary-general of the left-leaning Magistrates Union. "I have never seen so many resources put in place for a car accident, It's absurd. It's indecent compared to the lack of financing and the difficulty judges have in carrying out other investigations. If such vast means are deployed for one person, they should be for everyone. I don't care if it's royalty or not."

Critics pointed out that the Fiat inspections alone immobilized nearly a quarter of the criminal brigade's staff. On all aspects of the case, there were times when as many as 60 of the Crim's 110 detectives were working on the investigation (though this number fluctuated greatly). Some press reports put the total cost of the probe at more than $350,000; one disgruntled investigator complained it was "going to be the most expensive probe into a traffic accident in history."

At the height of this controversy, a colleague encountered Stephan in the hallway and joked that he had become "the most expensive judge in France." "The hell I am," Stephan shot back. "So far, the whole investigation has only cost the taxpayer $5,000." That figure corresponded to the amounts billed to the Justice Ministry by the gendarmes vehicle department, as well as to overtime paid to the various investigators, all of whom were civil servants and would have received their regular salaries no matter what cases they were working on. "If they hadn't been doing this, they'd have been drinking coffee and smoking cigarettes," quipped a jurist who found the whole debate out of place.

Michel Lernout, secretary-general of the Syndicated Magistrates Union, and a personal friend of Stephan's, argues that the judge had no choice but to pull out all the stops given the exceptional nature of Princess Diana's death. "Of course they wouldn't use such vast resources to investigate an ordinary accident," he says. "But this is not an ordinary accident. The victim is the Princess of Wales, after all. There is huge pressure on the judge to leave no stone unturned. If he did less, he would be blamed for not being thorough enough." In searching so assiduously for the Fiat's owner, Lernout believes, Stephan "seeks to avoid the charge that he held back on the investigation in order to cover up a plot.

As long as he does not find the owner, people will say maybe it's an agent of the secret services of this or that country.''

Indeed, that suspicion had hovered over the whole investigation from the very beginning. Investigators said they gave it little credence. Sources close to Stephan said it was not a ''hypothesis'' that he took very seriously: Prosecutor Coujard was said to find it ''laughable.'' But many troubling questions remained unresolved. In addition to the identity and role of the Fiat driver, there was that mysterious motorcycle that passed the Mercedes and disappeared seconds after the crash; there were the reported light flashes that corresponded to no photos in the police's possession; there were reports, albeit vigorously denied, that the Princess had been pregnant. That alone, in the eyes of plot theorists, would have been a powerful motive to eliminate her before her condition, and her impending marriage with Dodi Fayed, became known.

Whatever the investigators made of all this, there reigned an extraordinary atmosphere in the halls of the criminal brigade. Inspectors took to locking up their file cabinets and offices at night, even though no one but their own colleagues were present on their floor. Confided one Palais de Justice insider: ''There is a terrible secret that weighs on this case.''

13

In Search of Lost Memories

Two days after he was named to head the Diana investigation, Stephan went to the Paris morgue to witness the drawing of new blood samples from the body of Henri Paul. Profoundly annoyed over the doubts that the Fayed camp and the Paul family had raised about the validity of the first alcohol tests, Stephan was determined that the new round of analyses would be unassailable.* In addition to personally observing the procedure—a highly unusual step for an investigating magistrate—he ordered that the operation be duly photographed. The results, which confirmed and amplified the original data, proved beyond any doubt that Paul was more than three times over the limit. "Enough is enough!" grumbled a US-based member of the Fayed organization. "Every time they give the guy another test he gets drunker."

On September 9, Stephan and Devidal made their first visit to the tunnel, an introductory walk-through to familiarize themselves with the contours of the accident scene. That was a warm-up for the partial reconstruction of the accident that was performed on the night of September 29 in the presence of the two judges, prosecutor Coujard, criminal brigade chief Monteil, and a dozen police experts. The investigative team arrived at 8:30 P.M., after police had closed the tunnel to traffic and cordoned off the area. At 9:15, a flatbed truck

---

*The new tests had formally been requested by Jean-Pierre Brizay, attorney for the Paul family.

bearing the twisted hulk of the Mercedes under a black plastic tarp backed into the tunnel.

With the help of a crane, workers placed the death car in three separate positions: near the entrance, where the Mercedes lost control; against the 13th pillar, whose rectangular form was still etched into the car's front end; and nosed up to the right-hand wall, where the vehicle had spun to a stop. Three other cars were sent slowly through the tunnel to act out various scenarios. Others were driven through the opposite lane to determine exactly what witnesses could have seen from various vantage points. Using a theodolite on a yellow tripod, technicians measured angles and trajectories in an effort to calculate and reconstruct the precise movements of the Mercedes in the final seconds before the crash. For a time, the magistrate considered ordering a full-scale reenactment of the accident, starting from the back of the Ritz. They subsequently decided against this, but held open the possibility of doing a computer simulation.

In late September, the two judges focused on interrogating and reinterrogating key witnesses. Of these, none seemed more important than bodyguard Trevor Rees-Jones (a.k.a. Dodi's shadow), the lone survivor of the accident and thus the only person alive who could possibly know what was going on inside and immediately outside the Mercedes in the critical final moments. But the plucky young rugby player and ex-paratrooper was unable to speak for more than two weeks after the accident.

Since the early morning of August 31, Rees-Jones had been recovering in the intensive care unit of Pitié-Salpêtrière hospital. The first medical bulletin stated he was suffering from a "moderate cerebral contusion, a severe maxillo-facial trauma and a pulmonary contusion." His right wrist had also been badly broken. On September 4, the bodyguard underwent a 10-hour operation to reconstruct his shattered face; three weeks later, he had more surgery to realign his left cheekbone. A bulletin on September 10 described him as "improving," fully conscious, but still unable to speak. Six days later, doctors said he had been taken off the respirator and was now "able to communicate, but tires easily."

As Stephan prepared to question the bodyguard, he was warned by medical experts not to expect too much. Victims of severe head trauma, they said, typically developed partial amnesia, a phenomenon that would have been aggravated by heavy use of anaesthetics during his two operations. The condition was explained with great lucidity by Dr. Philippe Azouvi, a specialist in post-trauma therapy at Garches hospital. "These memory holes, in general, come after a cranial trauma sufficiently severe to cause a loss of consciousness," he said. "These amnesias are due to a commotion of the brain, which has been shaken up. Too-rapid acceleration or deceleration of the brain stretches the cells, which no longer function and no longer record information. The shock thus blocks the process of memorization." Azouvi said he expected the instants immediately preceding and following the accident to be "definitively lost" to Rees-Jones.*

At 11:45 on Tuesday, September 19, Stephan arrived at the hospital accompanied only by his secretary. They were taken by hospital security agents to the second-floor intensive care unit. Dr. Jean-Jacques Rouby met them outside Rees-Jones' room, guarded round-the-clock by two uniformed police officers, and laid down the ground rules. The patient tired very quicky, he explained, so the duration of the questioning must be determined uniquely by Rees-Jones' condition. That meant the doctor himself would have to be present to monitor the patient's physical state. It was a highly unusual situation, but Stephan agreed and swore Rouby in as a witness.

Rouby was not the only one who needed to be sworn in. Trevor's stepfather, Ernest Jones, and mother, Gillian "Gill" Blackborn Rees, also had to be present because the patient had trouble articulating and they were used to communicating with him. Also present was an interpreter, who translated Stephan's questions. The parents repeated Trevor's mumbled

---

*Interview in *Le Figaro*, September 18, 1997.

answers, which were then translated back into French. Because of all these complications, the whole interview was tape-recorded, contrary to normal procedure, and the final transcript had to be handwritten out in the hallway so that Rees-Jones could read and sign it.

Speaking generally in the third person, Stephan asked 30 questions before Rouby ruled the patient too tired to continue after 25 minutes. Herewith the entire transcript:

Q: Does he remember what happened after the departure from the Ritz?

A: I remember getting into this car, and I do not remember anything else.

Q: Concerning the accident, he has no memory of what happened?

A: No.

Q: Does he have any memory of what happened earlier at the Ritz?

A: Yes.

Q: Can he tell me?

A: When we arrived [at the hotel] there were numerous photographers and numerous cameras that bothered us. That really upset the Princess and Dodi . . . I went to see the photographers. I asked them to move back. They were trying to enter the Ritz by the front door . . . [The couple] were eating their meal and we [Wingfield and Rees-Jones] had eaten our meal. Dodi changed the plan. The Princess, Dodi, Henri Paul, and I left through the back exit. There were more photographers in the back.

Q: From that point, he has no memory of the journey?

A: I remember that we were followed, that's all.

Q: Where were they going?

A: We were going to the apartments.

Q: On the Champs-Elysées?

A: Yes.

Q: Does he remember how far they were followed, and by whom?

A: There were two cars and a motorcycle. I do not remember the route.

Q: Can he provide any details about the cars and the motorcycle?

A: It seems to me there was one white car with a boot which opened at the back, and three doors, but I don't remember anything else.

Q: So the cars followed after the departure from the Ritz?

A: Yes.

Q: Does he remember how Monsieur Paul was called and by whom?

A: Dodi called him so he could drive us from the back of the hotel.

Q: Can he tell me why?

A: No. It was Dodi who changed the plan, not I.

Q: Then what was the original plan?

A: The original idea was to leave from the front with two cars, so we could keep the photographers as far away as possible. They were there in any case. I thought it would be better to have two cars rather than one.

Q: Does he know the Place de la Concorde?

A: Next to the Ritz?

Q: No. Next to the Ritz is the Place Vendôme. The Place de la Concorde is next to the Champs-Elysées.

A: I don't remember. Everyone was driving fast.

Q: Does he remember who was the closest [to the Mercedes] when he saw the cars and the motorcycle?

A: I don't remember. It changed.

Q: It changed during the journey?

A: Yes.

Q: Does he remember if any photos were taken?

A: I don't know.

Q: Would he be able to recognize the white car?

A: I don't think so.

Q: Was this car behind them when they left the Ritz?

A: It crossed the street when we left and then followed us.

Q: Had he seen it earlier?

A: I don't know.

Q: Does he remember other photographers' cars? Those, for example, that followed them during the day?

A: Yes.

Q: What kinds of cars?

A: There was a Jeep and two motorbikes and a little three-door car. I think the car was dark-colored.

Q: Does he remember the attitude of the Princess and Dodi Al Fayed towards the journalists who were surrounding them?

A: They were not pleased. They were too close.

Q: Even during the drive in from Le Bourget?

A: They followed us.

Q: And later at the Ritz, they were there, too?

A: Yes, always.

Q: Does he remember an incident with the photographers?

A: . . . It was not [with] us. It was a man who takes care of the apartment [a Ritz security agent]. He stepped in front of the photographer and pushed him, and this photographer got angry and I tried to calm everything down.

Q: Does he remember how Monsieur Paul was that night, since he knew him from before?

A: He seemed fine.

Q: Does he remember whether Dodi asked him to change the route back to the apartment?

A: No.

Q: So he has no memory of the accident itself?

A: No.

The bodyguard had tried valiantly, but the results were disappointing. Apart from his confirmation that it was Dodi who planned the rear exit and chose the driver, and some vague recollections about the vehicles he saw during the first moments of the drive, Rees-Jones had told the judge nothing he did not already know.

A second interrogation, performed at the hospital on October 3 by two police detectives, was much longer and a bit more productive. Rees-Jones could now recall the journey up to the Rue de Rivoli, two blocks from the hotel. When investigators showed him photos of the photographers, he was able to identify two of them who had been following the couple during the day and hanging around the Ritz that night. He reiterated that it was Dodi who concocted the getaway scheme, and said he had recommended using two cars but was overruled.

Rees-Jones provided other details about the day's events and the goings-on at the hotel just before the departure. He remembered seeing Henri Paul drink two glasses of a "yellow liquid," but again insisted that he had seemed "fine" that night. "At no time during the discussion I had with Paul," Rees-Jones declared, "did he indicate that he was not on duty. He was at the Ritz, for me he was on duty." Diana, said Rees-Jones, took no role in organizing the departure, but waited "passively." Asked why he had been wearing a seat belt, contrary to normal procedures for bodyguards, Rees-Jones said he didn't remember putting it on but explained that "in general, in town I don't wear a seatbelt unless we're obliged to go fast." (Photos show he did not have the belt on when the car left the Ritz.) Investigators, suspecting that his earlier description of a white "three-door" car could possibly refer to a Fiat Uno, showed him three pictures of Unos; the witness, however, said they "didn't bring anything to mind." Nor could he provide any information on the critical final moments.

On October 4, after 34 days in the hospital, Trevor Rees-Jones finally left Pitié-Salpêtrière in a French government helicopter and was flown to a heliport at Issy-les-Moulineaux on the southwestern edge of Paris. Wearing dark glasses, a baseball cap, and sneakers, with a heavy cast on his arm, he walked unaided to a larger helicopter provided by Mohammed Al Fayed and was taken back to England. Following his return, he spent most of his time at his parents' home in Oswestry, 150 miles northwest of London. His mother, a registered nurse, helped him with his physical therapy.

A fellow member of Al Fayed's security force in London describes Rees-Jones as being on a "slow mending curve." Though the French doctors performed what his parents called an "absolute miracle" in putting his face back together, he still has a lot of physical problems to deal with. He has lost one-third of his former bodyweight, the orbit of his left eye is damaged and he has a large scar on his face. He needs extensive dental work, corrective glasses to deal with an eye-muscle problem, and intensive physiotherapy on his shoulder and damaged vertebrae.

Rees-Jones returned briefly to Paris in late October for an outpatient checkup by doctors at Pitié-Salpêtrière, who gave him a clean bill of health. At his initiative, he returned again on November 6, this time by Eurostar with some friends from his hometown. They drove him along the route from the Ritz to the Alma tunnel, hoping to jog his memory. "He came up zero, I'm afraid," says a member of the Al Fayed organization. "What he can remember, which isn't a great deal, he's already told the French." Indeed, when Rees-Jones returned to Paris on December 19 for another session with Stephan, he added little to what he had previously told the judge and still did not remember the accident.

Associates say the bodyguard has said nothing to suggest he feels at fault over the accident, but one of them confides, "If I were he, I'd certainly feel very badly about what happened." So might Mohammed Al Fayed: since Rees-Jones formally became a civil plaintiff in the investigation on October 16, he has become eligible to receive damages from those deemed responsible—possibly including Al Fayed's Ritz hotel.

After remaining off-limits to the press since the accident, Rees-Jones suddenly broke his silence with a five-part interview that ran in the London *Mirror* starting on March 2, 1998. Claiming that psychiatrists had helped him recover some of his lost memories, the bodyguard now said he recalled hearing Diana crying out for Dodi after the crash. "I have flashes of a female voice calling out in the back of the car. First it's a groan. The Dodi's name is called . . . And that can only be Princess Diana's voice." The bodyguard still had no memory of the decisive moments just before the accident. But his claim, if accurate, would add credence to the notion that the Princess was still conscious after the impact and could possibly have survived if operated on sooner.*

As for the other bodyguard, Kes Wingfield, French investigators questioned him for some five hours on September 2. A former S.A.S. commando and five-year veteran of the Al Fayed security force, Wingfield, 32, provided a richly detailed account of the day's events. He described being tailed by paparazzi during the drive in from Le Bourget, the altercation with photographers outside Dodi's apartment, the crowds outside the Ritz, and the change of departure plans. Like Rees-Jones, he said it was all Dodi's idea and underscored the fact that he had expressed reservations about it. As for Henri Paul, who had apparently fooled the bodyguards into thinking his pastis was pineapple juice, Wingfield insisted that Paul's behavior was "completely normal." But Wingfield, whose memory seemed as sharp as Rees-Jones' was fuzzy, could say nothing about the final drive, since he had left with Jean-François Musa in a decoy car via a different route.

Mohammed Al Fayed believes that it was a fatal mistake not to have followed the Mercedes with a backup car. As a senior official of his security force bluntly puts it, "They deviated from standard procedure." After his return to England, Wingfield was temporarily "reassigned" away from close protection to general surveillance around Al Fayed's estate in Oxted, but he was back on bodyguard duty by December. "The [getaway] plan was completely acceptable if the principals felt the need to do it that way," says one security force officer. "Dodi Fayed—the owner's son—wants something done. What's Kes supposed to do, call London and get it countermanded?"

In the first days of October, the two judges began to focus on reinterrogating the photographers.† Sygma's Jacques Lan-

---

*On April 20, 1998, saying it was time to "move forward" with his life, Rees-Jones announced that he was resigning from his $37,000-a-year job with the Fayed security force.

†In June 1998 the judges assembled all ten photographers together with other witnesses in an attempt to reconcile contradictions in their accounts.

gevin was called in by Stephan one unseasonably warm afternoon and sweated through a five-hour grilling. It was so hot, Langevin recalls, that his lawyer soon took off his black robes and the judge himself doffed his jacket and worked in shirtsleeves.

Stephan focused the interrogation on three points: Langevin's background and career as a photographer, the events outside the Ritz on August 30, and the scene in the tunnel after the accident. The judge showed him several cropped photos, enlarged stills supplied by the Fayed lawyers from the Ritz videos, and asked if he could identify various people milling outside the hotel that night. Stephan seemed particularly interested in identifying a certain individual, possibly an Englishman, who did not belong to the group of French photographers.

The session was not without humor. "I told him some funny stories about my experiences as a journalist," says the photographer. "He would laugh sometimes. He was not intimidating or arrogant." At one point, Langevin recounted his imprisonment in Peshawar while on a reporting assignment. "I was interrogated by their criminal brigade," he told the judge, "just like here." Stephan laughed. "Not *exactly* the same, I hope," he replied. Halfway through the interrogation, Stephan called a break and smoked a cigarette.

When the deposition was finished, at 7:30 P.M., Stephan informed Langevin that he was lifting his judicial control, meaning that he was no longer forbidden to leave the country or talk to the other journalists involved in the case. "Thank you, Judge," said the journalist. "Don't thank me," replied Stephan, with a firm handshake. "A lot of people are accusing us of having been too rough on you guys already."

Langevin took that as an encouraging sign. Having arrived in the tunnel at least 10 minutes after the crash, when the medical workers were already on the scene, he felt confident that both the involuntary homicide and nonassistance charges would ultimately be dropped in his case. But he, like the other nine, would have a long wait before learning his fate: according to Palais de Justice insiders, the final decision on whether or not to try the suspects is not expected before October 1998. The suspense, and the memories of that awful night, was painful to live with. For Jacques Langevin, a little amnesia would be a welcome thing.

14

Skidmarks and Debris

JEAN PIETRI KNOWS SOMETHING ABOUT SPEED AND TRAJEC-
TORIES. A retired engineer and former army reserve lieutenant-
colonel with 40 years of experience in the French armaments,
aeronautics, and automobile industries, Pietri, 70, has flown
airplanes through violent storms and test-driven cars at
speeds of up to 130 m.p.h. He has seen his share of air and
road accidents. And as a consulting engineer for France's
P.S.A. corporation (manufacturers of Peugeot and Citroën)
from 1966 to 1980, he has had many occasions to contem-
plate the factors that send cars spinning out of control and
careening into oncoming trucks, stone walls, or the stately—
sometimes deadly—poplar trees that line rural French road-
sides. But something about this accident particularly intrigues
him.

His brown eyes gleaming under a shock of gray hair, a
clutch of felt-tipped pens protruding from the pocket of his
tweed jacket, Pietri leans over a diagram of the crash site in
the office of *Time*'s Paris bureau chief. He is fascinated by
the skidmarks. One glance at those curving black lines tells
him much of the story of what happened that night. "What
are skidmarks?" he asks rhetorically. "Deposits of melted
rubber. In cases of violent braking, the rubber can become
as slippery as ice." For Pietri, the two sets of marks—one
19 meters long curving to the left and back to the right, the
other 32 meters long slicing from the middle of the road into

the 13th column—read like a mathematical graph of the decisive last seconds.*

"The second marks are conclusive," he says, taking a capped pen from his pocket and tracing the line with the butt end. "At this point, you see, he hasn't lost control yet. He is stabilized, he apparently has all the room in the world in front of him. But he doesn't go back into the right lane. Why? He didn't have room, because there was another car in that lane."

Pietri touches his pen to the point where the second set of tracks begins. They start with a single mark on the right-hand side. "That's his front right tire starting to skid first," he says. "That indicates a leftward turn of the steering wheel followed by a violent application of the brakes. At this point, the Mercedes is in a position of oscillation, accompanied by a fusion of the tires, with an acceleration to the left. That's what caused it to hit the 13th pillar."

The former test driver is amazed by Henri Paul's performance at the wheel. "This poor fellow may have had a few drinks in him, but he was not without reflexes," Pietri marvels. "He has to pass the second car with only a few centimeters of room on either side. He has no margin of error, he needs extreme precision in order to pass. He nicks the other car, but still manages to get around it. Remarkable reflexes! He was totally in control of that car until the final leftward turn of the steering wheel."

There was more to the story than that, of course. There was the role of the second car, the precise nature of the collision, the significance of the debris on the roadway, the Mercedes' impact speed, the effects of the tunnel's distinctive configuration, marked by a leftward curve and a sharp dip at the entrance. Pietri found all this fascinating and agreed to produce an in-depth technical report based on the best available data on the accident, information provided by Mercedes-Benz and Fiat, and his own on-site observations.

---

*Because of the precise technical data contained in this chapter, all measurements are given in metric units.

The field research started right away. We hailed a taxi in the Avenue Montaigne and asked the driver to take us first to the Place de la Concorde, then down the riverfront expressway to the Alma tunnel. The driver, a North African in a Muslim prayer cap, looked puzzled; we were asking to go around a big circle and wind up basically where we came from. He shrugged. It was a fare, after all.

At the Concorde, we made our first important observation: there was no traffic light at the entrance to the Cours la Reine, meaning that the Mercedes could have wheeled onto the express road with a full head of steam and accelerated to very high speed by the time it reached the first tunnel that cuts under the twin Alexander III and Invalides bridges.

The straight-line passage through that long tunnel, with its fairly gentle descent and ascent, Pietri remarked, would have slowed the Mercedes only slightly, and it had plenty of time to regain speed during the final 480-meter stretch leading towards the Alma bridge. In contrast to the first underpass, the road descending into the Alma tunnel veers to the left. The engineer smiled and made a mental note. "With that curve and dip, there is no way this tunnel can be negotiated at high speed."

As we proceeded slowly through the tunnel, we noticed that the alignment of the central pillars made it impossible to see the cars in the eastbound lane until they were roughly at our level. Our taxi slowed down so we could take a close look at the 13th pillar. It had grafitti scrawled on it and a few bunches of wilted flowers at its base. Apart from some crumbling of the concrete along its northeast edge, it showed surprisingly little damage considering the impact it had received from the Mercedes. "Steel-reinforced concrete," said Pietri. "It would take an atom bomb to knock that down."

If those solid, and deadly, columns had been protected by steel guard rails, it is quite possible that the Mercedes would have slid or bounced off it without taking the horrific frontal shock. So why no rails? Socialist deputy François Loncle posed that very question in a September 3 letter to Paris police chief Philippe Massoni. Massoni replied that the Alma tunnel was "an urban road belonging to the public domain of the City of Paris" and that the responsibility for deciding all such security measures resided with the mayor. It is worth noting that the Mayor of Paris, from 1977 to 1995, was French President Jacques Chirac.

Chirac, or course, bears no personal blame either for the absence of protective rails—legally optional in urban areas where the speed is limited—or for the curve-and-dip configuration. One hundred forty-two meters long and 15 meters wide, the Alma tunnel was built between 1954 and 1956 as part of the attempt to modernize postwar Paris and relieve traffic congestion. The engineers who designed it were obliged to trace a curve in order to avoid the number 9 Métro line and the Alma-Marceau station. Paris officials insist that the tunnel is not particularly dangerous. According to the city's central accident bureau, there have been six accidents involving bodily injury (including one death) since January 1994, not counting the crash of August 31. Those statistics, say officials, are within the "Parisian average." In at least four of the six cases, the accidents were caused by excessive speed, which confirms Pietri's observation: it's not a good place to step on the gas.

The taxi drops us off at the Place de l'Alma next to the golden torch statue that has become the focal point of a Parisian Diana cult. Flowers are still heaped at its base and handscrawled notes proliferate. "Diana, you have given meaning to my life," says one. Across the Seine, a sign on the illuminated Eiffel Tower continues to tick off the days until the year 2000. At Chez Francis, the art nouveau–style, glass-enclosed restaurant that dominates the Place, the tables are starting to fill up. In the deepening dusk, Pietri notes that the light is now perfect for observing how different witnesses would have seen the road under night-time conditions.

We cross the road, carefully avoiding the fast-moving Paris traffic, and walk to the Place de la Reine Astrid. This grassy triangle, named for a Queen of Belgium who died in a 1935 auto accident at the age of 29, sits on the edge of the Place de l'Alma some 50 meters from the tunnel entrance. It was here that two key witnesses, the chauffeurs Olivier P. and Clifford G., were standing when they saw the Mercedes approach at high speed, then swerve to the left to pass a "dark-colored" slow-moving car.

To our surprise, we observe that the field of view is extremely limited. Passing cars disappear from sight well before they actually enter the tunnel because the descending road is obscured by a retaining wall. To the left, the field of vision is blocked by a row of trees. In fact, Olivier and Clifford could only have seen about a 100-meter swath of road from where they were standing.

From that vantage point, moreover, it is very difficult to distinguish the colors of cars. Because of a back-lighting effect caused by street lamps and the headlights of oncoming cars, every vehicle appears dark until it reaches the level of the observer. As car after car passes, we note to our amazement that what we took for black or dark blue was often red, green, or white. Because of the oblique perspective, moreover, it was virtually impossible to tell whether an approaching car was in the left or right lane. Conclusion: apart from confirming that the Mercedes arrived at high speed, the testimony of Olivier and Clifford was highly unreliable as to the color of the second car, the lanes the cars were in and their respective positions during the final 10 or 15 meters before entering the tunnel.

Another detail strikes us. In the branches of the trees that line the Seine, there are hundreds of sparkling white lights that flicker on and off. They look like Christmas-tree lights but function year-round to decorate the riverbank for tourists. These lights could explain one confusing account.

In his initial deposition on August 31, Clifford had described a motorcycle with two passengers "snapping pictures in the direction of the [Mercedes]." Reinterrogated by Judge Stephan on September 17, he was no longer so sure of what he saw. "If I declared to the policemen that there were two people on the motorcycle and that the passenger was shooting pictures, today I cannot affirm that there were two riders ... Nor can I say that a passenger took pictures." Probably an honest mistake, in the heat of the moment, by a witness who had subsequently been to the accident site and observed the photographers behaving obnoxiously. But one explanation for his uncertainty about the picture-taking could have been the flickering white lights that would have appeared in his line of vision exactly behind the Mercedes and the motorcycle.

We cross the access road leading onto the expressway and find ourselves on a long grassy traffic island that separates the main thoroughfare from the parallel road, the Cours Albert 1er. It was here that David L., a Paris student, and his girlfriend Marie-Agnès C. were walking with her parents on August 31 at a distance of 30 to 50 meters from the tunnel entrance. That is a far better vantage point than the Place de la Reine Astrid. To the left, there is an unobstructed line of sight to the Invalides tunnel; to the right, there is a clear view of the entrance to the Alma tunnel but little of the interior due to the curve in the road. Another important detail: from this perspective, it is much easier to tell what lane an approaching car is in. On the face of it, then, the testimony of David and Marie-Agnès should be far more reliable than that of the two chauffeurs with their limited view.

What they saw, in sum, was a Mercedes approaching at very high speed in the *left* lane followed at a certain distance by a motorcycle with two men aboard. They both described a second vehicle in the right lane that was passed by the Mercedes; David told investigators that his girlfriend's parents had the impression that there was a collision between the two cars near the tunnel entrance. Their testimony was highly significant, as we shall see in detail later on, and corroborates a sequence of events that Pietri subsequently established, based on a series of scientific calculations. For now, it was sufficient to note that these witnesses were perhaps the best placed of all for observing the trajectory of the Mercedes in the final seconds before entering the tunnel.

From the grassy strip, we crossed the expressway (a foolhardy and dangerous exercise, but essential to our investigation). We proceeded towards the tunnel entrance along the narrow 1.5-meter central walkway with cars whizzing by on both sides. Pietri stopped and looked back to observe the approaching cars. "Look," he said, his face flushed with excitement. "There is a sudden dip in the road surface there, about forty meters from the entrance. You can see the headlights drop when the cars pass over it." Sure enough, the beams bounced down then back up again. "At high speed," said the engineer, "that's a destabilizing factor." So was the sharply descending entrance ramp. "Trampoline effect," he said shaking his head. "A car driving too fast over that incline would lose traction, or even leave the road like a ski jumper."

We made it as far as the third pillar before the honking cars streaking past convinced us that, even in the interests of science, it would be rather stupid to die while investigating an automobile accident. As we crept gingerly back towards the entrance, we noted that the artificial lighting in the tunnel played tricks with colors, making black cars look blue and white cars gray. Both inside and outside the tunnel, it appeared, color perceptions were unreliable at night.

We walked up the Avenue Georges V, like Holmes and Watson, talking excitedly about our findings. Before taking leave of each other, we stopped at Fouquets on the Champs-Elysées and had an espresso in its bustling bar. Pietri was drawing diagrams and making calculations on a napkin and talking in run-on sentences full of terms like "rotational speed," "oscillation," "forward momentum," and "centrifugal force." "There are several scenarios," he remarked, stroking his chin and studying his scribblings. "And every time you introduce a new assumption, the whole thing can change. That's the scientific method. You can't stay wedded to fixed ideas."

Figuring out exactly what happened, he said, would require a lot more thinking, observing and calculating. But the wheels were already turning in the engineer's mind and the Diana case became his unique obsession for the next few weeks. By early December, after numerous visits back to the tunnel, and countless faxes and phone calls between us, Pietri delivered his completed 52-page report on the physical phenomena that sent Princess Diana and Dodi Fayed to their deaths.*

Herewith a summary of Pietri's findings:

SPEED OF THE MERCEDES APPROACHING THE TUNNEL

The distance from the Place de la Concorde to the entrance of the Alma tunnel is 1.2 km. It is divided into three segments: 1) Concorde to the Alexander III bridge, 390 m., 2) the tunnel under the Alexander III bridge and the Invalides bridge, 330 m., 3) Invalides bridge to Alma tunnel, 480 m. This is a straight-line route which, in spite of the long Invalides–Alexander III tunnel, affords excellent visibility and driving conditions. Pietri assumes that Henri Paul would have logically driven the car as fast as possible under those circumstances: "The driver of the Mercedes," he wrote, "seeking to get the distance on his pursuers to the point of getting out of their line of sight, and favored by the long straight 1.2 km line between Concorde and Alma, would have sought to push his car to the extreme limits of speed." The relatively gentle slopes into and out of the Invalides tunnel would not have appreciably slowed or destabilized the car. Given the performance of the S280 (0 to 60 mph in 11 seconds; maximum speed 135 mph), concludes Pietri, "nothing opposes the hypothesis of a very high speed—on the order of 160 km/h (100 mph), on the last 480-m. stretch preceding the descent into the Alma tunnel."† At that speed, the Mercedes would be covering 44 meters per second.

---

*D. Jean Pietri, *Accident du Passage Souterrain de l'Alma. Paris, Dimanche 31 Août 1997, 0h25. Proposition d'Analyse Scientifique et Technique. Synthèse et Conclusions.* Report commissioned by the authors, December 1997.

†This is very roughly corroborated by eyewitness testimony estimating the Mercedes' speed at anywhere between 100 km/h and 180 km/h.

THE INHERENT DANGER OF THE
ALMA TUNNEL AT HIGH SPEED

The curve-and-dip configuration of the Alma tunnel, Pietri maintains, makes it impossible to negotiate at speeds of 100 km/h or more "without grave risks." This is not true of the straight-line, gentle-sloped Invalides underpass, which can support speeds of up to 160–170 km/h. The relative ease of passing the preceding tunnel at high speed, Pietri surmises, may have fooled Henri Paul into thinking the Alma tunnel posed no problem. A fatal error! Only an experienced professional driver could negotiate the descent into the tunnel at speeds of over 100 km/h, says Pietri, and only by cutting directly from the left to the right lane to reduce the degree of the curvature. Henri Paul had taken special driving lessons with Mercedes in Stuttgart, but even if he had the skills to execute that dangerous passage, he did not have the essential condition for success: a free right lane. Thus even without colliding with the Fiat, Pietri maintains, the Mercedes would probably have had an accident in the tunnel. The presence of a car in the right lane would alone have virtually insured a devastating crash. Writes Pietri: "The driver of the Mercedes was blocked by a presence in the right lane, which in reality provoked the catastrophe."

DISTANCE BETWEEN THE MERCEDES
AND THE FIAT UNO

From the point of the supposed collision near the tunnel entrance, Pietri traces the two cars back to the point where the Mercedes entered the expressway at the Concorde. Assuming the Fiat Uno also joined the road at the Concorde, or further to the east,* and assuming a constant speed of 80

---

*The Fiat could theoretically have entered the expressway from a right-hand access road just before the tunnel entrance, though several witnesses said that they saw the smaller car in front of the Mercedes as it approached the Alma tunnel.

km/h (50 mph) for the Fiat (the average speed of cars using the expressway), Pietri calculates the distances between the two cars as follows:

1. At the Concorde: 507 meters*
2. At the entrance of the first tunnel: 388 meters
3. Leaving the first tunnel: 240 meters

It is only at this point, when the Fiat is halfway between the first tunnel and the entrance to the Alma tunnel, that it becomes visible to the Mercedes (the smaller car was presumably already in the Invalides tunnel, thus not visible, when the Mercedes entered the expressway). The Mercedes now has some ten seconds to go before it enters the Alma tunnel. That still would have given Henri Paul plenty of time to ease into the left lane and pass the Fiat. If the accounts of David L. and Marie-Agnès C. are to be believed, he may already have been in the left lane. But Pietri speculates that he might have been driving down the center of the dual-carriageway.

When the Mercedes is 150 meters from the tunnel entrance, the Fiat Uno is about 75 meters ahead of it. The smaller car is now on the gentle 100-meter-long slope that precedes the curving descent into the tunnel. In less than four seconds, they will collide.

Why? One explanation is that Henri Paul was not able to pass around the Fiat because his excessive speed had robbed his front wheels of traction at that critical instant.

TRAMPOLINE EFFECT

Any vehicle encountering a downward slope will tend to rise off the road (actually it is the road that falls away under the vehicle) due to its own inertial force. If the speed is

---

*I.e., as the Mercedes enters the express road; the Fiat at this point is presumably well ahead of it.

sufficient, the vehicle will actually leave the ground. In most cases, the vehicle will remain on the road, but its weight, and thus its traction, will be diminished. The effect is most pronounced on the front wheels, which control the steering. If a driver, at this critical point, must change direction (to negotiate a curve or avoid an obstacle, for example) he will have to turn the steering wheel more than normal in order to get a response. Very quickly, however, the front end of the car will settle back onto the road with a force superior to its normal weight, thus greatly increasing the adherence of the tires on the road. Under these conditions, writes Pietri, "the car can suddenly find itself catapulted out of its normal trajectory." According to Pietri's calculations, on the relatively steep 50-meter descent into the Alma tunnel, a car traveling at 100 km/h would lose all effective traction on the front wheels over a distance of 20 meters; at 160 km/h, that distance would be 32 meters.

HOW THE COLLISION HAPPENED

Pietri reasons that the driver of the Mercedes, pushed to the right by centrifugal force, and with reduced or zero traction due to the trampoline effect, would have overcompensated in his attempt to steer to the left and avoid a collision with the Fiat. In spite of this effort in the last fraction of a second, Paul is unable to avoid clipping the left rear end of the Fiat Uno. The Mercedes then falls with its full weight onto the front tires, sending the car veering to the left. It is at that point—not before the collision—that Paul hits the brakes and leaves the first 19-meter skidmark. Why just one mark? Because the car is curving back to the right as Paul seeks desperately to avoid hitting the central pillars, a movement that reduces the weight on the right wheels.

WHERE THE COLLISION TOOK PLACE

Based on the location of the debris on the road surface, Pietri calculates that the collision actually occurred some 5 meters *outside* the tunnel entrance, at least 10 meters east of the "probable collision zone" designated on the police diagram. How is this possible? The "probable collision zone" is the area where the white glass from the Mercedes headlight and the red polycarbonate plastic from the Fiat's taillight were found. But the elementary laws of physics, says Pietri, tell us that those fragments were moving at the same speed as the vehicles when the collision took place. They therefore retained their forward momentum as they fell, and then rolled or slid some distance on the ground before they came to rest. Allowing for air resistance, and estimating a "roll" distance, Pietri puts the total distance travelled by the various fragments at 10 meters (assuming a speed of 100 km/h); 13 meters (assuming 130 km/h); and 16 meters (assuming 160 km/h).

If Pietri's calculations are correct, then the collision took place before the Mercedes entered the tunnel. This version of events is supported by testimony from David L. and Marie-Agnès C., the best-placed witnesses to see what was happening as the Mercedes approached the underpass.* "I saw a big dark car arrive, driving very fast in the left lane," David told Judge Devidal on September 24. "At the moment when it passed in front of me, I turned to the people who were with me and remarked that he was crazy to go that fast. At that instant, I distinctly heard the sound of a small shock, then a very hard application of brakes . . . and then a much louder noise behind me [i.e., from the tunnel]." In his original deposition, on September 4, David had spoken of "a large, dark-colored car, in the right-hand lane, [that was] passed by the other car [the Mercedes]." The young man was looking in the opposite direction at that point. But he said that his girlfriend's parents, facing the tunnel, "remember that this car in the right lane was passed by the Princess' vehicle. They even think a collision happened at the moment

---

*Throughout this chapter, the use of eyewitness testimony is inserted by the authors to illustrate or support Pietri's points. There are no such citations in his technical report.

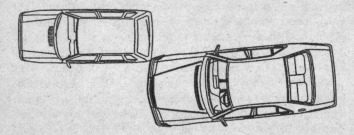

FIG. 1: While attempting to swerve around the slower-moving Fiat Uno, the speeding Mercedes hits the Fiat's left rear corner at a distance of some five meters outside the tunnel entrance. The shock sends white fragments of the Mercedes' headlight and red fragments of the Uno's taillight flying into the tunnel, where they come to rest in the right lane.

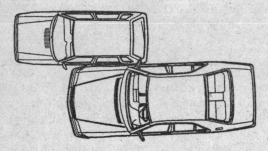

FIG. 2: The Mercedes' right external mirror smashes into the side of the Fiat Uno, ripping off the mirror's plastic housing and shattering the glass. The Fiat, its front end nudged some five degrees to the left by the force of the tangential rear-end collision, leaves the Mercedes only the narrowest of passages between it and the central walkway.

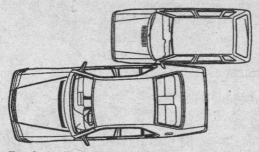

FIG. 3: As driver Henri Paul pulls ahead, his off-balance left wheels tracing a single curving skidmark, the left external mirror of the Fiat brushes the right rear of the Mercedes.

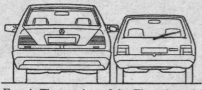

FIG. 4: The passing of the Fiat, viewed from the rear. According to Pietri's calculations, the two cars advanced side by side for at least 26 meters before the Mercedes cleared the Fiat. In the accident's second phase, several fractions of a second later, a "presence" in the right lane forced Henri Paul to jerk the wheel to the left and jam on the brakes, causing the final, fatal slide into the 13th pillar.

it was passed. They said it was passed near [i.e. outside] the tunnel."

The placement of the debris, writes Pietri, indicates that "the contact between the two cars took place when the Mercedes was toward the middle of the dual-carriageway; the presumed Fiat Uno at this moment was slightly to the left side of the right lane [but not over the center line]."

WHAT HAPPENED IN THE MERCEDES-FIAT COLLISION?

Finding the Fiat in its path, the Mercedes suddenly veered to the left, but not enough to avoid a tangential contact. Its front right fender hit the rear left corner of the Fiat, breaking the Mercedes headlight and the Fiat taillight. At that point, says Pietri, the momentum of the heavy Mercedes against the Fiat's rear would have caused the front end of the smaller car to veer some five degrees to the left, further reducing Henri Paul's maneuvering room and causing the two cars to brush against each other. That lateral contact shattered the Mercedes' right rearview mirror and ripped off its plastic housing. (From this point on, it should be noted, Paul no longer has any view to his right rear.) During this brush-by phase, which lasted less than one second according to Pietri's calculations, the Mercedes advanced some 26 meters before it cleared the Fiat just to its right.

Though no one has yet been able to examine the Fiat (which may in fact never be found), the impact of a 1.9-ton Mercedes against a 780-kilogram Uno must have caused far more serious damage than the loss of a taillight. At a minimum its rear bumper and fender were likely bashed in, and there would logically be scrapes on its left side caused by the Mercedes mirror. But it was clearly not immobilized, since it was able to drive away from the scene.

THE FINAL SECONDS

After colliding tangentially with the Fiat, Henri Paul, to whom Pietri attributes remarkable reflexes, managed to negotiate the narrow space between the Fiat to his right and the line of support pillars to his left. Although his front left wheel hit the central walkway (and according to police reports the bumper may actually have nicked the third post) Paul was able to keep the car on the road and head back towards the center of the left lane at a speed Pietri estimates as superior to 100 km/h. "The driver of the Mercedes having regained control of his car, as shown by the nineteen-meter trace," writes Pietri, "one must infer that the real cause of the fatal accident came several dozen meters further on and several fractions of a second later.

"At this point," the engineer's report continues, "the driver of the Mercedes finds himself confronted by two obstacles on his right: one preexisting, the other new. Behind the Mercedes, the Fiat Uno is still close. In front of the Mercedes is a Citroën BX [driven by witness Mohammed M.] driving at about 90 km/h, but which the Mercedes, still moving very fast, cannot help either passing or running into from behind if the Mercedes enters the right lane.*

"The driver of the Mercedes then executes a second countermaneuver [of the steering wheel] towards the left, to avoid at all costs spilling over into the right lane, a countermaneuver accompanied by a simultaneous and desperate application of the brakes to avoid hitting either the dangerously close Citroën BX in front or . . . the Fiat Uno arriving behind.

"From this moment, the fusion of the tire rubber causes a considerable loss of adherence to the road, and the Mercedes finds itself in a double, and definitively catastrophic, situation: 1) the emergency braking maneuver does not have the expected effect and the residual speed remains high . . . , 2) the rotational speed of the Mercedes is not significantly reduced and the Mercedes pursues its movement of rotation towards the left.

"Against this movement of leftward rotation, which sends the Mercedes straight into the line of central pillars . . . the driver of the Mercedes should have turned the wheel back

---

*It will be remembered that Mohammed M., in his testimony, told investigators that "I was quite afraid that this car would hit me, and for this reason I accelerated." Mohammed's passenger, Souad M., estimated the distance between the Mercedes and the BX at this point to be 30 or 40 meters (a distance that the Mercedes would cover in less than two seconds at its high rate of speed).

to the right in an attempt to realign his car along the axis of the road. But at this instant, there remains less than one second before the final shock and the unfortunate driver of the Mercedes does not have the time even to begin this gesture.''

When the Mercedes strikes the 13th pillar, the report continues, ''the center of gravity of the car turns around the shock point. During this rotational movement, the residual elasticity of the structural steel sends the Mercedes backwards on its axis. Continuing its simultaneous movements of rebound and gyration, the Mercedes finally immobilizes itself against the north wall of the tunnel, having marked a rotation of some 180 degrees.'' This 180-degree rotation, incidentally, explains why the Princess was found facing the rear of the car: in effect, her body continued on its initial trajectory and the car turned around her!

IMPACT SPEED

Contrary to claims that the Mercedes hit the 13th pillar at speeds of up to 196 km/h (123 mph), Pietri estimates the speed on impact at no greater than 95 km/h (59 mph). From his long experience testing automobiles, he knows that when cars hit immovable objects head-on at speeds over 100 km/h they tend to disintegrate. Though badly deformed, the Mercedes did not sustain that kind of damage; indeed the rear passenger compartment was intact and the back end of the car virtually untouched. Though it left an impressive rectangular gap in the front end, the pillar did not actually cut through the massive engine, but shoved it over to the right side of the car and penetrated the less resistant steel of the body and chassis.

Backing up these qualitative observations, Pietri looked at how far various bits of debris (interior rearview mirror, front left turning signal, front right headlight parabola) had been projected into the eastbound lane, then calculated the energy generated by the crash. The results indicated an estimated speed on impact of 95 km/h or less.* This was possible, despite the Mercedes' much higher speed on the tunnel approach, because the successive braking movements would have substantially slowed the car before the final crash. The winner in that was Trevor Rees-Jones, who would almost certainly have been killed, even with a seat belt, at speeds over 100 km/h.

WHAT HAPPENED TO THE FIAT UNO?

This is one of the greatest mysteries of the whole Diana affair. Pietri presents two possible scenarios. The first supposes that the Fiat, after being hit from behind, accelerated brutally, perhaps in an attempt to get the Mercedes' license number or prevent it from getting away from the accident scene. According to this scenario, the Fiat would have kept pace with the Mercedes, which would further explain why there was no room for the Mercedes in the right lane. If the Uno was going fast enough, it could have slipped past the Mercedes on the right during the split second when Henri Paul was executing his turning and braking maneuver and before the car rebounded off the pillar and back to the right.

Several things make this plausible. First, though the lower-end Fiat models are no match for a Mercedes, the top-of-the-line Uno 70 SL can almost equal the S280 in acceleration (0 to 100 km/h in 11.5 seconds, compared with 11 seconds for the Mercedes) and the Uno Turbo I.E. actually *out-accelerates* the German car (0 to 100 km/h in 8.3 seconds). Thus it would have been entirely possible for some Unos to catch and even surpass the Mercedes.

Second, some eyewitness testimony supports this thesis. Olivier P., for example, spoke of hearing the driver of the Mercedes ''downshift to pick up speed in order to pass the

---

*Interestingly, Richard Cuerden, head of the University of Birmingham's Accident Research Centre, estimated an impact speed of about 70 km/h because the car did not come to a halt after hitting the pillar but kept on moving before coming to rest against the opposite wall. Thus both these experts put the final speed far below the level that has been generally reported.

car in its way" as it approached the tunnel. Standing next to him on the Place de la Reine Astrid, Clifford G. also described the Mercedes as "accelerating sharply to pass this car." But it has already been established that these two men could not see the final approach to the tunnel from where they were standing. Since the Mercedes had an automatic shift, and since it is a famously quiet car, it is doubtful that the downshifting and engine roaring they heard came from this vehicle—especially since Henri Paul's problem at the entrance to the tunnel was excessive speed, not insufficient speed. A Fiat Uno 70 or Turbo, however, would have made a considerable noise had it downshifted and sharply accelerated.

Gaëlle L., a key witness who saw the crash at close range from the eastbound lane, seemed to corroborate this version when she was reinterrogated by Stephan on September 12. As in her original testimony on the morning after the accident, she described how she had heard squealing tires in the opposite lane and looked up to see the Mercedes hurtling in her direction. In front of it, she told Stephan, was a "small dark-colored car . . . [and] when the Mercedes tried to pass it on the left, it hit something [i.e., the 13th pillar] at that point, then went into the wall on the right. *The little car, seeing that, accelerated. I don't know what became of it.*"*

That account would seem to be contradicted by Mohammed M., whose Citroën BX was just ahead of Henri Paul's car and who claimed to see no other vehicle between his and the Mercedes. But it has already been established that Mohammed was looking in his left external mirror and could not see the right lane behind him.

The other scenario Pietri postulates is that the Fiat, instead of accelerating after the collision, hit the brakes. The engineer estimates that within 10 meters, the smaller car could have decelerated from its presumed 80 km/h to some 60 km/h, and would thus have found itself between 15 and 20 meters behind the Mercedes at the moment of the shock.

*Authors' italics.

"The driver of the presumed Fiat Uno would then have just enough time to go around the wreck that had just come to a stop against the north wall." This version finds some support from Mohammed's girlfriend, Souad M., who was a passenger in his Citroën BX and reported seeing "six or seven" cars pass around the wreck immediately after the crash and continue on their way. If the Fiat Uno remained invisible for most witnesses, Pietri observes, that is partly explained by the fact that the alignment of the central pillars blocked much of the action from the view of those in the eastbound lane.

As informative as Pietri's report is on the immediate causes and physical circumstances surrounding the crash, it sheds no light (that was not its mission) on the baffling question of who was driving the Uno, why he fled the scene, and how he escaped. We have already seen that a U-turn in the tunnel was impossible and that no car in any apparent hurry to leave the scene passed Mohammed's BX or Peyret's Saab as they proceeded towards the Place du Trocadero 600 meters to the west of the tunnel. Where did it go?

According to the witnesses Georges and Sabine D., the only ones who specifically mentioned a white Fiat Uno in their testimony, the vehicle in question emerged from the tunnel between 12:20 and 12:25 AM and passed their car just as they entered the dual carriageway from the right. The Fiat zigzagged and the driver appeared confused. These witnesses said the Fiat nearly hit them because the driver was looking at the rearview mirror instead of the road. The couple passed the Fiat and continued heading west. Georges said the Fiat, which appeared to have a damaged exhaust, parked briefly on the right then continued on its way.

Although the car Georges and Sabine saw seems to fit the description of the mysterious Fiat Uno, nothing proves it actually was the second car in the collision. They said they had not heard the noise of the crash or of the Mercedes' blaring horn, that they noticed no signs of agitation around the tunnel, and that there seemed to be no damage to the Fiat's tail lights. All of which suggests that they may have passed through the Place de l'Alma shortly before the accident actually took place, and that the car they saw might not have been the one that was rear-ended by the Mercedes.

After some details of their testimony were first leaked in the January 1, 1998 edition of *Le Parisien*, which identified them only as "François" and "Valérie," the couple's lawyer began negotiating "exclusive" interviews and photo sessions via the Paris-based ABACA agency. Asking price: $40,000 to $60,000 per interview. As of mid-January, interviews had been sold to France (*Voici*), Britain (*Hello*) and Spain (*Hola!*), with more negotiations underway in the U.S., Italy and Germany.

There is another possible scenario, not necessarily incompatible with François' and Valérie's version. At the time of the crash, Gary Hunter, 41, a British solicitor, was in his third-floor hotel room in the Rue Jean Goujon, about 100 meters from the Place de l'Alma. "I was watching television when I heard the crash at exactly 12:25 A.M.," he told Britain's *Sunday Times*. "There was an almighty crash followed by the sound of skidding, then another crash. My initial thought was that there had been a head-on collision. I went to the window and saw people running towards the tunnel."

Several seconds later, Hunter continued, "I heard a screeching of tires. I saw a small dark car turning the corner at the top of the road. I would say it was racing at 60 to 70 mph. My own feeling is that these were people in a hurry not to be there. I am confident that car was getting off the scene. It was obvious they were getting away from something and that they were in a hurry. It looked quite sinister. I can't recall the type of car but it was a small dark vehicle. It could have been a Fiat Uno or a Renault." He added that the small car was being tailed by a "white Mercedes."

No one can say for sure whether the Fiat Uno Hunter saw was indeed the one involved in the accident. Admittedly, the color he remembers seeing was not white, but he shares that contradiction with most other witnesses who described the second car. Bafflingly, the French police do not seem the least bit interested in following up this lead. After returning to England and telling his story to the *Sunday Times,* Hunter was put in touch with Mohammed Al Fayed's security chief John MacNamara, an ex–Scotland Yard chief superintendent. MacNamara, who is heading Al Fayed's private investigation of the accident, urged Hunter to go back to Paris and tell the story to the French investigative team. Hunter did go to Paris on September 7, but French judicial authorities declined to take his deposition.

That is a great pity. Because Hunter's testimony, says a French judicial source not involved in the case, is something to be "handled with extreme care." Some investigators laughingly dismissed Hunter's story by saying he couldn't even see the tunnel from his hotel window. True enough. But a close look at a street map, or better still, a drive through the tunnel, shows just how easily a car fleeing the scene could have wound up speeding under Hunter's nose. Twenty meters from the tunnel exit, perpendicular to the expressway, is a one-block street called Rue Debrousse. A car turning right onto that road would reach the Avenue du Président Wilson within seconds. A right turn from there would take him into the Place de l'Alma. With a little luck on the lights, and by taking a 90-meter wrong-way shortcut through a bus lane, an escaping vehicle could cut down the Rue Jean Goujon within about one minute of leaving the tunnel.

Why a getaway driver would necessarily choose such a complicated route, when he could just as easily have turned left on the broad Avenue du Président Wilson, remains a mystery. No less puzzling is why such a car should be tailed by a white Mercedes. But as Gary Hunter aptly put it, it looked sinister.

15

Was It Murder?

LESS THAN 10 DAYS AFTER THE FUNERAL OF PRINCESS DIANA in London, a new book by an Egyptian writer hit the shelves in Cairo. It was called *Who Killed Diana?* The question was quickly answered in the subtitle, *Order from the Palace: Execute Emad Fayed.*

As preposterous as the idea sounded to many in Britain, it was taken very seriously in Egypt. Millions of Egyptians, and large numbers of Arabs generally, believed that Diana and Dodi were murdered because her marriage to a Muslim would have threatened powerful British interests. *Who Killed Diana?* sold 20,000 copies, a bestseller in the Egyptian market. And it was not only the Middle East. Conspiracy theorists began popping up everywhere, notably on the World Wide Web.

As with any good conspiracy theory, there seemed, at first glance, to be a strong foundation for the belief that somebody wanted Diana and Dodi out of the way: a Muslim marrying into the top ranks of the British monarchy threatened to undermine the Christian basis for the nation that a king or queen of England is sworn to uphold. At the very least, it could bring further damaging embarrassment to the embattled House of Windsor. As British author Anthony Sampson says, in the latter part of the twentieth century "the constitutional role and the soap opera came into total conflict." Given the controversies involving his father, Mohammed, Dodi's becoming the stepfather of the future king promised the tabloid press sensational front-page headlines far into the future.

Yet there is no convincing evidence that Diana's union with an adherent of the Islamic faith would in itself have posed a direct, mortal threat to Britain's monarchy, political system, or way of life. For one thing, it is far from clear that Diana would have converted to Islam. In Muslim tradition, if a Christian man wishes to marry a Muslim woman, he must adopt Islam himself. In Islam, children born of a Muslim woman must be raised Muslims. Since the children derive their faith from their father, however, he must also be a Muslim.

It is not the case in reverse. A Christian woman, for example, can marry a Muslim man without taking his religion, although she must accept that her children by him will be raised as Muslims. Particularly in countries where Islamic culture pervades every aspect of life, in Saudi Arabia, for instance, non-Muslim women tend to convert anyway. Diana's close friend Jemima Goldsmith, daughter of Sir James Goldsmith, converted to Islam after marrying Pakistani cricketer Imran Khan, who was embarking on a political career.

Diana's case was very different. There is no evidence that she was attracted to Dodi for religious reasons. For his part, Dodi was not the sort of person who would have applied pressure on her to convert. Although he was born a Muslim, he was a secular man of the world, who had gone to a Catholic school in Egypt, and had not lived in a Muslim country since he was 13. At one point, probably because of his education at the hands of French monks, he joked to former wife Suzanne Gregard that he was Catholic. During their ten-month marriage in 1987 (after a civil ceremony at a ski resort), he made no effort to make her convert to Islam. Mohammed Al Fayed's wife Heini did not convert to Islam.

Scholars agree that Diana's future choices presented no immediate constitutional challenge, as she was technically no longer a member of the royal family. She may have continued to reside in Kensington Palace, enjoy more popularity than her former husband, and go abroad on missions for British charity, but when she divorced the future king, she was stripped of her royal title, "Her Royal Highness," and thus lost her formal role. From that point on, she was simply "Diana, Princess of Wales."

At issue, rather, was her 15-year-old son, William, second in line to the British throne. The scenario, highly speculative, was that Diana would not only convert to Islam, but in time would persuade William to do so, too. In that event, the problem would still not necessarily be catastrophic for the monarchy. Being a Muslim would make William ineligible to be in the line of succession. His younger brother would ascend instead. (Unless Harry, too, had converted by then.)

The most serious trouble would come if William converted to Islam after he became king, or did so secretly beforehand and announced the adoption of his new faith after ascending to the throne. If William then wished to remain king, it could have precipitated a full-blown constitutional crisis.

The British monarch's relationship with the established church has evolved from a series of historic conventions. It was the Bill of Rights of 1619 that established the Anglican Church and decreed that the monarch must be the head of both church and state. Later, the Act of Settlement in 1701 said that the heir to the throne could not be a Catholic, or married to one, although he or she could be a Protestant of another denomination. The 1910 Accession Declaration Settlement then stated that the heir must "meet the provision of communion with the Church of England," which indicated again that the future king must be Anglican. The Accession ceremony is an Anglican religious rite in which the king or queen must take part.

Thus if William converted to Islam, Parliament and probably other members of the royal family as well would almost certainly have demanded his abdication. That in turn would have opened the way for republicans to press for the abolition of the monarchy. At the very least, the crisis could have prompted stronger calls for the disestablishment from the Church of England.

The remarkable outpouring of grief in Britain after Diana's

death suggests, perhaps, that the country stands behind "the firm," even if it could do without certain members of its top brass. But certainly the monarchy has been steadily weakened, not least by centuries of political evolution that has created a vibrant parliamentary democracy. The collapse of the House of Windsor would hardly signal profound political or economic change in Britain. The main loser, besides those Britons who still see the monarchy as an essential part of their national identity, would be the institution itself: the members of the royal family and its courtiers. William, trying to cling to his throne, would be no Henry VIII, the Tudor king who renounced his official Roman Catholic faith and still managed to remain in power (in his case, after Pope Clement VII refused to nullify his marriage to Catherine of Aragon so he could marry Anne Boleyn).

Thus the House of Windsor, goes the argument, decided to get rid of Dodi and the Princess because, in the purple prose of *Who Killed Diana?* author Mohammed Ragab, their "declared love for one another, which was on every tongue, threatened to shake the foundations of the Palace and bring down the Crown."

In Egypt, conspiracy theories began circulating immediately after the crash. Within days they were splashed in the columns of government-owned dailies as well as sensational tabloid-style weeklies. In the first month after the crash, Saad Eddin Ibrahim, a sociologist at the American University in Cairo, estimated that the theories were believed by 80 percent of Egyptians. Among them: seasoned diplomats, army generals, police officials, heads of public sector companies. Anis Mansour, once an advisor to President Anwar Sadat and now a popular commentator, wrote in *Al Ahram,* Egypt's most authoritative daily: "Diana was killed by British intelligence to save the monarchy." Egyptian film director Khairi Besheva is making a movie about Diana called *The Last Supper,* and although he doubts the conspiracy theories, he explains they are so prevalent in Egypt he will not be able to ignore them.

Of course, none of the Egyptian reports provided any material evidence. They were hastily compiled studies that relied on an assumption of motive, a belief in the cold-hearted ruthlessness of British spies, and a raising of unanswered (at least to the conspiracy theorists) questions. Most of the press stories, as well as *Who Killed Diana?* and several other books on the affair, agreed that the couple was assassinated by MI-6, Britain's foreign intelligence service, to prevent the mother of the future king of England from marrying, as Mohammed Ragab put it, "a Muslim Arab whose veins do not carry the blue blood."

This type of comment was prevalent in the chatter of Cairo and Alexandria, and probably explains why so many Egyptians were so quick to accept the murder hypothesis. Racist attitudes towards them during the colonial period so wounded their national psyche that Egyptians have little trouble believing the British would be capable of the ugliest crime against an Egyptian if it suited a British interest. Through schoolbooks and storytelling, underlying attitudes towards the British as a cunning yet treacherous people have been handed down from generation to generation.

Thus the cover of the September 8 *Rose al Youssef,* the most popular national weekly, ran the headline "Racism Against Diana" over a photograph of the Princess wearing a headscarf, to suggest that she had adopted Islamic virtue before her death. "For the British monarchy, it was totally unthinkable that the mother of the future king could be married to a Middle Eastern Muslim," wrote the Cairo magazine *Al Mussawar,* which put on its cover that week a computer-generated image of Diana and Dodi dressed as bride and groom.

For Egyptians, the stark differences in attitudes toward the romance before the crash only helped fuel the logic of a plot. When the love affair became known, Egyptians were euphoric, extremely proud that one of their own had stolen the heart of the world-famous Princess. As Hadia Mostafa of *Egypt Today* magazine put it, "Egyptians followed the relationship as if they were watching a foreign soap opera in which the leading man was an Egyptian.'' Cairenes spoke of the romance as a glorious Egyptian victory over the former imperial power, and the photos of Dodi embracing Diana became the new standard of Egyptian virility.

In contrast, as Egyptians saw it, the British press was filled with hurtful and essentially racist remarks about why Dodi was unfit to be Diana's beau. For them, there was nothing surprising in this. Egyptians had closely followed the trials and tribulations of Dodi's father, and believed that British prejudice was responsible for the denial of his citizenship application. Following the crash, therefore, Egyptians made an effortless leap: the anti-Fayed campaign in the British press (which in Arab countries is indistinguishable from the government) was part of a British government plot to break up the romance. When that didn't work, Buckingham Palace resorted to assassination. ''It was clear from the beginning,'' sighs Egyptian writer Sabry Hafez, ''that the relationship would not be allowed to continue.''

The violent deaths of Diana and Dodi had fallen on particularly fertile ground. Egyptians were prone to conspiracy theories anyway, thanks to an inward-looking culture that lacks standards of factual reporting, and has long blamed foreign spy agencies for everything from the founding of Israel and political assassinations to outbreaks of disease and failed crops. Within a week of the crash, Saad Eddin Ibrahim had identified no less than four separate theories making the rounds in Cairo:

1. Britain did it to save the monarchy from Islam.
2. Britain did it out of racism.
3. Britain did it to prevent the scandal of Diana's pregnancy.
4. Israel, through its Mossad spy agency, did it to prevent Diana from championing Arab causes.

In death, the most-photographed woman in the world quickly acquired another fin-de-millennium superlative: Queen of the

Internet. News of Diana's death hit the World Wide Web at 06:40:59 Greenwich Mean Time on Sunday August 31 with a Reuters bulletin headlined: "Princess Diana Dies After Car Crash in Paris." Thirteen minutes later, the first Web discussion board went up in Australia, appropriately calling itself "The First Diana Conspiracy Site." Within 100 days of the crash, a Yahoo search engine probe for the words "Diana conspiracy" could yield more than 31,000 entries. These ranged from essays numbering thousands of words, adorned by photos and even video clips, to one-line blurbs by Web surfers depositing their two-cents' worth on the subject at bulletin boards with names like *alt.conspiracy.diana* and *www.mcn.org/b/poisonfrog/diana.*

There is nothing parochial about the global village: the Web abounded in theories that went beyond the narrow Egyptian line that MI-6 in cahoots with Buckingham Palace had arranged the hit to protect the monarchy from Islam. With ascribed motives that were not always apparent, the Vatican, the Irish Republican Army, and the global arms industry (worried about Diana's highly publicized and effective recent campaign against antipersonnel land mines) joined the list of suspects in the crime.

Armchair conspiracy theorists armed with few facts and vivid imaginations amused themselves by spinning scenarios about how the assassination was actually carried out. One story had it that one of the paparazzi was an MI-6 agent who shot Henri Paul or the Mercedes' tires. In another, photographers were taken into police custody so that they could be hypnotized by French police (who were in on the plot) and made to forget what they had seen.

Another identified bodyguard Trevor Rees-Jones as the MI-6 agent, explaining that he wore special protective gear to survive his murder mission. Then there was the *Manchurian Candidate* scenario, which contended that Dodi, Henri Paul, or Rees-Jones had been brainwashed so he would respond to death orders. Other scenarios held that the car had been bombed (though there was no trace of explosives), a rival car manufacturer engineered the crash to discredit Mercedes, that Hollywood studios orchestrated it to create the story of the century, or that the spirit of slain designer Gianni Versace had returned to whisk his best client up to heaven with him. There was, finally, the happy-ending theory: a truck was waiting in the Place de l'Alma tunnel and spirited the lovers safely away, to a place where they would never be bothered by paparazzi again. Di and Dodi sightings, like Elvis visitations, could not be far behind.

There have been some attempts to document the conspiracy case more thoroughly. A publication called the *Executive Intelligence Review*, for example, has published a long investigation by Jeffrey Steinberg. He has also discussed his theories on a U.S. television program hosted by Geraldo Rivera, pointing to the inconsistencies of what, he argues, should have been conducted from the beginning as a murder investigation by French authorities. Steinberg's reasonable-sounding arguments are somewhat undermined by the fact that they appeared in a review associated with Lyndon Larouche, a marginal ex-Presidential candidate and convicted felon who also reportedly believed that the Grateful Dead were a British intelligence plant to corrupt American youth.

Then there was the October cover story in *Ici Paris* claiming "It Was an Attack!" But *Ici Paris* is a preposterous French scandal sheet that published what it purported to be an "interview" with the authors of this book without ever having spoken to them!

"Sometimes, a car crash is just a car crash," says John Whalen, author of *The Sixty Greatest Conspiracies of All Time,* who runs a Web site called alt.conspiracy but does not believe Diana was a victim of one. He says, however, the case has three important elements that "appeal to the conspiratorial mind": she was a celebrity, an opponent of powerful forces, and the victim of an incident in which there were conflicting news reports in the immediate aftermath.

The proliferation of conspiracy theories, he says, has more to do with the medium than the message. Using the incredible powers of the Internet to communicate, conspiracy buffs have made almost a contest of putting plots and suspicions on the Web. "Any idiot with a loud mouth who can type fast enough can get a theory out there, and once it begins to reverberate around the Internet, it doesn't tend to go away no matter how much it is debunked," says Whalen. "This incident is an example of how the Internet combined with fascination with powerful figures can spin a basic story way out of control."

But not all the doubts are being raised by indignant Egyptians or Internet nutcases. Persons close to Mohammed Al Fayed with knowledge of the official investigation warned him that a variety of problems make it as yet impossible to conclude that Diana and Dodi died in an ordinary traffic accident. They claim that the crime scene was not properly preserved, that the Mercedes was removed from the tunnel with "indecent haste," and that initially the French police either were ignorant or lied about a collision with a second car, the mysterious Fiat Uno. They continue to insist, though without concrete evidence, that the postmortem on Henri Paul was botched and thus led too easily to the drunk-driver conclusion.

Serious unanswered questions, they say, include why it took medical rescuers nearly two hours to get the Princess to a hospital; why French authorities have not made available tapes from surveillance cameras outside the ministry of justice (just next to the Ritz) and along the Mercedes' itinerary;* and why MI-6, which would have been alerted to Diana's presence in Paris that evening, has failed to come forth with what they know about the crash. Investigators, they add, are closely examining enlarged stills taken from the Ritz security videotapes to identify suspicious men in the crowd outside the hotel, apparently neither photographers nor tourists, shortly before Dodi and Diana fled from the rear.

---

*There are a number of traffic monitoring cameras along the route, but French authorities insist that they were not recording any images at the time. There were also widespread press reports that a mobile police radar near the tunnel clocked the Mercedes speeding at 196 km/h (123 mph), but Police Chief Philippe Massoni has denied that any radar unit was operating in that sector on August 31.

Seeking to get independent information on the case, Mohammed Al Fayed launched his own investigation. It is headed in Britain by Harrods Security Chief John MacNamara, an ex–Scotland Yard inspector, and in France by Pierre Ottavioli, a former chief of the criminal brigade and now the head of a private French security firm.* A retired C.I.A. agent with links to Ottavioli's network has also been brought into this private probe. In addition, Scotland Yard has assigned one of its own inspectors, Jeffrey Rees, to serve as an official liaison with the French investigation.

Neither Rees nor Al Fayed's bloodhounds have the right to interrogate witnesses in France, nor do they have any direct access to the official investigative dossier. Al Fayed's people receive periodic briefings through his French lawyers and a British barrister, Hodge Malek, who provides them with English-language summaries of the dossier's key findings. "We are only privy to information provided by the judge," says MacNamara. "If we go near a French witness, we're in contempt of court. I can't even interview employees of the Ritz!"

A jurist who is familiar with Al Fayed's investigative efforts feels they may be more psychologically than scientifically motivated. "He would find moral comfort in the idea that Dodi and the Princess died in a dramatic attack," confides this source, "because the Princess was in love with Dodi and the British Establishment couldn't accept it. I don't rule anything out, but I can't buy into that line of thinking. You'd have to have the imagination of a le Carré to believe it."

There is no protection from the whims of a psychopath, especially if he is a rogue MI-6 agent. "It doesn't need Queen Elizabeth to order a murder, it merely needs an agent or officer from one of the 16 [Commonwealth] countries to *think* she ordered it," wrote Anthony Gentles, a retired British barrister, in a letter to the authors. "If, for example,

---

*Compagie Française de Protection Privée.

someone disaffected about landmines should arrange for a sworn servant of QE II to believe that she ordered Di's demise, the said sworn servant would believe that it was a lawful order carrying total immunity from prosecution or guilt.''

Intriguing tales of rogue operations have been spun by master spywriters like John le Carré and Len Deighton, and have provided the plots for countless movies from *The Three Days of the Condor* to *Mission: Impossible*—not to mention whole libraries full of Kennedy assassination literature. The beauty of rogue spy operations is that if successful, they are impossible to prove. Thus there is no knowing whether or not the death of Diana and Dodi could conceivably have resulted from an unauthorized intelligence mission, however absurd it may seem.

As for the admittedly far-fetched possibility that William might convert, there is a recent although not perfectly analogous precedent for a clash between a monarch's personal desires and the requirements of state. The rapid abdication of King Edward VIII, later Duke of Windsor, suggests that constitutional crises involving the monarchy can be resolved quickly and safely, without need of an assassin.

After Edward VIII became King in January 1936, his relationship with Wallis Simpson, an American divorcée, was opposed by the Church of England and the government. In October, Mrs. Simpson obtained a divorce from her second husband, and in November the King informed the prime minister he wished to marry her. Meeting strong resistance, he abdicated a month later.

A murder, however, would probably be less hastily arranged. The news that Diana and Dodi were even dating did not break until August 7. There is no evidence that they informed anyone else of their marriage plans before the morning of August 29, and they died less than 48 hours later. Certainly a well-trained and experienced special forces squad could, with little advance notification, carry out an assassination against a target that had only light bodyguard protec tion, but the decision process preceding such a mission would, one surmises, have taken far longer.

There was no serious fear that Diana's marriage to a Muslim posed a political, rather than constitutional danger, for instance becoming a trigger for Christian-Muslim tensions in Britain. The country's 1.5 million Muslims, mainly immigrants from the subcontinent, not Arabia, are reasonably well integrated in British society. Prince Charles in particular has been a leading proponent of interfaith understanding, praising Islam's contribution to Western civilization, decrying ''unthinking prejudices'' against Islamic customs and coming to the support of suffering Muslims in Bosnia. He has met with the Sheikh of Al Azhar, Egypt's supreme religious authority, in Britain and on a visit to Cairo. Historian David Starkey of the London School of Economics says conspiracy theorists betray a basic misunderstanding of British tolerance. ''I don't think marriage with a Muslim is seen as fundamentally undesirable at all,'' he says. ''We have been remarkably open about cross-marriages. Everything depends on individuals and how they behave.''

A case can just as easily be made that Diana's marriage to Dodi, Muslim or not, might have pleased rather than alarmed the Establishment: given the controversies swirling around his father, her star could have fallen in public esteem. That would have put other members of the House of Windsor in a more favorable light. By killing her, the palace would have achieved the opposite: does anybody doubt that, because of her untimely and tragic death, she will forever be Saint Diana?

''My own belief, everything I conclude from my knowledge of this country, is that all these stories are bullshit,'' says veteran political commentator Hugo Young, author of a distinguished biography of Margaret Thatcher. Lord Blake, a constitutional historian, is equally blunt: ''This is utter drivel from start to finish. Total rot.''

*   *   *

Based on the available evidence—the presence of the pursuing paparazzi, the excessive speed of the Mercedes, the alcohol and drug intake of driver Henri Paul, the dangerous configuration of the Alma tunnel—it now seems likely that Diana and Dodi died in a tragic accident. And even if someone did intend to murder the couple, as implausible as that seems, there were presumably more efficient and sophisticated methods than a car crash.

Intelligence services could have resorted, for example, to the chemical Fentanyl, a traceless poison absorbed through the skin and deliverable via a surreptitious spray on the arm; operatives of Israel's Mossad spy agency used this approach in a September 1997 assassination attempt against a Palestinian leader on a street in Jordan. Or why not sink the *Jonikal* on the high seas and blame it on IRA or fundamentalist Egyptian terrorists? After all, the IRA did bomb Lord Mountbatten's *Shadow V* in 1979, killing the British war hero and his grandson.* In 1985, frogmen from France's DGSE used a limpet mine to sink the *Rainbow Warrior* in the port of Auckland, New Zealand, killing one person on board, in order to prevent the Greenpeace flagship from leading a protest against French nuclear tests.

Evidence and logic, therefore, point to the conclusion that the crash in the Alma tunnel was simply a traffic accident. Nonetheless, as with any good conspiracy theory, many of the facts surrounding the Paris crash can be arranged to fit plot scenario. But even if one accepts the hypothesis that the British Establishment (or whoever) had sufficent motive to assassinate Diana and Dodi, the seeming randomness of the events makes it difficult to imagine how anyone could have controlled such an operation.

Who could have orchestrated a plot that depended on last-minute change of escape plans; a substitute car,

---

*Diana herself, in fact, had previously been targeted in an aborted 1983 assassination attempt. According to a new book by convicted IRA hitman Sean O'Callaghan, his bosses ordered him to kill Diana and Prince Charles by placing a bomb near their box in a London theater. O'Callaghan, then working as a double agent, tipped off the police and fled the country before the plan could be carried out.

drunken, medicated, off-duty driver; a pursuit by a disparate band of French paparazzi; and a chance collision with a small car that just happened to find itself in the path of a speeding Mercedes that was not following its normal itinerary?

For such a complex plot to succeed, there would have had to be a number of operatives involved. The most effective operative would have been inside the Mercedes. There are two possibilities: Henri Paul and Trevor Rees-Jones.

Driver Henri Paul would have been the one best placed to bring about the accident. As we have seen in a previous chapter, he was a former military man who had regular links with French intelligence services; as the hotel's acting security chief, he would also have been in contact with British and other services in connection with visits to the Ritz by foreign dignitaries. But for him knowingly to execute an order to crash the car, it would have had to be a suicide mission. Even for a single man, nursing a broken heart, under treatment for depression, and overstressed by his job, that hypothesis is difficult to accept though not theoretically impossible.

There remains the possibility that Henri Paul was impaired physically to make him lose control of the vehicle. Apart from the alcohol he had consumed and the prescription medicines he was taking, the postmortem analyses found no drugs in his system. But the autopsy revealed a troubling fact, which for now defies explanation: his blood contained an abnormally high level of carbon monoxide (CO). At high concentrations, CO can be lethal: smaller doses can cause drowsiness or unconsciousness. Paul died instantly in the crash, so he could not have breathed automobile exhaust fumes present in the tunnel. Was the Mercedes' engine exhaust seeping into the interior of the car? Could that have been arranged?

As for Trevor Rees-Jones, the ex-paratrooper and breakneck rugby player, his witting involvement in such an operation also seems highly implausible. The authors are not in any way affirming that this was the case—on the contrary—but one hypothesis making the rounds would have

Rees-Jones, whose job would have made him a useful agent for keeping an eye on the troublesome and politically dangerous Mohammed Al Fayed, enlisted in such a plot.

According to this theory, Rees-Jones could have changed the departure plan, chosen Henri Paul as the driver, and made sure he got drunk while sitting with the two bodyguards in the Vendôme bar. Whoever actually made the plan, Mohammed Al Fayed is known to consider it a disastrous blunder not to have used a backup car. None of which remotely proves that Rees-Jones or Wingfield were the originators of the rear departure idea. The authors of this book, in fact, believe that Dodi himself had the idea and chose Henri Paul as the driver.

The hypothetical Rees-Jones-as-operative scenario, like the Henri Paul version, would require a huge leap of faith: acceptance of the idea that a strapping young man in the prime of life would accept a suicide assignment. It is hard to imagine even the most disciplined paratrooper or intelligence agent willingly doing that in peacetime. Unless there was a high payoff (about which no shred of proof exists) and/or a reasonable chance of survival. A frontal airbag and a seat belt would have increased that chance—and did, in fact, save his life. Rees-Jones, contrary to normal practice for bodyguards, was the only one in the car with his seat belt buckled. As noted in a previous chapter, he did not have the belt on when the car pulled away from the Ritz, but buckled up somewhere en route to the Alma tunnel.

If one were to accept, on any level, the purely theoretical notion that Rees-Jones might have been on such a mission, it would seem logical that he may have pursued it by instructing Paul to drive at increasingly high speed, and perhaps distracting him or even grabbing the steering wheel at the last minute. The latter gesture would have been very risky, however, since it would have left fingerprints on the wheel and, in the event any of the others survived to tell their tale, would have incriminated the bodyguard. As intriguing as it is to speculate about, though, this whole scenario is implausible.

*   *   *

Somewhat more believable is the notion that operatives outside the Mercedes might have engineered the crash. One possible suspect is the driver of the Fiat Uno. We have seen in the previous chapter that the Fiat appears to have been driving towards the middle of the road, partially blocking the path of the Mercedes. That there was a tangential collision between the two vehicles just outside the tunnel entrance leaves little doubt at this point. But as the Pietri report has demonstrated, the critical and determining events took place in the second phase, after Henri Paul had apparently regained control of the Mercedes.

At that point, it will be remembered, Paul suddenly turned his wheel to the left and jammed on the brakes, prompting his fatal slide into the pillar. As Pietri wrote, it was a "presence" in the right lane "that in reality provoked the catastrophe." Pietri suggests that the "presence" may have been a twofold danger from the Fiat just behind the Mercedes in the right lane and the Citroën BX just in front of it.

But one can also suppose that the Fiat had pulled up alongside the Mercedes after the initial fender-bender. There is, in fact, some evidence to suggest that the two cars may have collided a second time at this juncture. Did the Fiat in fact move into the left lane during the second phase? Was it even with, or ahead of the Mercedes by the time of the final impact? In her September 12 interrogation, it will be remembered, Gaëlle L. gave Stephan the following account: "This [smaller] car, in my opinion, was never passed by the Mercedes. I should specify that, for me, the small car was in the left lane as well, and when the Mercedes tried to pass it on the left, it hit something at that point [namely, the 13th pillar] then went into the wall on the right. The little car, seeing that, accelerated. I don't know what became of it."

Gaëlle's boyfriend, Benoît B., in his first deposition of August 31, described an apparent collision between the two vehicles during this second, critical phase: "I think the Mercedes, which was moving very fast, hit the sedan and then lost control.'' Stephan reinterrogated him on this point on September 17. ''At the moment when the Mercedes lost control,'' he told the judge, ''this car I am speaking of was just in front of the Mercedes in the same lane. The vehicle accelerated at the moment of the loss of control of the Mercedes. I then saw it take off and when I pulled even with the Mercedes, [the other car] was already far away. We did not see it after that.''

Stephan then asked Benoît about his earlier statement that the Mercedes struck the other car before losing control. ''I confirm that. I specify that, for me, the Mercedes hit the first vehicle that preceded it and after that lost control and crashed into the pillar.'' Benoît describes his position at the time of the impact as being some 35 or 40 meters west of the 13th pillar. Thus it is clear that the collision he witnessed was a *second* contact, not the original shock that took place outside the tunnel entrance, more than 70 meters east of the crash point.

What about that mysterious motorcyclist that several witnesses reported seeing just behind the Mercedes? Benoît, Gaëlle, and Grigori R., all of whom were in the eastbound tunnel, described seeing a large motorcycle slow down and pass the wreck just instants after the crash. Jean-Pascal Peyret, headed west in his Saab, was passed by a single motorcyclist just seconds after hearing the final impact.

Before the Mercedes reached the Alma tunnel, it will be recalled, several witnesses described one or more motorcycles close behind it. Clifford G., for example, reported seeing a single motorcycle 30 or 40 meters behind the Mercedes just as the car entered the tunnel. Several moments earlier, and further to the east, California businessman Brian Anderson's taxi was passed by the Mercedes closely tailed by two motorcycles. One of them seemed headed ''in a direction to get in front of the car,'' said Anderson. ''I felt that the one motorcycle, certainly without hesitation and any doubt whatsoever, was driving aggressively and dangerously.''

It is quite clear at this point that the motorcyclist closest to the Mercedes—the one who slowed down, drove around the wreck, then accelerated and took off—was not one of the photographers arrested that night. It was definitely not the Honda 650 bearing Romuald Rat and Stéphane Darmon, who were the first of the 10 arrested photographers to arrive on the scene. Several witnesses described what appears to be the Rat/Darmon motorcycle as being at least a few hundred meters from the tunnel entrance at the time of the final crash. Marie-Agnès C., standing on a grassy strip some 40 meters east of the entrance, saw a motorcycle with two riders arriving "in front" of her, that is, coming from the direction of the Concorde, at the moment she heard the noise. This is corroborated by other testimony. Rat himself claimed that he and Darmon were far behind the Mercedes, and that their motorcycle could not have been the one that was tailing the car closely. "There was perhaps another motorcycle in front of ours," said Rat.

There definitely *was* a motorcycle right behind the Mercedes, and it does not appear to have been driven by a photographer.* Let us suppose, just for the sake of argument, that this motorcycle was working in tandem with the Fiat Uno. Its role might have been to pursue the Mercedes doggedly and aggressively from the Place de la Concorde, forcing it to drive faster and faster as it approached the Alma tunnel.

In this context, the testimony of the much-maligned François Lévi bears a closer look. Lévi, it will be recalled, told police he had entered the expressway from the right-hand access road as the Mercedes was approaching from some distance behind. The Mercedes was closely followed by two motorcycles, Lévi said, and "there was a white car between

---

*On February 10, 1998, the French celebrity magazine *Voici* published an interview with Eric Petel, a 28-year-old Parisian cook, who claimed he was the motorcyclist who had been following close behind the Mercedes. Petel told the magazine that he stopped his motorcycle just behind the wrecked car, opened the door, and recognized Princess Diana. He also claimed to have reported the accident to police, who did not take him seriously. Petel's version of events, in which no other car was driving in front of the Mercedes as it entered the tunnel and he was the only person on the scene after the crash, conflicts with multiple eyewitness acounts and, in the opinion of the authors, lacks credibility.

the convoy and myself." In his rearview mirror, he claimed to see one of the motorcycles "cut in front" of the Mercedes just before the car crashed. The police discounted Lévi's claims, which admittedly didn't take account of the presence of Mohammed M.'s Citroën BX and were not corroborated by other close observers of the scene, none of whom saw a motorcycle cut in front of the Mercedes.

But writing off Lévi's whole testimony may be a case of throwing the baby out with the bathwater. Though mistaken on the precise details, it is possible that he did glimpse the movement of a motorcycle close behind the Mercedes and was fooled by the perspective and parallax into thinking it was in front. Or maybe the movement he vaguely perceived as he was ascending the exit ramp was that of the white car, which he mistook for a motorcycle, cutting in front of the Mercedes. Maybe he was making the whole thing up. But maybe not. It is interesting, though, that Lévi is the only witness who reported seeing a "white" car ahead of the Mercedes—and this at a time when neither the press nor the investigators were talking about any white vehicle or Fiat Uno.*

If the mystery motorcyclist's mission was indeed to tail Henri Paul and force him to speed, the presence of numerous photographers on motorcycles following in the Mercedes' wake would have provided an ideal cover. Indeed, an intelligence service could have made sure that such a cover existed by tipping off the photo agencies—and they were indeed tipped, some of them via London—about the impending arrival of Diana and Dodi in Paris.

There may well have been agents milling about among the paparazzi outside the Ritz that night. Mohammed Al Fayed's lawyers submitted to Judge Stephan 13 photos, enlarged from Ritz security videos, showing several unidentified individuals

---

*The fact that most of the others spoke of a "dark" car could suggest that they were describing a different vehicle, that their color-perception was distorted by the lighting conditions, or, just possibly, that they were seeing a dark Fiat Uno with a white mirror housing.

in the crowd. They have no cameras and are not dressed like tourists; they appear to be surveying the scene, their eyes looking intently in different directions. The photos have been included in the dossier. During his reinterrogation in early October, says photographer Langevin, he was asked by Stephan if he could identify any of these individuals. Investigators are also looking for an English photographer, unknown to the French journalists, who was said to be hanging around outside the Ritz.

Did this mysterious English "photographer," like the French paparazzi, scramble for his motorcycle and take off after the Mercedes? Maybe, maybe not. If the motorcyclist was an intelligence agent, he would have known about the rear exit in advance: Dodi discussed his plan on the phone with his father just before leaving the hotel; assuming one or both phones were tapped (a virtual certainty if there was a plot), the secret service in question would have relayed that information to their operatives on the scene. The motorcyclist could thus have followed them from the rear or been pre-positioned along the route.

At this point, it is useful to recall Trevor Rees-Jones' statement to Stephan on September 19 that the Mercedes was followed by "two cars and a motorcycle" upon leaving the hotel via the Rue Cambon. He specified that one of the vehicles was a "white car with a boot which opened at the back"—a description that could apply to a Fiat Uno. It seems more likely, however, that the Uno in question would have been pre-positioned closer to the tunnel. It might, in fact, have been waiting in the parallel road, the Cours Albert 1er, entering the expressway from the right at the last minute and taking the Mercedes by surprise.

In any event the mystery motorcyclist would have blended right in with the French paparazzi. But this particular motorcycle would not be shaken off by the Mercedes because it would have been more powerful than the ones used by the journalists, and its driver would be a highly trained and experienced operative. Furthermore, this motorcyclist would have known the route ahead of time.

The choice of the route, in fact, would have been an essential element of a plot to engineer an automobile accident. The ideal itinerary would be a road that would allow for high-speed driving. The normal route back to Dodi's apartment was no good: on a Saturday night, the Champs-Elysées was bumper-to-bumper. So the westbound riverfront expressway was the logical choice. And the Alma tunnel, with its curve-and-dip configuration, its lack of guard rails, and its record of high-speed accidents, would be the ideal spot to plan the crash.

It would not even be necessary to bump or ram the Mercedes at that spot. As Pietri's report makes clear, it would be impossible to pass into the Alma tunnel at speeds over 100 km/h without "grave risk." Describing a situation that would be well understood by technical experts working for an intelligence agency, Pietri writes: "Under conditions of extreme speed . . . a passage like the descent into the Alma [tunnel] could only be negotiated . . . by rectifying the curve that descends to the left by cutting directly from the left lane to the right lane."

In other words, by forcing Henri Paul to speed and by blocking the right lane, one could virtually guarantee a crackup. After which, the motorcyclist might be expected to slow down briefly, inspect the damage, and take off—which is exactly what this one did. And there would normally be a backup car watching the whole operation and waiting to spring into action if necessary—for example, to pick up the driver of the Fiat Uno if it became damaged and incapacitated in the accident. And that would probably be a heavy, powerful, and fast car—like the white Mercedes Gary Hunter saw speeding down the Rue Jean-Goujon after the crash in the wake of what appeared to him to be a Fiat Uno.

It is interesting to note, in this context, that the Rue Jean Goujon and its extension, the Avenue du Général Eisenhower, are the shortest straight-line routes from the Alma tunnel to the British embassy at 35 Rue du Faubourg–St. Honoré. The distance is only six blocks, or 1.5 km. By running the two sets of lights they would have encountered—

or, of course, if the lights were in their favor—the two vehicles could easily have made the trip in a minute or two. The embassy has a large drive-in door on the Rue du Faubourg–St. Honoré which opens onto an interior courtyard. The authors are not affirming that this is where those cars were headed, merely stating what anyone with a map and a knowledge of Paris could easily observe. This intriguing scenario, however, appears to be contradicted by the September 18 testimony of François and Valérie, who reported seeing a white Fiat Uno with a damaged muffler continuing westward along the expressway just after the accident.

If the choice of the death route seems obvious in retrospect, how could the putative plot organizers be sure the Mercedes would go down the riverfront expressway and not the Champs-Elysées? With Dodi hyped up over the paparazzi, with Henri Paul hopped up on booze and antidepressants and eager to show his pursuers a thing or two about his Stuttgart-honed driving skills, it might seem logical that they would head down the expressway. But that was not good enough. In an operation of this nature, nothing can be left to chance.

There might have been an order to follow that itinerary. It could have come, for example, to Henri Paul, who, as we have seen, had a military background and may be presumed to have links to the services. Accepting a prescribed itinerary would not require him to know the deadly nature of the mission—and its suicidal implications for himself. Disciplined security professionals are trained to carry out orders without asking questions. Alternatively, the putative plot organizers could have had backup plans allowing for a different route.

It is also possible that the motorcyclist and Fiat Uno driver were intelligence agents engaged in a close surveillance operation that went terribly wrong. In which case, unlike most normal drivers, they would have fled the scene. Which is precisely what these drivers did. None of this speculation, of course, remotely proves the existence of a conspiracy.

*   *   *

What of the role of the French in all this? Wouldn't their full-throttle investigation, and their assiduous hunt for the Fiat Uno, expose a plot if one existed?

There are some surprising inconsistencies—at least in the initial phases of the French investigation.

As the first details began to filter out from police investigators, for example, there was no reference to white paint anywhere on the car. As earlier noted, they spoke of dark blue, black, gray, red—anything but white. Until the gendarmes' spectrographic analysis revealed—deus ex machina—that the paint was in fact white. Despite all the fuzzy talk about blue and blue-green primers, the story about the changing paint colors remains bizarre. One explanation, of course, could be that investigators didn't want to divulge too many details about what they knew in order not to alert the Fiat's driver and allow him to slip the net.

There is no proof whatsoever that MI-6 or any other secret service had the slightest involvement in the crash. But there is some evidence, as we have seen, that British intelligence may have secretly raided the home of the Sipa agency's London-based photographer, Lionel Cherruault, on the night of September 1 and made off with his computer equipment.* According to Cherruault, the intruders were apparently seeking to locate and destroy the five graphic images of the crash scene that LS Presse director Laurent Sola had transmitted to London via computer in the early hours of August 31. Sola had taken his photos off the market on learning of Diana's death—and Cherruault, in any case, had never received them. But the images that Sola had sent to potential buyers, in many cases, remained in their computer memories.

Were the intruders simply trying to snuff out an offensive traffic in crash photos? Or were they seeking to destroy incriminating evidence? In either case, this possible involvement of British intelligence in the Diana case raises unsettling questions. No less disturbing is the fact that an MI-6 agent called one of his journalistic contacts just days

---

*See Chapter 11, The Paparazzi.

before the accident and warned him not to follow Dodi and Diana to Paris.* According to Italian intelligence sources, moreover, several MI-6 agents checked into the Ritz on the weekend of the accident.

None of which proves any direct British intelligence role in the accident. And even if the British services did have something to hide, it was the French authorities who were leading the investigation and had the Mercedes, with its potentially incriminating marks, in their possession—not to mention all the other forensic evidence and the eyewitness testimony. Surely the French services would not have condoned or abetted the assassination of a British Princess and the son of an Egyptian millionaire on their own soil; they had no stake in Diana's marital plans and would never have risked involvement in a potentially disastrous scandal. Particularly since President Jacques Chirac was a personal friend of Mohammed Al Fayed's and a great admirer of the Princess.

It also seems highly unlikely that the French services would have aided a cover-up after the fact. The domestic branch of French intelligence, the Direction de la Surveillance du Territoire (D.S.T.), is under the authority of the ministry of the interior, which also oversees the police. Thus any request from British intelligence for cooperation from their French counterparts on a matter of that importance would have to be presented at the highest level.

To pursue the purely hypothetical—and admittedly farfetched—notion of French complicity in a cover-up, one would have to imagine that a French official was discreetly contacted, perhaps during the long August 31 vigil at the hospital, by certain British officials. There are said to be at least six MI-6 agents working undercover at Britain's Paris embassy. Was one of them present at Pitié-Salpêtrière on August 31? If a high-level French official did issue a coverup order, it would have to have been transmitted to others involved in the investigation and the postmortem exams.

---

*The authors must remain vague on this point so as not to compromise a source.

All this is pure speculation, for which no evidence exists. Two things are certain: 1) no autopsy was performed on Diana in France and 2) no blood sample was taken by the French pathologist, "in accordance with instructions received," as a police report later put it. Among other things, the absence of an autopsy and blood sample would have insured that no mention of a pregnancy, with all its explosive implications for plot theorists, would ever find its way into the French postmortem report.

In any event, once Judge Stephan was named to head the investigation on September 2, it would have become far more difficult to sustain a cover-up, if there ever was one. Stephan is not under the authority of the interior minister and enjoys a large degree of independence even from the justice minister, his nominal boss. The naming of the second investigating magistrate, Marie-Christine Devidal, on September 5 reinforced Stephan's independent position and added another pair of eyes that would make a cover-up far more complicated.

At that point, administrative authority over the police side of the investigation (assigned to the criminal brigade) would formally have shifted from the Interior Ministry to the Justice Ministry, and specifically into the hands of the two judges. In practice, however, according to a veteran Palais de Justice insider, the police detectives would continue to report to their own immediate bosses.

But even if the Interior Ministry chose to interfere with the investigation—and there is no evidence of its intervention in this case—there are limits to its authority. Once these judges assigned the examination of the Mercedes to the gendarmes' vehicle department at Rosny-sous-Bois, which is under military authority, any attempt by the interior ministry or the D.S.T. to influence the probe would have run into serious administrative obstacles. It is interesting to note that it was the police side of the investigation that initially expressed skepticism over the existence of a second car and discredited the testimony of Lévi and Gary Hunter. It was the gendarmes who finally proved the existence of a Fiat Uno and discovered the color of the paint.

But even the gendarmes refused to let anyone outside their ranks even see the wreck: according to Jean Rol-Tanguy, a French spokesman for Mercedes, the company has repeatedly offered to send technicians from Stuttgart to assist in examining the car, but their proposal has been ignored. During the week of October 27, a promised visit by the authors of this book to the gendarmes' vehicle department in Rosny-sous-Bois was abruptly called off for "legal reasons." The same week, a previously scheduled interview with Police Chief Philippe Massoni was also canceled, as was a visit to the Gaston-Cordier wing of Pitié-Salpêtrière hospital, where Princess Diana died. (Interior Minister Chevènement had earlier turned down a request for a background interview.)

None of this, of course, even remotely indicates the existence of any coverup. But the canceled appointments spoke eloquently about the lid of secrecy that was clamped down on the case just as the hunt for the Fiat was about to begin. It was at that point that our judicial source spoke to us of the "terrible secret that weighs on this dossier."

As of this writing, the Fiat has not been found. Nor, if it played any sinister role, will it ever be discovered. "The last thing a professional would do would be to let the car be found," says Mohammed Al Fayed's entourage. "They would never abandon that car. They'd take it to the crusher. The fact that the car has never been found—that's what rings my bell."

The now-historic Fiat Uno may well have been driven by an innocent, if clumsy, Parisian who just didn't want to be bothered with an accident report. It might have been a teenager out for a joyride in his dad's car. If the driver is found, some of these troubling questions may be answered. If not, the events of August 31, 1997, will continue, at least among the conspiracy-minded, to feed speculation about plots and coverups for the next hundred years. Either way, the Place de l'Alma will be France's Dealey Plaza. And its golden flame will forever remind Parisians of the dreadful night when the world lost Diana, Princess of Wales.

Epilogue

IN THE CLASSIC 1950S AMERICAN TELEVISION SERIES *Drag-net*, each installment would end by saying what became of the various suspects. It is still too early to pronounce on the fate of the nine photographers and one photo agency motor-cycle driver under investigation in the case of the "Fatal Road Accident, 31 August 1997, 00:30." But here seems what is likely to happen:

With the meticulous nut-by-bolt examination of the Mer-cedes expected to last until the autumn of 1998, the judges will probably not be able to hand the completed dossier over to prosecutor Maud Coujard before November or December. At that point, Coujard will sift through the thousands of pages of depositions and expert reports, then draft her ré-quisitoire, a judicial document summarizing the case and rec-ommending what action to take vis-à-vis each suspect. Coujard will then return her findings to the judges, who will be guided, but not bound, by the prosecutor's opinion.

The final decision on whom to prosecute and on what charges will be taken jointly by Judges Stephan and Devidal. In the event that they decide to drop charges, the civil plain-tiffs and the prosecutor can appeal that decision under French law. And if the case does go to trial, the photographers would have the right to appeal any guilty verdict.

At this point, according to informed sources in the pros-ecutor's office, it seems likely that the involuntary homicide (manslaughter) charges will be dropped for all 10 photog-raphers, but several of them may be sent before the correc-tional court on nonassistance charges in the first half of 1999 at the earliest. In that event, the defendants will be publicly tried by a panel of three judges with no jury, no expert defense witnesses, and no television cameras. In contrast to America's O.J. Simpson extravaganza, such trials typically last only a few days, and are heavily based on the findings of the investigating magistrates.

The current thinking of French judicial experts is that any convictions are likely to draw fines and suspended jail sentences, without any of the photographers facing a serious risk of going to prison. In the event of a conviction, the same three judges will then hear a civil case, in which the current civil parties to the investigation, Mohammed Al Fayed, the Spencers, Trevor Rees-Jones, and the parents of Henri Paul could be awarded damages.

Other actions could be brought, for example, against the management of the Ritz for allowing their employee to take the wheel without the proper license and while under the influence of alcohol. Misdemeanor charges for reckless endangerment are theoretically possible but considered unlikely. In the event of a civil suit, the defendant would not be Ritz owner Mohammed Al Fayed but rather the French-based Ritz corporation, whose chief executive is Frank Klein. In the end, it would be up to the hotel's insurance company to pay any civil damages, which are far more modest than in the U.S.—typically under $20,000 and rarely more than $1 million.

"The responsibility of the Ritz is secondary to Mohammed Al Fayed," said his attorney Georges Kiejman, a former cabinet minister under François Mitterrand and one of France's most prominent lawyers. "That is not his problem. The only thing that concerns him is finding out why his son died." Nor does Al Fayed care about a monetary award in the event that any of the photographers are found responsible for the accident. "He has a right to seek damages in the event of a conviction," says Kiejman, "but it would probably only be one symbolic franc. What he wants out of this is moral satisfaction, not money."

If the Ritz were the target of a successful civil action by

the family of Henri Paul, the hotel management would have to pay damages as defined by French labor law, since he was their employee. The amounts would be set within the limits of a standard scale, unless the plaintiffs could prove a "grave fault" on the part of the hotel.

The other potential plaintiffs against the Ritz are Trevor Rees-Jones and the Spencer family. Rees-Jones, whose medical expenses are being entirely paid by Mohammed Al Fayed, seems an unlikely claimant. The Spencers, however, were said by Britain's *Sunday Times* on December 21 to be preparing to sue Al Fayed for at least $12 million, reportedly the amount of inheritance taxes owed by Princess Diana's estate.

The Spencers' French attorney, Alain Toucas, refused to confirm or deny the story, but lawyers for Al Fayed and the Ritz said that no writ of any kind had been filed as of the end of December. "Knowing the British as I do," said Kiejman, "I would be amazed if the Spencers did not try to work things out solicitor-to-solicitor rather than filing a suit. In any case, Mohammed Al Fayed has always said that he would bear his responsibilities."

Kiejman stresses the fact that, under French law, Al Fayed cannot be personally sued in this case. Moreover, he insists that the Ritz' responsibility is far from proven. "One could argue," he says, "that Henri Paul was asked to work extra hours, that he was not really a chauffeur, that the management of the Ritz should have stopped him. But who would that be? No one who was there that night could have imagined that he was under the influence of alcohol. Their fear of Mohammed Al Fayed was such that they would never knowingly have taken such a risk." Besides, he argues, "Paul's alcohol level does not change the problem. Certainly alcohol played a role in the sharing of responsibilities. But the initial responsibility is that of the photographers whose behavior required him to take a route that was not the normal route, at a speed that he should not have been driving at. No paparazzi, no accident." And just in case the paparazzi beat the manslaughter rap, Kiejman and his partner Bernard Dartevelle have filed invasion of privacy charges against those who photographed the victims in the car.

Other lawyers involved in the case fully expect a civil suit against the hotel management. "If it is established that Paul's drunkenness was the principal cause," says one jurist, "they will look for who committed a fault at the Ritz. If it is established that the Ritz knew that Paul was sick, fragile, depressed, and alcoholic, then the Ritz is in trouble. If it can't be shown that the Ritz knew about Paul's state, however, it will be hard to prove their responsibility." In the end, the only ones who are likely to pay for the death of Princess Diana and Dodi Fayed are the insurance companies.

René Delorm is expecting us. He opens the door of the third-floor apartment and ushers us into the foyer, with its geometric black, white, and pink marble floor and crystal chandelier. At 55 years old, standing about five foot six inches, René is trim and fit, elegantly dressed in a light gray raw silk jacket, maroon turtleneck, black wool pleated trousers, and black tasseled loafers. Wire-rimmed glasses frame his lean, tanned face. His slightly bouffant brown hair is brushed straight back. There is warmth and sadness in his brown eyes. It is a slightly lost look.

"We didn't touch anything since that night," he explains in his French-accented English. "We just cleaned up. Mr. Al Fayed wants the apartment to stay just the way his son left it, as if he were coming back."

René is proud to show off the ten-room apartment on the Rue Arsène-Houssaye. He takes us through a small salon to the left of the foyer and out onto a wide wrought-iron balcony. Just to the right stands the Arc de Triomphe. To the left is the broad expanse of the Champs-Elysées. Its bare trees, now bright with white Christmas lights, form a glittering cordon all the way to the Place de la Concorde, about a mile to the east. Looking out on that panorama, one can't help thinking how different things might have been that night if Henri Paul had just taken this stately thoroughfare, for all its traffic lights and bumper-to-bumper traffic. The champagne could have waited twenty minutes more.

Next to the salon is the green living room, where Diana left her luggage and dressed for dinner on that Saturday evening. René can't say for sure where she would have slept that night. One might suppose it would have been in Dodi's bedroom. But, as the butler points out, "They never spent the night here. They never came back."

René takes us through the main living room, an immense space with a view onto two streets, high ceilings, two large sofas, a pink marble-topped coffee table, a white marble mantelpiece. A large-screen Philips TV, one of at least half a dozen scattered through the apartment, stands blank and mute in the corner. Here and there, there are framed pictures of Dodi with movie stars.

But it is in the intimacy of the master bedroom that Dodi's spirit seems most present. A king-sized bed with a gold bedspread dominates the room. Heavy brocade and silk curtains frame the tall windows. On the mantelpiece is a collection of medicine bottles—Vitamin E-400, folic acid, Super Hy Vites, Tylenol, Tums—that bear witness to Dodi's health mania. There are three stuffed bears on a table by the marble fireplace; stuffed animals are to be found all through the apartment, a throwback perhaps to that magical menagerie he left back in Alexandria.

One by one, René opens the mirror-covered doors to the clothes closets that line the south wall. In one, there are fifteen suits—all Armani and all dark. On the floor, neatly arranged, are three or four pairs of cowboy boots. To the left, a narrow chest of drawers, labeled by category: "boxer shorts," "underwear," "socks," "shorts," "sweat pants." "He asked me to put labels on the drawers because he's very meticulous," says René, still speaking in the present tense. "He's very organized, very neat."

In the next closet, the shelves are stacked high with designer jeans, slacks, elegant wool and cashmere sweaters. Lined up on hangers are a half-dozen jackets and a dozen flowery silk shirts. It is from these very closets that Dodi chose the suede jacket, jeans, and cowboy boots that he wore that night. We stare in silence for a moment, then René closes the closet doors.

The rest of the visit takes us through cavernous marble bathrooms, guest rooms, an exercise room, two kitchens, the butler's quarters. There are more framed pictures, more TVs, more stuffed bears, more exquisite *faux marbre* walls, tapestries, Persian carpets.

There are no Rosebud revelations here. Only silence, and space, and the sadness of René Delorm. His eyes tear up a bit when he tells how Mohammed Al Fayed came to the apartment the night his son died. "He said, 'René, you took care of my son. Don't worry, I'll take care of you.' How can a man think of the worries of someone else when his son has just died? I couldn't believe it."

But René says he can't accept Al Fayed's offer to take him on as his own butler. "I cannot work for anyone else, only for Dodi. I cannot picture doing that job with anyone else. I spent eight years of my life with Dodi. I left everybody in L.A., my son, my girlfriend, my friends, my family. When I heard he died, I cried like a baby."

René is heading back to California, the warm, sunny haven that this wandering Moroccan Jew long ago decided to call home. He had left it all behind to accompany a lonely Egyptian playboy on his quest for happiness and paternal approval. Dodi almost had both in his grasp. "It was a wonderful life," says René. "There were dinner parties, cruises, movie stars. And the Princess was going to come into his life. Then . . . psssht! It all went away."